Visions of Filth

Deviancy and Social Control
in the Novels of Galdós

Visions of Filth

Deviancy and Social Control
in the Novels of Galdós

Teresa Fuentes Peris

LIVERPOOL UNIVERSITY PRESS

First published 2003 by
Liverpool University Press
4 Cambridge Street
Liverpool, L69 7ZU

British Library Cataloguing-in-Publication Data
A British Library CIP Record is available

ISBN 0–85323–718–2 cased
ISBN 0–85323–728–x paper

Typeset in Monotype Apollo by Koinonia, Bury
Printed and bound in the European Community
by Bell and Bain Limited, Glasgow

To my mother, Teresa Peris Arrufat

Contents

Preface and Acknowledgements

The word 'filth' conjures up a variety of images. In late-nineteenth-century Spain, industrialization and urban growth provided a fertile breeding ground for such images. The explosion of poverty in the country's cities, along with the growth of related social problems of mendicity, vagrancy, prostitution, alcoholism and the spectre of racial degeneration, generated both fears of social instability and disorder and strategies aimed at containing the threat posed by marginal and deviant social groups. The anxieties sparked by these groups found expression in the images of 'filth' – a metaphor for immorality, vice, disorder and deviant behaviour generally – that appeared around them.

The association established in the imagination during that period between 'immoral' and 'infectious' contagion is reflected in the various discourses of control and science – seen not only in Spain but also elsewhere in Europe – that emerged during this time. In this book I set a selection of Galdós's novels in the context of discourses on public health, domesticity and philanthropy, emphasizing in the process the way in which these were constantly interwoven. My intention is to show how bourgeois and expert-professional ideas on, and attitudes to, deviancy were reproduced by Galdós, and how he positioned himself in relation to these. In doing so, I hope to add a new perspective to the existing critical material on Galdós.

During the course of my research I found especially significant the desire of public health experts – and criminologists – to assume responsibility for, and pronounce on, moral and social matters that did not necessarily fall within their domain of expert knowledge. Their construction of an interventionist medico-moral discourse was based on the link they were concerned to establish between *physical* and *moral* health. In medicalizing social issues, Spanish public health experts devoted large parts of their texts to the various aspects of deviancy – mendicity, vagrancy, prostitution, alcoholism, madness and other 'immoral' behaviour – that were perceived at the time as 'social pathologies', or 'enfermedades del cuerpo social'. In the mentality of the period, social abnormality was seen as constituting an important branch of public hygiene, as valid as the sanitation of public space or the control of disease. In the hygienic manuals and treatises of the day it is not surprising to find, for example, that a section dealing with the urban drainage system is closely followed by one on prostitution: both areas were perceived as being in need of sanitation, or regulation, and thus became objects of inquiry, supervision and control for hygienists seeking to give social relevance to their scientific knowledge and teaching. Given the paucity of secondary material devoted to deviancy, and certainly to its association with 'filth', I found such primary sources not only revealing but also highly valuable in seeking a fresh analysis of Galdós in the light of contemporary discourses related to deviancy and control. In addition, the work by the social commentator and philanthropist Concepción Arenal, and in particular the ideas expressed in *La Voz de la Caridad*, the journal she edited, proved to be an equally valuable source of information.

This study began life as a doctoral thesis, written at Birkbeck College (University of London) between 1993 and 1997. My primary thanks go, therefore, to my supervisor, Jo Labanyi, for her enthusiasm and efficiency, as well as for being a constant source of inspiration. I could not have wished for a better supervisor. I would also like to express my gratitude to those scholars who have personally offered ideas and material: Ricardo Campos Marín and Rafael Huertas, from the Consejo Superior de Investigaciones Científicas, who provided me with useful information on alcoholism and degeneration; Ramón Castejón Bolea, for his comments on prostitution and venereal diseases; Akiko Tsuchiya, for her interest and support; Antonio Sánchez; and Catherine Jagoe. I should also like to thank many others for the encouragement they gave me at various stages of the research, among them Anny Brooksbank-Jones, Rhian Davies, Alex Longhurst, John Macklin and Chris Murphy. In addition I wish to express appreciation for the assistance afforded to me by the staff of those libraries and repositories that I visited in the course of my research, most notably, in Madrid, the Biblioteca Nacional, the Hemeroteca Municipal and the Real Academia de Medicina (special thanks here to Nacho Díaz-Delgado Peñas); as well as the British Library, the Wellcome Institute and the Casa Museo de Pérez Galdós, Las Palmas de Gran Canaria. I am also grateful to the British Academy for providing me with the research grant that made this book possible. For his constant encouragement and patience, I would especially like to thank my husband, Alistair.

Note, finally, that parts of Chapter 2 and Chapter 3 have already appeared, in a similar form, as the following articles: 'The Control of Prostitution and Filth in *Fortunata y Jacinta*: The Panoptic Strategy in the Convent of Las Micaelas', *Anales Galdosianos*, XXXI–XXXII (1996–97);

'Drink and Degeneration: The "Deserving" and "Undeserving" Poor in *Angel Guerra'*, *Romance Studies* (Spring 1997); and 'Drink and Social Stability: Discourses of Power in Galdós' *Fortunata y Jacinta'*, *Bulletin of Hispanic Studies* (Liverpool University Press) LXXIII, No. 1 (January 1996). I thank the editors of these journals for allowing me to rework this previously published material and integrate it into this book.

Ilkley Teresa Fuentes Peris
March 2001

Introduction

Social deviancy is a crucial aspect of Galdós's work, yet one that has been largely ignored by critics. Although several have addressed the subject of the working classes in Galdós's novels, no major study has been devoted to the wider issue of social deviancy and its various forms or, it follows, to the strategies and techniques designed to control it. This study examines notions of deviancy and social control in a series of Galdós's novels of the 1880s and 1890s. Deviancy is defined here as behaviour that is seen to be diverging, or deviating, from the accepted social norm and is therefore considered to be in need of regulation or control – deviancy and control being inevitably intertwined. In addition, I also explore the associations of deviancy with 'filth', a conceptualization arising from the images of dirt and disease generated by social abnormality. Attention is focused in this study on several deviant groups much publicized by Galdós: prostitutes, drunkards, beggars and vagrants. Analysis of these categories necessarily requires discussion of ideas on, and attitudes to, poverty and the working classes especially the working-class groups considered less deserving or less respectable.

The first novel I analyse, *Fortunata y Jacinta* (1886–87), has received considerable critical attention in respect of social class. Studies have tended to concentrate on the working-class figure of Fortunata and her relationship with the bourgeois world. Less has been written about other working-class characters in the novel, especially those at the very bottom of the social scale, generally associated with dissolute and debauched behaviour. Those studies that do exist do not relate their discussion of working-class characters in the novel to contemporary perceptions of deviancy and to the associated notion of filth.[1] The other four novels I analyse – *Angel Guerra* (1890–91), *Nazarín* (1895), *Halma* (1895) and

---

1 Akiko Tsuchiya ('"Las Micaelas por fuera y por dentro": Discipline and Resistance in *Fortunata y Jacinta*', in Linda M. Willem [ed.], *A Sesquicentennial Tribute to Galdós 1843–1993* [Newark, DE, Juan de la Cuesta Hispanic Monographs, 1993], 56–71) has explored how the disciplinary mechanisms of control work in *Fortunata y Jacinta*; however, hers is a purposely focused and restricted study, upon which I hope to build by looking at the novel within a wider, alternative theoretical framework.

Misericordia (1897) – have tended to be seen as novels belonging to Galdós's 'spiritual period', dealing less with social than with non-material matters. *Nazarín*, *Halma* and *Misericordia* have often been regarded as forming an organic whole, and analysed in relation to one another. I argue that there is much common ground in all four novels, and that rather than being a product of Galdós's 'spiritual' tendencies they are firmly grounded in the social context in which they were produced.

My methodology is, thus, fundamentally socio-historical. But my emphasis is not so much on the particular social and historical circumstances of the period in which these novels were written as on the contemporary discourses of control generated by these circumstances. My methodology has therefore been defined by a close analysis of the attitudes that developed around this time to activities considered socially dangerous such as prostitution, excessive drinking, mendicity and vagrancy. These attitudes manifested themselves clearly in a series of social, medical and moral debates among the professional and middle classes that circulated in Restoration Spain, as elsewhere in Europe, at a time when views on poverty had begun perceptibly to change. The analysis of attitudes towards deviancy inevitably leads to an exploration of the images of filth that, at the time, were projected on to marginal groups of the population, especially on to elements of the working classes. By the late nineteenth century filth had become a powerful metaphor for immorality and social disorder. The images of filth constructed around prostitution, drunkenness, mendicity and vagrancy in contemporary discourses – most notably discourses on public health produced by medical experts – testify to the social threat that deviant, marginal groups were felt to pose to the emergent capitalist order.

Discourses have a regulatory dimension that naturally invites an exploration of theories of social control. This study approaches the notion of social control – called the 'dominant ideology thesis' in Marxist terminology – in a critical way.[2] Marxist thinking concerning the imposition of

2 Early twentieth-century theorists of social control studied the concept exclusively in the context of deviant behaviour such as crime, delinquency, perversity, immorality and so on. Later, social control took on a wider meaning, associated with the domination of the majority by power elites: hence its adoption by Marxists and their articulation of the dominant ideology thesis. Clearly, there is an overlap between these two perceptions of social control. In this study, the choice of subject areas conforms to the traditional view of social control, but attention is also paid to the later dominant ideology notion, the critique of which offers theoretical perspectives relevant to an analysis of Galdós's treatment of deviant groups. For a discussion of the development of the concept of social control in the twentieth century, see Anne R. Edwards, *Regulation and Repression: The Study of Social Control* (London, Allen and Unwin, 1988), Chapter 1.

a dominant ideology might be considered too simplistic an interpretation. According to the dominant ideology thesis, the class that controls the means of economic production also controls the means of ideological production. Thus, the ideas and values of ruling elites become the ruling ideology that dominates a particular historical period. In keeping with this thesis, the ideas and values of the bourgeoisie – which had assumed the position of the most powerful social class by the end of the nineteenth century – became the *dominant ideology*. This ideology, it is argued, was disseminated downwards to other social groups in an attempt to maintain a social order that was constantly perceived as being in danger of collapse as a result of the ongoing processes of urbanization, industrialization and concentration of ownership.

This thesis has been found wanting on a number of counts.[3] Firstly, disciplinary and authoritarian strategies almost inevitably generate resistance in the recipient, rather than acquiescence or submission. Control can thus be counter-productive, leading to further problems of control. Secondly, it has been argued that values traditionally held to be bourgeois in complexion – such as respectability, independence, improvement, thrift, self-help, cleanliness, hard work and temperance – were not exclusively middle class but had a long tradition within the working class. This indicates a degree of autonomy that does not fit with the proposition of effective social control. Thirdly, the working classes have never been simply helpless and naive victims of bourgeois indoctrination. They might have assimilated certain influences unintentionally, but they have also accepted others because it suited their own interests. In other words, control can be exploited, and often has been. It is clear, therefore, that theories concerning social control should not be taken at face value. This is not to say that concerted attempts by sections of the middle class to exercise control over the classes beneath them did not occur. However, what is significant about arguments against the social control thesis is that they question the bourgeoisie's success in imposing its ideology on other classes.

Having summarized the main counter-arguments to the dominant ideology thesis, and in order to be able to analyse how the disciplining and indoctrination of the working classes in Galdós's novels was either absorbed or deflected by them, it is necessary to examine precisely how these disciplinary mechanisms work. In recent years, ideas about the exercise of control by dominant social groups have been given a sophisticated

3 For a succinct critique of the dominant ideology thesis, see Nicholas Abercrombie, Stephen Hill and Bryan Turner, *The Dominant Ideology Thesis* (London, George Allen and Unwin, 1980).

edge by the work of the French philosopher Michel Foucault and those who have developed his insights. Hesitancy concerning the dominant ideology thesis is expressed here through the adoption of a Foucauldean perspective on the operation of power, in which emphasis is placed more on the cultural than the economic power of experts, professionals and social elites. In *Discipline and Punish*,[4] Foucault explores the transformation in penal practices and the emergence of new disciplinary techniques of power. With the birth of the modern prison, the public spectacle of torture was replaced in the early nineteenth century by the appearance of the soul or the mind as a primary target of punishment. About this time the body began to lose its importance as a major object of penal repression. In place of the executioner a whole body of technicians, or experts, took over: wardens, doctors (hygienists among them), psychiatrists, psychologists, chaplains and educators. These new 'technicians of power' did not employ violence or physical coercion so much as mental coercion, which was based on the subjection of the individual to an expert system of constant supervision and regulation. Foucault argues that this shift in the concept of punishment was aimed not so much at leniency and humanity as at greater efficiency in penal practices. Systems of disciplinary control instituted by the state, with the support of social elites, depend for their efficiency on the surveillance and moralization of deviant, or potentially deviant, groups. Foucault has viewed this process of surveillance as 'panoptic', referring to the prison scheme drawn up by the moral philosopher Jeremy Bentham in his *Panopticon; or the Inspection-House* (1791). Foucault observed that the penal disciplinary techniques of power – for training and transforming the individual, and making him/her more docile and useful to society – were to be found not only in prisons but beyond the frontiers of penal incarceration, propagating themselves outside the limits of the enclosed institution and permeating the whole of the social body: hence Foucault's image of a 'carceral network' operating throughout society.

This extension of the disciplinary mechanisms through society is defined by Foucault as the 'surveillance society'. Such a society has two fundamental facets. Firstly, the creation and implementation – the physical writing, printing and dissemination – of rules, procedures and regulations, which can operate inside or outside enclosed institutions, and which are used to log and track citizens, especially deviant citizens, by means of bureaucratic practices and structures. Examples of this view of surveillance, in the context of this study, include the 'invasion' of the homes of

---

4 Michel Foucault, *Discipline and Punish: The Birth of the Prison* (London, Penguin, 1991).

the poor by regulating, moralizing philanthropists; institutions imposing a strict and rational regime, such as the convent of Las Micaelas in *Fortunata y Jacinta*, which was used for the rehabilitation of prostitutes; the state regulation of prostitution through the enforced registration of prostitutes; and the licensing of beggars by local authorities. Secondly, it is possible to conceptualize the surveillance society in terms of the way in which power is exercised through discourses (essentially social or human science discourses, which often dovetailed with knowledge in the pure sciences) produced by experts. In fact, both notions of surveillance are closely interconnected, since systems of rules, procedures and regulations emerge as a result of the discourses of control: for example, the legal regulation of prostitutes and the creation of institutions for their regeneration emerge as a result of the discourse on public hygiene, which regarded prostitution as a source of infections and diseases and therefore as a real social threat. Foucault also argued that power is exercised through an interplay of different discourses. Thus, in the nineteenth century the discourse on hygiene intersected with that on gender, which constructed marriage and domesticity as the norm and classified any digression from this norm, such as prostitution, as abnormal behaviour in need of reform.

Although the theory of control through disciplinary practices did not originate with Foucault, recognition should be given to his identification of discourses – particularly those with a social dimension – as key sites of power. Foucault defined discourses as ways of specifying particular 'truths', or bodies of knowledge, at particular times in history. However, the 'truths' produced by discourses cannot be neutral or objective since the formation of this knowledge is, according to Foucault, essential to, and inseparable from, the exercise of power. The ideas embodied in a discourse are generated by the socio-political interests of a group, which defines what is 'normal' (conforming to an established norm of behaviour) and what is 'abnormal' (in need of normalization through mechanisms of control). Discourses are therefore social constructs containing a control dynamic wrapped in a language of neutrality. The formation of a regulatory discourse constructs as the objects of power those who have been excluded from its production, and categorizes them as 'abnormal' or 'deviant'; that is, it submits them, through a series of regulatory practices, to a system of constant supervision and moralization aimed at their 'normalization' or 'reform'.[5]

5 For a discussion of Foucault's notion of 'discourses', see Caroline Ramazanoğlu, 'Introduction', in Caroline Ramazanoğlu (ed.), *Up against Foucault: Explorations of some Tensions between Foucault and Feminism* (London, Routledge, 1993), 18–20; and Stuart Hall, 'The West and the Rest', in Stuart Hall and Bram Gieben (eds), *Formations of Modernity* (Cambridge, Polity Press, 1992), 291–95.

During the Restoration, Spanish society was structured around a series of mechanisms – based on the surveillance and moralization of the poor – designed to maintain social stability.[6] The development of capital-sm brought with it a series of conflicts that crystallized at the time of the Restoration. Some of these conflicts were related to public health, to the geographical proximity of the working classes to the middle classes, and to prostitution; as well as to the need for a skilled work force and for a programme of regulation and 'fixing' of the population that was per-ceived to be floating. Following a Foucauldean line, Varela argues that the emergence of these conflicts resulted in a series of disciplinary strategies aimed at neutralizing the dangers posed by those sectors of the population – often seen as represented by the working classes – that threatened the social norm and the capitalist order, and that were conse-quently categorized by dominant groups as 'deviant'.[7] Order had become, asserts Varela, 'la categoría privilegiada sobre la que se construyen los discursos de poder en la Restauración'.[8]

According to Shubert,[9] the solutions offered in Spain to the problem of the poor (the workers and the poor were increasingly seen as synon-ymous in the second half of the nineteenth century) differed little from the measures taken elsewhere – in Britain and the United States, for example – to deal with the 'social question'. These measures were of two basic kinds. Firstly, lifting the poor from the streets and putting them in moralizing institutions where they would be subjected to discipline and work. This institutional solution grew out of the fear of a floating popu-lation which did not work and out of the accompanying desire to 'fix' this population at a time when idleness had become associated with immorality: 'el ocioso ataca directa y gravemente a la sociedad', stated the nineteenth-century social commentator Concepción Arenal.[10] Secondly, a common solution to the problem of poverty was the creation of volun-tary charitable associations, which entailed the surveillance of the homes of the poor by women considered respectable, who sought to rearrange their lives in accordance with established morals. Charitable associations and institutions were part of the formation of what Foucault calls the

6 Julia Varela, 'Técnicas de control social en la "Restauración"', in Julia Varela and
    Fernando Alvarez-Uría (eds), *El cura Galeote asesino del obispo de Madrid-Alcalá*
    (Madrid, La Piqueta, 1979), 210–11.

7 Ibid., 211.

8 Ibid., 215.

9 Adrian Shubert, *A Social History of Modern Spain* (London, Unwin Hyman, 1990),
    52–56.

10 Concepción Arenal, *Cartas a un señor* (1880), in *Obras completas*, ed. Carmen Díaz
    Castañón (Madrid, Atlas [Biblioteca de Autores Españoles], 1994), II, 245.

'disciplinary society'. Moreover, philanthropic societies were an example of the diffusion of the disciplinary mechanisms of power beyond the enclosed institution: in other words, the de-institutionalization of discipline. In this sense, philanthropy provided a powerful instrument for the control of the lower classes.[11]

This study analyses how control is imposed on and/or deflected by Galdós's working-class characters (and other social groups perceived as deviant) by addressing contemporary cultural and medical discourses – especially those on public hygiene, class and gender – that emerged in Restoration Spain. I concentrate not only on the ways in which Galdós's novels reproduce contemporary perceptions and attitudes towards deviancy, but also on Galdós's position in these debates. I hope to show how Galdós's representation of these contemporary discourses often subverts them through the use of narrative point of view and of verbal and situational irony. The establishment of a historical and theoretical framework enables the reader to appreciate the significance of Galdós's critical focus and personal contribution to such discourses.

Chapter 1 examines the changing attitudes towards poverty and the dispensation of charity that developed in the second half of the nineteenth century in particular, as a consequence of the transformations wrought by industrial and urban expansion. This entails an analysis of the role played by philanthropy in the moralization of the lower layers of the population, those living at both the moral and economic margins of society. Emphasis is placed on the association established in the bourgeois mind between the poorer classes on the one hand and filth, savagery and pre-civilized behaviour on the other. My focus is here on one chapter of *Fortunata y Jacinta*, 'Una visita al Cuarto Estado'. This episode provides a useful introduction to themes developed in later chapters, since it offers a vision of poverty in relation to the working classes in general, rather than concentrating on specific aspects, such as drunkenness or prostitution. Furthermore, it highlights the fact that problems that arose when dealing with the working classes were not the same as those posed by beggars or vagrants, although in practice often only a thin line was drawn between workers and the casual or nomadic poor.

Chapter 2 analyses the control of prostitution in *Fortunata y Jacinta* and *Nazarín* by drawing on the images of filth that emerged around the figure of the prostitute. Stress is laid on the ways in which working-class prostitutes were categorized as 'deviant' (and thus seen in need of moral

11 Within the 'carceral network' penalties could be imposed in more or less obvious ways. According to Foucault, charitable institutions and associations constitute particularly subtle instruments of power.

reform) by associating them with infection, both physical and moral. In this respect, special attention is given to the discourses on public hygiene and domesticity as instruments of control and, similarly, to the regulatory role played by philanthropy. In my analysis of *Fortunata y Jacinta*, I focus critically and in detail on the issue of social control and, similarly, on resistance to it, both within the convent of Las Micaelas (an example of a controlling institution organized according to the principles of the panopticon scheme) and outside the institutionalized milieu of the convent. Although in this chapter I mainly concentrate on *Fortunata y Jacinta*, I discuss *Nazarín* where relevant, particularly in connection with associations established in the period between prostitution and foul odours.

Chapter 3 explores the issue of drink in *Fortunata y Jacinta* and *Angel Guerra*. After examining various contemporary discourses on drink, and how these are reproduced in *Fortunata y Jacinta*, this chapter turns to the burning issue of alcoholism as a major factor in the degeneration of the human race, as developed by Galdós in *Angel Guerra*. Within the context of working-class drinking, attention is given to the problem of alcoholism in relation to gender. This is achieved by reference to the contrasting attitudes adopted towards male and female alcoholism.

Chapter 4 focuses on the concept of the 'deserving' and the 'undeserving' poor and the related themes of mendicity and vagrancy. The contemporary concern with differentiation between categories of poor, and growing fears about the consequences of the indiscriminate dispensation of charity, are key features of the four novels analysed in this chapter: *Angel Guerra*, *Nazarín*, *Halma* and *Misericordia*. Similarly, *Nazarín* and *Misericordia* echo anxieties about a nomadic urban population that refused to be 'fixed'.

Finally, in respect of my choice of novels generally, I have limited myself to those novels by Galdós that illuminate most clearly the various issues of deviancy I seek to discuss in this book. The exception is *La desheredada* (1881), which also deals with certain aspects of deviancy (prostitution and vagrant criminality) and raises the question of hereditary degeneration. The reason for excluding *La desheredada* is based on the fact that the theme of prostitution does not feature in a significant way, and is mentioned only at the end of the novel. Similarly, the problem of vagrancy in this novel is covered merely in relation to criminality, a facet of deviancy not included in this study.

Chapter 1

The Miasmas of Poverty:
The Lower Classes in
'Una visita al Cuarto Estado'

From the perspective of contemporary images of the poor and attitudes towards poverty and charity, 'Una visita al Cuarto Estado'[1] is one of the most significant and illustrative chapters in *Fortunata y Jacinta*. During the second half of the nineteenth century in Spain, the incipient process of industrialization and urbanization brought with it not only a change in the concepts of poverty and charity as they had been traditionally understood by the wealthier classes but also new ways of dealing with the needy. In particular, a new system of philanthropy gained ground over old charitable practices. To understand how new attitudes to poverty and, similarly, changed perceptions of the poor are reflected in 'Una visita al Cuarto Estado', it will be useful to analyse the historical context in which these developed.

From the 1830s, the liberal revolutionary process initiated a series of social transformations – including the dismantling of the guilds, proletarianization and increased migration from an impoverished countryside to the towns. The growing numbers of immigrants flocking to the cities exacerbated the long-standing problem of mendicity, especially in Madrid, whose industrial structures, still underdeveloped, were unable to absorb a rapidly expanding labour force. The widening gap existing between demographic and economic growth generated increasing numbers of unemployed, many of whom were forced into mendicity.[2] Almost from

---

1 Caudet notes that the term 'cuarto estado' is used by Galdós to refer to the world of poverty of the Madrid slums; see the Introduction to his edition of *Fortunata y Jacinta*, 315, note 225. At the end of the Ancien Régime, French society was divided into three estates or orders. The first estate was the clergy, the second the nobility, and the third – which comprised the vast majority of the population – was formed by many different social categories, from the well-to-do bourgeois to the very poor, the only link between them being the fact that they were all base commoners. It has been argued that the poorest sections of the community hardly belonged to this group, in the sense that they were, in a way, outside the social order and may, therefore, be seen as forming a fourth estate; see Georges Dupeux, *French Society 1789–1970* (London, Methuen, 1976), 46–62.

2 Angel Bahamonde Magro ('Cultura de la pobreza y mendicidad involuntaria en el Madrid del siglo XIX', in *Madrid en Galdós, Galdós en Madrid* [Madrid, Comunidad

the outset of industrialization, from about 1840, unemployment – or at best occasional employment – became a permanent feature of urban Spain. As a result, from mid-century onwards unemployment and mendicity became intimately associated, as street begging by the unemployed increased.[3]

The problem of mendicity in Spain's larger cities not only renewed interest in the relatively narrow issue of poverty, it also sparked a broader concern for social stability. Poverty and other related issues, such as the insanitary living conditions of the poor, increasingly came to be viewed as a problem closely linked to the wider and more threatening 'social question'. Social and economic change meant that the ancient perception of the destitute as 'Christ's poor ones' was gradually displaced by a more negative image. The poor became associated, especially in the last third of the century, with the emergence of mass, violent protest and with the new socialistic ideas that propounded a radical transformation of the existing order. Thus, attitudes towards the poor underwent an important change. Scepticism grew about the providential origin of poverty and the traditional deferential figure of the poor resigned to their lot and dependent on the charity of the rich.[4] Poverty now came to be more widely regarded as a moral failing arising from what was believed to be the dissolute nature of the lower classes.

Alongside this shift of attitude, the giving of alms to beggars began to be criticized, by government officials and social commentators, for its indiscriminate nature. Similarly, the traditional moral obligation to help the poor was questioned. Writers on social and moral issues, as well as dispensers of charity, increasingly felt that a discriminatory process was

---

de Madrid, Consejería de Cultura, May 1988], 164) has observed that mendicity was a pressing issue throughout the nineteenth century in Spain. Most Madrid news-papers devoted more space to the beggar – or the unemployed forced into begging – than to the working classes.

3 Angel Bahamonde Magro and Julián Toro Mérida, 'Mendicidad y paro en el Madrid de la Restauración', *Estudios de Historia Social*, 7 (1978), 353–54 in particular; and Adrian Shubert, *A Social History of Modern Spain* (London, Unwin Hyman, 1990), 52–56. According to Bahamonde and Toro (353) Madrid doubled its population between 1857 and 1890, in spite of its high mortality rate. In 'La cuestión social' (17 February 1885), Galdós raises the issue of the unemployment crisis in Madrid – which particularly affected the building industry – and deplores the fact that healthy, hard-working men were forced to have recourse to charity, as noted by Peter B. Goldman, 'Galdós and the Nineteenth-Century Novel: The Need for an Inter-disciplinary Approach', in Jo Labanyi (ed.), *Galdós* (London, Longman, 1993), 143.

4 This was a slow process, however, since, as Bahamonde has shown ('Cultura de la pobreza', 163–82), there survived in nineteenth-century Spain old conceptions of charity, which regarded the right to be poor as 'un elemento más de la ética cristiana'.

essential, since not all the poor could be considered as belonging to one category. It followed that they had to be dealt with in different ways. This changing attitude to poverty, which was not exclusive to Spain, strengthened considerably the older classification of the poor into two broad categories: the deserving and the undeserving.[5] The deserving poor were those who were considered to possess, or to have the potential to possess, respectable values, such as self-improvement, cleanliness, hard work, thrift, temperance and, especially in the case of women, chastity. This category of poor found themselves living in poverty – or falling on hard times – due to circumstances beyond their control, but could be assisted back to independence and self-reliance. This category stood at the opposite pole to the undeserving poor, whose impoverishment was widely seen as self-inflicted, that is, resulting from their dissolute ways of life, or from their inbuilt propensity for 'vices' such as neglect of cleanliness, idleness, reluctance to work, improvidence, drinking, gambling, general fecklessness and, again, especially in the case of women, sexual waywardness. With regard to this category of poor, charity given indiscriminately and thoughtlessly was believed to produce a damaging demoralization (in the sense of moral debasement).

Donzelot has observed that this process of discrimination between those who were in real need and those who were not was a core characteristic of nineteenth-century philanthropy and a departure from older forms of charity.[6] The essential role of philanthropy was to separate the deserving from the undeserving poor. In this way, the poor became a site

---

5   The notion of 'pobres verdaderos' and 'pobres fingidos' was already present in legislative texts of the sixteenth and seventeenth centuries. Similarly, Constancio Bernaldo de Quirós and José M. Llanas Aguilaneido (*La mala vida en Madrid* [Madrid, B. Rodríguez Serra, 1901], 323) refer to a book by a sixteenth-century Spanish doctor entitled 'Amparo de los legítimos pobres y reducción de los vagabundos'. Later, the reasoning of the Enlightenment brought with it more ordained and discriminatory charitable practices, the need to differentiate between the 'ociosos' and the 'pobres verdaderos' being thus reinforced. During this period economists generally insisted on the disastrous consequences of unthinking charity. Bernardo Ward declared categorically that 'la sopa de los conventos' was the main obstacle to Spain's process of industrialization; see, in this regard, Jacques Soubeyroux, 'Pauperismo y relaciones sociales en el Madrid del siglo XVIII', *Estudios de Historia Social*, 12–13 (1980), 161–65 in particular; and Pedro Trinidad Fernández, *La defensa de la sociedad: Cárcel y delincuencia en España (siglos XVIII–XX)* (Madrid, Alianza, 1991), especially 29–34. But it was in the nineteenth century that the exacerbation of the mendicity problem as a consequence of industrialization and urban growth accentuated the distinction between the deserving and the undeserving poor.

6   Jacques Donzelot, *The Policing of Families: Welfare versus the State* (London, Hutchinson, 1980), 64–70.

of power and an object of control for the bourgeoisie. Deciding which
poor were deserving of assistance was not, however, an easy task, as the
dividing line between the deserving and the undeserving was often
blurred and individuals over time might have easily shifted, in terms of
their character, from one category to another. Thus, although it was felt
that the deserving poor were more likely to conform to bourgeois
standards, and therefore to be reformed, there were also some attempts at
reaching and influencing the very lowest layers of the population,
precisely because of the difficulty in knowing which individuals could
be successfully reformed or, in other words, restored to the norm of
accepted behaviour through a moral regime imposed from above. This
desire to discriminate and categorize was in keeping with the social context of the second half of the nineteenth century, a time when the bourgeoisie sought to reinforce its power through the surveillance and control
of those social groups that did not comply with established social norms
and therefore represented a threat to the new order. As we shall see, the
arbitrariness and lack of logic in classifying the poor into categories is
highlighted by Galdós in the novels considered in this study.

Another important factor that differentiated new philanthropy from
old charity was that the new system was not restricted solely to the
distribution of material aid but also used moral advice and exhortation as
a major instrument of control. Thus philanthropy deployed, as Donzelot
suggests, new forms of power, these being 'effective advice rather than
humiliating charity, [and] preserving the norm rather than destructive
repression'.[7] The new system of philanthropy sought to convey an image
of benevolence and a more humane approach. Benevolence became a disguised or less obvious technique of exercising power, replacing repressive and authoritarian methods of control. Advice had to be given in a
subtle way, so as not to make recipients feel that they were obliged to
accept it, thereby avoiding feelings of resentment arising from the
philanthropist's interference. The relationship between giver and recipient
– between controller and controlled – had to be not one of dependence
but one of 'legitimate influence'.[8]

However, it is possible to argue that disguised, or subtle, control was
not always successful in that the working classes were not necessarily

---

7 Donzelot, *The Policing of Families*, 57.
8 Ibid., 64–65. Concepción Arenal was aware of the need of the philanthropist to
   legitimize her activities. In *El visitador del pobre* (1860) she emphasized that home
   visitors had to be tactful and diplomatic with the poor. She advised, for instance,
   that, 'Hemos de conducirnos de tal modo, que el pobre no diga: "*en todo se mete*";
   sino "*De todo se ocupa*"'. See Concepción Arenal, *Obras completas*, ed. Carmen Díaz
   Castañón (Madrid, Atlas [Biblioteca de Autores Españoles], 1993), I, 17.

duped by it. As Summers has noted, if the poor willingly allowed philanthropic visitors into their homes it was often 'in order to gain the benefits of patronage rather than to accept the dubious and somewhat double-edged "friendship" which was on offer'.[9] The main aim of late-nineteenth-century philanthropy was to reform and improve the character and habits of the poor and, from this perspective, philanthropy necessarily implied a certain degree of interference, since the notion of improving character 'presupposed an agreed moral code'.[10] Because of the difficulty in maintaining a balance between benevolence and authoritarianism, between the humanitarian and disciplinary approaches, it would be difficult to subscribe to the simplistic idea of philanthropy as the successful imposition of control.

The concern of philanthropists to change or improve character has often been criticized as an attitude to poverty that denies social causes, stressing instead the importance of weak character and the moral failings of the individual as the main determinants of destitution. Such an attitude ignores the need for structural reform and simply insists on the need to indoctrinate the poor. In Spain, the approach to poverty was similar to that seen elsewhere. However, Spanish philanthropy towards the end of the century has to be seen in the context of the Catholic revival of the 1870s, which emerged as a conservative reaction to the 1868 Revolution and the liberal Constitution of 1869. This made the moralizing dimensions of Spanish philanthropy especially intense.[11] Most moral and social commentators of the period – among them Concepción Arenal, a leading advocate of nineteenth-century philanthropy – believed that philanthropy could serve, through moral and religious indoctrination, as an instrument for social stability.[12] Religious indoctrination in this respect manifested itself in a series of philanthropic societies (or 'juntas de señoras') run by upper-class women – what Carr calls 'the elegant sanctimonious swarm of aristocratic ladies'[13] – often mocked by Galdós in his fictional works.

9 Anne Summers, 'A Home from Home – Women's Philanthropic Work in the Nineteenth Century', in Sandra Burman (ed.), *Fit Work for Women* (London, Croom Helm, 1979), 45–46.

10 Stefan Collini, 'The Idea of "Character" in Victorian Political Thought', *Transactions of the Royal Historical Society*, 35 (1985), quoted by Jane Lewis, 'Women and Late-Nineteenth-Century Social Work', in Carol Smart (ed.), *Regulating Womanhood: Historical Essays on Marriage, Motherhood and Sexuality* (London, Routledge, 1992), 83.

11 This is in keeping with Raymond Carr's general observation that 'every tension in Spanish society was refracted through the prism of the religious issue', *Modern Spain: 1875–1980* (Oxford, Oxford University Press, 1980), 40.

12 As discussed by Shubert in *A Social History of Modern Spain*, 54.

13 Carr, *Modern Spain: 1875–1980*, 40.

Arenal's approach to poverty, although more humane, differed little from contemporary attitudes to poverty elsewhere. In *Cartas a un obrero* (written in the 1870s) she stressed the importance of elevating the moral and intellectual standards of the working classes in order that their social and economic standards could also be improved.[14] Similarly, in *El pauperismo* (1897), she stated that 'la situación económica de los miserables es consecuencia de su estado moral e intelectual', and that 'la raíz primera y más profunda de la miseria física es espiritual'.[15] Although this approach was rather limited, in the sense that it failed to take into account the wider socio-economic dimensions of poverty, concentrating as it did only on the lack of morality and religious feelings of the working classes, it has to be given some credit for dismissing the proposition that the poor were *intrinsically* immoral, innate moral corruption being seen as the root cause of destitution. However, moral indoctrination can be resisted. The view of poverty that fed on the notion that lack of morals was at the root of destitution thus allowed for the possibility that some of the poor were not amenable to moral reform or did not want to improve, and must therefore be intrinsically corrupt, innately immoral and unredeemable.

This ambiguous bourgeois attitude to the poor can be detected throughout 'Una visita al Cuarto Estado'. The most obvious example is seen in José Izquierdo's relationship with the philanthropist Guillermina. To Guillermina, the working-class drinker Izquierdo represents the idleness and unwillingness to work that tended to be associated with the undeserving poor. Guillermina comments, in her usual recriminatory manner, that Izquierdo 'es hombre de poca disposición: no sabe nada, no trabaja' (I, 371). At a time when the image of poverty had begun to change, work was increasingly considered to be of paramount value, since idleness had become linked with immorality. Like Arenal, Guillermina seems to recognize the importance of certain external factors, such as lack of education, as determinants of the degradation of the poor: '¿qué destino le van a dar a un hombre que firma con una cruz?' (I, 372), she says to Izquierdo. Earlier in the novel she had similarly put the blame for poverty on a lack of education (which for her usually meant *religious* education). As she observes, 'La falta de educación es para el pobre una desventura mayor que la pobreza. Luego la propia miseria les ataca el corazón a muchos y se los corrompe' (I, 272). Poverty is the cause not only of moral but also of mental deterioration. When Guillermina

14 Concepción Arenal, *Obras completas*, II, 15–213. Although *Cartas a un obrero* was written in the early 1870s, it was not published until 1880.
15 Quoted by Díaz Castañón in her introduction to Arenal, *Obras completas*, I, lxv.

rebukes Izquierdo for the fantasies he has invented about his own past, she comments, 'Veo que entre usted y don José Ido, otro que tal, podrán inventar lindas novelas. ¡Ah! la miseria, el mal comer, ¡cómo hacen desvariar estos pobres cerebros! ...' (I, 373).

However, in spite of these declarations, Guillermina's lack of recognition of the existence of wider economic and structural factors of poverty renders her vision, like Arenal's, very narrow in scope.[16] As mentioned above, this restrictive approach to the causes of poverty could easily lead to the assumption that the corruption of the poor results from their intrinsic immoral nature. Thus, Guillermina seems to regard Izquierdo's defects as emanating from innate moral weaknesses, rather than seeing him – at least partially – as a victim of misfortunes beyond his control. It has to be noted, in this regard, that Izquierdo is a drinker, the causes of drunkenness often being ascribed during this period to the perceived immorality and dissolution of the poor, rather than to environmental and structural factors. Excessive drinking came to be regarded as a main cause of poverty and other social problems related to it, including unemployment, absenteeism from work, subversion, criminality and idleness (as we will see in Chapter 3). Guillermina sees Izquierdo as entirely responsible for his own situation. Ignoring the socio-economic conditions that forced many unskilled workers into unemployment or begging, she accuses him of being an idler and not having done a decent job in his life: 'Usted se ha pasado la vida luchando por el pienso y no sabiendo nunca vencer. No ha tenido arreglo...' (I, 371), she scolds him.

Guillermina's words echo the individualism of a period in which competition and market economics had led to the extolling of personal success and, equally, to the belief that personal failure resulted from individual vices or defects. This value system was in keeping with contemporary social Darwinist thought, which transferred the struggle for life of the species in their physical environment to the fight for survival among humans in their social environment. Although Guillermina shows a certain degree of pity for Izquierdo's struggle, for her Izquierdo represents the undeserving poor, unwilling to seek self-improvement. Despite the fact that some of Guillermina's statements place part of the blame for the degradation of the poor on their lack of education, the reader is left with the

16 It needs to be noted, however, that Arenal's approach to philanthropy was more humane than that shown by Guillermina in this episode, particularly in her dealings with Izquierdo. In *El visitador del pobre* she advises home visitors to be humble and insists that they should never humiliate the poor or make them feel inferior. As she writes, 'Si hemos de rehabilitar a un hombre a los ojos del mundo, es preciso rehabilitarle antes a sus propios ojos; porque no puede inspirar aprecio si antes no se aprecia él mismo', *Obras completas*, I, 43–44.

impression that to her, Izquierdo's idleness and his failure in life are a function of his immoral nature, too deeply rooted in him to be removed, as her recrimination, 'no ha tenido arreglo', suggests. The bourgeoisie was aware of the existence of a residual element among the working classes: individuals who were beyond reform, in the sense that they rejected basic values of morality and improvement. In Guillermina's eyes, Izquierdo appears to occupy this residual level. She draws the line between the deserving and the undeserving poor when, to Izquierdo's claim that '[l]a probeza no es deshonra', she retorts, 'No lo es, cierto, por sí; pero tampoco es honra, ¿estamos? Conozco pobres muy honrados; pero también los hay que son buenos pájaros' (I, 369). She places Izquierdo in the undeserving – and hence, unreformable – category when, to his claim of being 'todo lo decente', she replies: '[t]odos nos llamamos personas decentes; pero facilillo es probarlo' (I, 369). For the bourgeoisie, Izquierdo is basically an unreformable 'bruto' who refuses to follow a civilized, ordered and moral life.

In *Fortunata y Jacinta* working-class people are often described by bourgeois characters, and the bourgeois narrator himself, as brutal and savage, that is, lacking the benefits of civilization. In 'Una visita al Cuarto Estado' they are frequently associated with filth, rubbish and foul odours, an association related to nineteenth-century beliefs about disease and sanitation.[17] In the late nineteenth century, the principle of the germ transmission of disease had yet to be fully established. Many diseases were still thought to be caused by the polluting 'effluvia' or 'miasma' emanating from decomposing organic refuse, from stagnant water and from damp and filth – problems often arising from dilapidated and over-crowded dwellings. This miasmatic theory of disease coexisted with the still rudimentary germ theory until the end of the century, when the latter was proved and no longer seriously contested in the wake of Pasteur's discoveries. Since foul emanations often occurred in environmental conditions – notably in working-class areas – which favoured the transmission of infection and the spread of epidemics, the pre-Pasteurian correlation between foul odours and disease was established on the grounds of simple observation, without scientific rigour.[18]

17 In connection with this, see Alain Corbin, *The Foul and the Fragrant: Odor and the French Social Imagination* (Leamington Spa, Berg Publishers, 1986).

18 See G. Melvyn Howe, *Man, Environment and Disease in Britain: A Medical Geography of Britain through the Ages* (Newton Abbot, David & Charles, 1992), 186; and Perry Williams, 'The Laws of Health: Women, Medicine and Sanitary Reform, 1850–1890', in Marina Benjamin (ed.), *Science and Sensibility: Gender and Scientific Enquiry 1780–1945* (Oxford, Basil Blackwell, 1991), 69–70. For a detailed account of the origins of the miasmatic theory of disease, see Carlo Cipolla, *Miasmas and Disease: Public Health and the Environment in the Pre-Industrial Age* (New Haven, CT, Yale Univer-

For much of the nineteenth century in Europe, miasmatic theory helped generate anxieties concerning a submerged and morally unreachable element of the population. Foul smells and their rapid spread in the atmosphere were a vivid symbolic manifestation of the immorality of the working classes and, similarly, of the risks of immorality spreading through the population. For example, in the *Report on the Sanitary Condition of the Labouring Population of Great Britain* (1842), whose main author was the public health reformer and proponent of the theory of utilitarianism, Edwin Chadwick, poisonous atmosphere was identified as the source of the physical, moral and mental deterioration of the poor.[19] The 'labouring population' of the title, or the 'poorer classes of the population', as they are described in its opening sentence, are identified by the report as being synonymous with the insanitary, filthy conditions in which they live, and with moral degradation also. Insanitary areas inhabited by the poorest classes were referred to as an 'unknown country' (*terra incognita*), and their inhabitants as 'foreigners', 'animals' and 'savages'.[20] Himmelfarb has highlighted the striking similarity between Chadwick's *Report* and the study undertaken by the mid-century English sociologist Henry Mayhew, *London Labour and the London Poor* (1851–62).[21] The Mayhewian poor were again described as living under the worst sanitary conditions; moreover, the poor themselves (those he describes are mostly scavengers) were depicted as being little different from the filth in which they lived. Words like 'residuum', 'refuse' and 'offal' were used by Mayhew to describe both the physical and moral condition of the poor.

'Una visita al Cuarto Estado' is particularly relevant from the point of view of these associations.[22] It is interesting to note that Galdós describes

---

sity Press, 1992). The issue of miasmas and their pernicious effects was often discussed by Spanish public health experts of the period. Juan Giné y Partagás, for instance, devotes a whole chapter to it; see his *Curso elemental de higiene privada y pública* (Barcelona, Imprenta de Narciso Ramírez y Cñía, 1872), II, 47–59.

19 As observed by Gertrude Himmelfarb, *The Idea of Poverty: England in the Early Industrial Age* (London, Faber & Faber, 1984), 357.

20 The metaphor of the 'unknown country' was generated by the fact that the abysmal living conditions of slum dwellers were completely unknown to the general public. For a discussion of the notion of the 'unknown country', see Christian Topalov, 'The City as *Terra Incognita*: Charles Booth's Poverty Survey and the People of London, 1886–1891', *Planning Perspectives: An International Journal of History, Planning and the Environment*, 8 (1993), 395–425.

21 Himmelfarb, *The Idea of Poverty*, 358.

22 Jo Labanyi ('The Raw, the Cooked and the Indigestible in Galdós's *Fortunata y Jacinta*', *Romance Studies*, 13 [1988], 55–66, 61–62 in particular) has noted the associations established in the novel between savagery, rubbish and putrefaction on the one hand, and the working classes on the other.

the slum area and, in particular, the tenement building, mainly through the eyes of the wealthy bourgeois character Jacinta. Jacinta is what Genette calls a 'focal character', the character from whose perspective the reader is made to view events, and through whom the author can regulate the information given.[23] What Jacinta sees is a panorama of filth that serves as a metaphor for poverty and its accompanying moral corruption. In her visit to the 'cuarto estado', one of the first things that catches Jacinta's attention is the scene where the children are playing with mud.[24] One of the children is making an oven out of rubble. When the two women move from the first 'patio' into the second, they also move into a different social layer. This second 'patio' represents the lower layers of the working classes. Here, the associations between rubbish, dirt and poverty become more disturbing. In this second 'patio': 'el aire [era] más viciado [y] el vaho que salía por puertas y ventanas más espeso y repugnante' (I, 323). Jacinta is disgusted by the 'olor nauseabundo' coming from the offal ('cueros, tripas u otros despojos') that had been hung up to dry (I, 323). When Guillermina and Jacinta are waiting for Izquierdo in Ido's house, it is also Jacinta who notices hanging from the ceiling 'el horrible tinglado [...] [de] cueros puestos a secar' (I, 331). The working classes are not just linked with dirt and rubbish, as before, but also with foul odours and the offal ('despojos') from which those odours emanate.

A related association at the time was that established between the working classes on the one hand, and savagery and lack of civilization on the other – in keeping with contemporary anthropological discourses that identified the poorer classes within the civilized world with non-European, 'uncivilized' races.[25] On their way to Ido's home, Guillermina and Jacinta are intercepted by a bunch of filthy-looking children (they have covered their faces and hands in ink so that they look like blacks) described by the narrator as 'una manada de salvajes' who 'no parecían pertenecer a la raza humana' (I, 324).[26] Even Guillermina, who has been

23 See Gerard Genette, *Narrative Discourse* (Oxford, Basil Blackwell, 1980), 185–94.

24 Corbin (*The Foul and the Fragrant*, 22–26) comments on the anxieties generated by mud (and the vapours emanating from it) that survived into the mid-nineteenth century. As he writes, 'The mud of Paris formed a complex mixture of sand, that had infiltrated between the paving stones, vile-smelling rubbish, stagnant water, and dung; carriage wheels kneaded it, spread it, spattered walls and passerby'. Stagnant water and organic waste were regarded as a main source of miasmas.

25 See, for instance, José Harris, 'Between Civic Virtue and Social Darwinism: The Concept of the Residuum', in David Englander and Rosemary O'Day (eds), *Retrieved Riches: Social Investigation in Britain* (Aldershot, Scolar Press, 1995), 67–68.

26 In connection with these images, Cynthia Eagle Russet (*Sexual Science: The Victorian Construction of Womanhood* [Cambridge, MA, Harvard University Press, 1989]) has noted that in the nineteenth century, children (and also women), like the poor, were

used to working among the poor, is repelled by the view and tells them to keep their distance. The association of the poor with savagery is underlined in this scene by Guillermina, who refers to the children as 'caníbales' (I, 324).

When Jacinta first meets Pitusín he is also covered in ink (I, 329). In *Fortunata y Jacinta* Pitusín often appears in connection with savagery, animality and rubbish. Also, the working-class drinker Izquierdo is seen by Jacinta and her maid and, at times, by the narrator, as a savage and a 'bestia'. Similarly, as will be discussed in Chapter 3, he is perceived as politically dangerous. This perception derives from the connection established by contemporaries between drunkenness and political subversion – the image of the violent and irrational drunken working-class male being easily linked with the rioting and the irrational and uncivilized uprisings of the working classes. The threat posed by working-class drinking is similarly reflected in Guillermina's comment on the large number of taverns she sees on her way to the tenement building: '¡Cuánta perdición! una puerta sí y otra no, taberna. De aquí salen todos los crímenes' (I, 318). Guillermina is here echoing contemporary views, which associated drinking with criminality and disorder. In the same passage, the narrator points to the adverse effect that the sight of so many taverns has on the upper-middle-class Jacinta ('Jacinta se asustaba de ver tantas tabernas' [I, 318]).

As argued above, the narrator makes the reader see the 'cuarto estado' mainly through the eyes of Jacinta. It could be said that the 'cuarto estado' represents for Jacinta the 'unknown country' to which reformers and the middle classes often referred. The narrator also notes the ignorance in which Jacinta had been living until that moment: 'En el seno de la prosperidad en que ella vivía, no pudo darse nunca cuenta de lo grande que es el imperio de la pobreza' (I, 363). Jacinta is undertaking her surveillance from a middle-class, and thus biased, standpoint. Poverty is being observed by an outsider, by someone who is a complete foreigner to the 'cuarto estado', and to whom the 'cuarto estado' appears completely foreign. This seems to be the reason why Galdós has chosen to describe the 'cuarto estado' though Jacinta's perspective rather than Guillermina's. By portraying Jacinta's view of poverty as limited, Galdós disengages himself from the associations – often endorsed by the bourgeois narrator – that arise from her surveillance of poverty, thereby avoiding complicity with contemporary ideas linking the poor with filth and immorality. Hence, in spite of the frequent associations between the

---

seen as being at a lower stage of human development, as was the case with the so-called inferior races.

inhabitants of the tenement building and the 'moral residuum', these associations are presented by the author as biased and unreliable.

It is noteworthy that in a recent study of the galley version of this episode, Linda M. Willem has observed that Jacinta's view of the slum area and its inhabitants is presented in a more threatening light than in the published version, in which Jacinta's exaggerated fears about her alien surroundings are diluted. In the galley version Jacinta imagines the drinking poor coming out of the taverns covered in blood and brandishing knives (an image prompted in her mind by Guillermina's association of drinking with criminality); similarly, she perceives the children playing in the patio as wild and dangerous, feeling hounded by them. As Willem notes, through the amendments to the galley version, Galdós played down the threat represented by the lowest layers of the urban poor.[27]

In 'Una visita al Cuarto Estado' Galdós links the brutal and savage aspects of poverty to the sanitary conditions of the working classes and broader socio-economic factors beyond the control of the individual (such as unemployment, low wages, family size, sickness and work accidents), rather than with their innate moral degradation. An obvious example of this is the scene in which Jacinta is waiting for Guillermina in the street and she is surrounded by a group of working-class women who tell her about their misfortunes:

> Esta tenía a sus dos niños descalcitos; la otra no los tenía descalzos ni calzados, porque se le morían todos [...] La de más allá tenía cinco hijos y vísperas,[28] de lo que daba fe el promontorio que le alzaba las faldas media vara del suelo. No podía ir en tal estado a la Fábrica de Tabacos, por lo cual estaba pasando la familia una *crujida* buena. El pariente de estotra no trabajaba, porque se había caído de un andamio[29] y hacía tres meses que estaba en el catre con un tolondrón en el pecho y muchos dolores, echando sangre por la boca. (I, 362–63)

27 Linda M. Willem, 'Jacinta's "visita al cuarto estado": The Galley Version', *Anales Galdosianos*, XXXI/XXXII (1996/1997), 97–103.

28 This reflects nineteenth-century anxieties about demography (the working classes can breed whereas Jacinta cannot), as expressed by the economist Thomas Malthus, who influenced Charles Darwin's theory of the survival of the fittest. Demographic concerns were thus linked to the racial question: the notion that the poor were an inferior race.

29 The issue of invalidity or death due to falls from unsafe scaffolding, which affected a great number of building workers during the late nineteenth century, is brought up again and again in the pages of the journal *La Voz de la Caridad* (1870–83), whose editor and main contributor was Concepción Arenal. There are also frequent references in this journal to the uncertain future of those affected by accidents and their families. The problem of the lack of safety of scaffolding and the financial

As far as the specific sanitary and environmental aspects are concerned, in the Spain of the Restoration, unlike in other European countries, little was done to improve the well-being of the working classes. The state tended to delegate social reform initiatives to private charities. For example, there were several projects in the late nineteenth century for building 'barrios obreros' in an attempt to find a solution to both the sanitary and the overall 'social question'.[30] The most important and effective organization in this respect was 'La Constructora Benéfica', created in 1875.[31] However, apart from the few districts built by this organization, most projects never became a reality or were hampered by speculative interests. The problem of workers' housing still remained. Charitable activity seems to have concentrated on building institutions (soup kitchens being a familiar example) for the poor, rather than on improving the workers' built environment. As Díez de Baldeón observes,

> El espíritu de auténtica reforma social fue desplazado o bien por el nihilismo más absoluto o por un paternalismo filantrópico. En la Restauración la Beneficencia se caracterizó por la fundación de asilos, hospicios, albergues, casas de dormir y comedores para los menesterosos. La 'sopa boba' se convirtió en la panacea milagrosa, en la componenda alicorta y reaccionaria con la que la clase dirigente tranquilizó sus conciencias. Pero el problema seguía latente. Las pésimas condiciones de habitabilidad de los sótanos, buhardillas, cuartos interiores y corralas fueron una realidad de la que muy pocos trabajadores pudieron sustraerse.[32]

The description given by Galdós of the appalling state of the interiors and exteriors of the tenements, and of the foul odours coming from them,

---

hardships faced by work invalids is also voiced by both workers and social commentators reporting to the Comisión de Reformas Sociales, the first official institution, created in 1883, for investigating and seeking solutions to the 'social question'. For an analysis of the origins, aims and achievements of the Comisión, which are further discussed in later chapters, see María Dolores de la Calle, *La Comisión de Reformas Sociales 1883–1903: Política social y conflicto de intereses en la España de la Restauración* (Madrid, Ministerio de Trabajo y Seguridad Social, 1989).

30 Clementina Díez de Baldeón, 'Barrios obreros en el Madrid del siglo XIX: ¿Solución o amenaza para el orden burgués?', in Luis E. Otero Carvajal and Angel Bahamonde Magro (eds), *Madrid en la sociedad del siglo XIX* (Madrid, Comunidad de Madrid, Consejería de Cultura, 1986), I, 118–34.

31 See, in this respect, Sonsoles Cabeza Sánchez-Albornoz, 'La Constructora Benéfica 1875–1904', in Otero Carvajal and Bahamonde Magro (eds), *Madrid en la sociedad del siglo XIX*, I, 136–58. The insanitary living conditions of the working classes was an issue often raised by workers giving evidence to the Comisión de Reformas Sociales. In *La Voz de la Caridad* there are numerous allusions to the achievements of La Constructora Benéfica during the 1870s and early 1880s.

32 Díez de Baldeón, 'Barrios obreros en el Madrid del siglo XIX', 134.

illustrates these 'pésimas condiciones de habitabilidad' of working-class dwellings. Similarly, the absence in the novel of charitable efforts directed towards solving either sanitary or larger environmental problems is a reflection of the socio-economic situation of the Restoration. Despite Guillermina's claim that 'la miseria' is the cause of the corruption of the poor, and despite the frequent associations between filth, immorality and poverty, she makes no suggestion that action needs to be taken with regard to sanitation. Guillermina seems to concentrate her philanthropic efforts on the distribution of material aid – mainly clothes and medicines – among the inhabitants of the 'cuarto estado', and on the building and mainten-ance of institutions for orphans and 'fallen women'. She is not seen giving advice about sanitary matters – such as cleanliness or ventilation – to the residents of the tenement building, despite the unhygienic conditions in which they live. A clear example of her lack of concern for workers' hous-ing conditions appears towards the end of the novel. When Fortunata, after her definite separation from Maxi, moves back to her aunt's house, the filth is invading everything, and she finds that there is not enough water to clean the house (II, 397–98).[33] The irony here is that she learns, through Estupiñá, that, after the death of Moreno Isla, Guillermina had inherited the property. However, she has done nothing to improve the insanitary conditions of the house. A further irony is that she has mort-gaged this house (and another that she has inherited) in order to complete her orphanage. Fortunata thus has to live in a 'basurero', as she describes the house, for the sake of the orphanage being finished (II, 406–07).

Guillermina's philanthropic efforts at home assistance are always subordinated to her concern for building institutions where the poor can be educated into the values of the Christian religion. Her persistence in completing the orphanage is often shown by Galdós in a negative light. Although Guillermina is initially described by the narrator as a woman of 'perseverancia grandiosa' (I, 264), this is discredited by the way she is depicted later in the novel.[34] The building of the orphanage appears, on

33 Shortage of water was another aspect of this lack of sanitation. In 'Una visita al Cuarto Estado', when Jacinta urges the neighbours to get some water in order to wash 'el Pitusín', the narrator points out that, 'unas no tenían agua y otras no querían gastarla en tal objeto' (I, 330).

34 The genuineness of Guillermina's charity has been questioned by several critics. See, for instance, J. L. Brooks, 'The Character of Guillermina Pacheco in Galdós' Novel *Fortunata y Jacinta'*, *Bulletin of Hispanic Studies*, XXXVIII (1961), 86–94; Ricardo Gullón, *Técnicas de Galdós* (Madrid, Taurus, 1980), 162–64; Denah Lida, 'Galdós y sus santas modernas', *Anales Galdosianos*, X (1975), 19–31; and John H. Sinnigen, 'Individuo, clase y sociedad en *Fortunata y Jacinta'*, in Germán Gullón (ed.), *Fortun-ata y Jacinta* (Madrid, Taurus, 1986), 78–79.

many occasions, as a calculating enterprise, or as one critic puts it, 'una especie de negocio de intercambio'.[35] Thus, when practising charity, Guillermina is usually seen trying to make a profit for her 'obra', often at the expense of the poor themselves.[36] Guillermina also tries to make a profit for her orphanage out of the purchase of 'el Pitusín'.[37] This episode highlights her self-interested motives; however, she thinks that she is performing 'dos obras de caridad' (I, 368–69), since she is not only going to put 'el Pitusín' in better hands, but will also try to help Izquierdo if he is not 'muy exigente' (I, 369). Guillermina's (and Jacinta's) self-interest and selfishness are emphasized by Izquierdo's relatively more ethical attitude. If it is true that he lied about the real parents of 'el Pitusín', his intention was to get a good job out of it, rather than to sell the child off. '[C]olóqueme a mí, y yo lo criaré', he tells Jacinta (I, 358), but Jacinta and Guillermina are not interested in this sort of deal. It is interesting here that, by suggesting that he is going to bring up 'el Pitusín' and at the same time become the breadwinner, Izquierdo subverts late-nineteenth-century gender roles. If Guillermina's intentions are clear to Izquierdo – '¿Cree que yo me vendo?' (I, 370), he replies to her suggestion of exchanging the child for money – she insists that 'esto no es compra, sino socorro' (I, 370). If it is true that in the end Guillermina finds Izquierdo a job posing as a model for a portrait painter, she does it as part of the deal. She is not shown trying to reform Izquierdo through work since, ironically, being a painter's model does not involve any demanding physical labour.

Guillermina's attitude to Izquierdo, and to other inhabitants of the 'cuarto estado', is authoritarian, paternalistic and elitist. In this interview

---

35 Lida, 'Galdós y sus santas modernas', 25.
36 Another obvious example of this, as critics have observed, is the episode when she gets Ido to carry seventy bricks from the factory to the orphanage on foot, promising him 'un sombrero casi nuevo' if he carries out the errand correctly. It is interesting to note here, as Lida has ('Galdós y sus santas modernas', 29–30), that this condition does not appear in the manuscript version of the novel. Galdós's addition thus emphasizes Guillermina's calculating and harsh outlook. The 'material aid' that she promises Ido is here dependent on his correct fulfilment of the mission entrusted to him. It could also be argued that the humorous way in which Galdós depicts the episode offers a counterpoint to Guillermina's belief in her elevated charitable work. When she tells Ido that he has to carry the bricks to her 'obra', Ido seems to be taken aback, not knowing what 'obra' Guillermina is talking about. Guillermina then tells him, in a tone of annoyed disbelief, that she is talking about her orphanage, to which Ido replies, '¡Ah! Perdone la señora… cuando oí la obra, creí al pronto que era una obra literaria' (I, 332).
37 Guillermina makes a profit of 3,500 reales for the purchase of Pitusín, as she manages to buy him off Izquierdo for 6,500 reales, rather than the 10,000 reales that Jacinta was willing to pay. As previously arranged with Jacinta, she keeps the difference, which she will put towards the building of the orphanage.

it becomes evident that there exists a relationship of superiority between the philanthropist and the poor. Izquierdo realizes that Guillermina is a powerful rival: 'Desde que se cruzaron las primeras palabras de aquella conferencia [...] cayó Izquierdo en la cuenta de que tenía que habérselas con un diplomático mucho más fuerte que él' (I, 368). The hierarchy established between the philanthropist and the poor becomes obvious from the outset. Rather than serve as an instrument of control, this hierarchy can work in the opposite direction, provoking a hostile reaction from the poor. Izquierdo is made to feel inferior by Guillermina, who degrades and belittles him. This awareness makes him feel awkward and, at times, hostile towards her. Izquierdo's attitude is, arguably, typical of the suspicion and dislike with which some members of the working class regarded the visiting philanthropist: 'La tal doña Guillermina, con toda su opinión de santa y su carita de Pascua, se le atravesaba' (I, 368). He is not very keen on receiving her visit, but if he does it is because he thinks that he can profit from it. Thus, although Izquierdo '[y]a estaba seguro de que [Guillermina] le volvería tarumba con sus *tiologías*' (I, 368), he accepts her visit because he knows that he can deflect the moralizing aim and obtain a tangible benefit instead. The humorous use of 'tiologías' (which suggests a hybrid mix of 'teologías' and 'tías') in this quotation suggests that Galdós is poking fun at Guillermina's indoctrinating mission. Clearly philanthropy, largely because of its authoritarian and disciplinary dimensions, was not necessarily an effective instrument of control.

Guillermina's interview with Izquierdo reveals the shortcomings of her philanthropic mission. Her moralizing speech to him is full of ironic comments and reproaches. Similarly, the piece of advice she gives him before leaving his house is characteristic of what she believes to be the right way of dealing with the less deserving poor: 'El consejo allá va. Tú no vales absolutamente para nada. No sabes ningún oficio, ni siquiera el de peón, porque eres haragán y no te gusta cargar pesos. No sirves ni para barrendero de las calles' (I, 376). Guillermina is never seen giving much moral support or constructive moral guidance to the poor. When she advises Ido and his wife that they should send their children to school, she does it in an authoritarian and reproachful tone: 'Pues lo primero que tienen ustedes que hacer [...] es poner en una escuela a esos dos tagarotes y a la berganta de su niña pequeña' (I, 328).[38]

The relationship between Guillermina and Severiana, although not made explicit, is suggested to be very different from the other less respect-

---

38 School, like work, was regarded as a weapon against idleness and the social evils attached to it. Concepción Arenal expresses this view in *El visitador del pobre*, in her *Obras Completas*, I, 52.

able poor.[39] Severiana stands at the opposite pole to the squalor and filth associated with the inhabitants of the 'cuarto estado'. Severiana and her family represent the upper layers of the working classes. They enshrine the values of respectability, order and cleanliness. Philanthropy has been viewed by Marxist historians as an imposition of values on the lower orders by a bourgeois class seeking to confirm its status and power. Contrary to this view, Prochaska, along with other historians, has argued that, although it is true that values can be imposed on the poor from above, it is also true that the desire for respectability and self-reliance occurs naturally in many people, independent of their social station.[40] Severiana's family epitomize this desire for self-improvement, and therefore it is not surprising that they are favoured by Guillermina and Jacinta, representatives of the bourgeoisie. Severiana is portrayed as thrifty and clean, virtues that were described in contemporary discourses on hygiene as desirable in the deserving poor generally, and in the deserving working-class female in particular. Severiana's house is depicted as the height of cleanliness and tidiness. Similarly, her husband is portrayed as an honest, sober and hard-working man. Severiana also displays her respectability as a woman by talking about her sister Mauricia as bad and disrespectful: 'pero si es muy mala…, señora, muy mala' (I, 365), she tells Jacinta.

If Severiana, unlike Izquierdo, represents for the bourgeoisie the highly attractive image of the deserving poor trying to improve itself and, therefore, worthy of assistance, in her turn she accepts their interference because she is aware of the favours that she can exploit from it. Thus, when she realizes that Jacinta is taking an interest in Adoración, the narrator observes that Severiana 'estimó en lo que valían las bondades de la dama para con la pequeña', inviting her into her house and offering her the best chair to sit on (I, 365). The narrator emphasizes Severiana's self-interested motives when, in a later visit that Jacinta pays to her 'protegida' Adoración, he points out that Severiana spoke to Jacinta 'con esa adulación de los humildes muy favorecidos y que aún quieren serlo más' (II, 66–67). Severiana's respectability is mirrored by Adoración's good manners and cleanliness. Adoración is proud to let Jacinta know that she has not been playing in the mud like the other children. She is shown taking pride in her cleanliness in the same way as Severiana. The

---

39 For instance, one of the neighbours of the tenement building tells Jacinta that 'la señorita Guillermina la quiere mucho [a Severiana]…' (I, 364).

40 Frank Prochaska, *The Voluntary Impulse: Philanthropy in Modern Britain* (London, Faber & Faber, 1988), 27; and F. M. L. Thompson, 'Social Control in Victorian Britain', *Economic History Review*, XXXIV (May 1981), 189–208.

narrator observes the impact that Adoración has on Jacinta and her maid:

> Jacinta y Rafaela estaban embelesadas. No habían visto una niña tan bonita, tan modosa y que se metiera por los ojos como aquella. Daba gusto ver la limpieza de su ropa. La falda la tenía remendada, pero aseadísima; los zapatos eran viejos, pero bien defendidos, y el delantal una obra maestra de pulcritud. (I, 364)

The text suggests that Adoración, who was brought up in her first years by Mauricia and who learnt bad habits from her and her friends, is taken away from her mother by an upper class that had established marriage and the family as a social norm. After Mauricia's 'encierro' in Las Micaelas, her 'deserving' sister, Severiana, is conveniently left in charge of Adoración's upbringing, a task that she has undertaken willingly, thereby assuming the elevating role of motherhood that her disrespectful sister is considered unable to fulfil (the integrity of the family, as the next chapter will show, was a chief concern of nineteenth-century bourgeois philanthropy, since it was believed to have a considerable effect on the formation of good or bad habits).

In the remaining chapters we shall see how Galdós continues to distance himself from the associations drawn by his bourgeois characters and, often, by the bourgeois narrator, between the deviant poor (whether prostitutes, alcoholics, beggars or vagrants) on the one hand, and immorality and filth on the other, thereby undermining the bourgeois attempt at categorizing the poor according to socio-moral criteria.

Chapter 2

The Control of Prostitution

This chapter analyses how attitudes towards prostitution, and the images of filth that were generated around it particularly in the last third of the century, are dramatized in *Fortunata y Jacinta* and, to an extent, in *Nazarín*. Galdós's reproduction of contemporary perceptions of prostitution and filth is examined in the context of the 'regulatory' cultural debates on public health, class and gender that emerged in Restoration Spain, as elsewhere at the time. Prostitution was perceived, during this period, as a threat to public health. In public health discourses, prostitutes became associated with filth and decomposing organic waste. Like dirt and refuse they were also seen as a source of polluting miasmas: as a source of physical and moral disease. Furthermore, the discourse on domesticity constructed marriage and the family as the norm of behaviour, thereby presenting the figure of the prostitute as abnormal or deviant and, therefore, in need of reform. Given this threat, the need arose to keep prostitution under constant surveillance, to control and regulate it through the deployment of a series of disciplinary strategies.

Tsuchiya has observed the 'panoptic' strategies developed in *Fortunata y Jacinta*.[1] I hope to build on her analysis of notions of control and resistance in the novel with reference to contemporary debates on domesticity and femininity by setting my discussion within a wider, alternative theoretical framework. This will also allow me to add to Jagoe's detailed examination of Fortunata's challenge to the bourgeois ideology of domesticity, middle-class morality and gender roles, as well as her subversion of the idea of true womanhood.[2] In order to appreciate how control works in the novel and, similarly, where Galdós stands in relation to bourgeois control, it is necessary to start by analysing contemporary discourses on class, gender and public hygiene and coverage of ideas on

1 Akiko Tsuchiya, '"Las Micaelas por fuera y por dentro": Discipline and Resistance in *Fortunata y Jacinta*', in Linda M. Willem (ed.), *A Sesquicentennial Tribute to Galdós 1843–1993* (Newark, DE, Juan de la Cuesta Hispanic Monographs, 1993), 56–71.

2 Catherine Jagoe, *Ambiguous Angels: Gender in the Novels of Galdós* (Berkeley and Los Angeles, University of California Press, 1994), 102–19, and 'The Subversive Angel in *Fortunata y Jacinta*', *Anales Galdosianos*, XXIV (1989), 79–91.

social regulation, as well as more recent discussions on discipline and control.

Regulating Deviant Femininity: The Role of Philanthropy

In his *History of Sexuality* Foucault examines the proliferation, during the nineteenth century, of a series of discourses on sexuality. In that period sexuality became a major social issue and source of knowledge for the human sciences – medicine, psychiatry, criminal justice – each of which produced its own discourse on sexuality and its own definition of 'acceptable' and 'deviant' sexual behaviour. Foucault argues that these scientific discourses created new sites of power – which, in turn, generated new forms of knowledge.[3]

The definition and categorization of respectable and non-respectable forms of femininity have to be seen within the wider process of the formation of the ideology of domesticity, resulting from the division of social space into two differentiated spheres – the private and the public. As Aldaraca and Jagoe have shown, this took place in Spain from the mid-nineteenth century and especially after the 1868 Revolution.[4] The separation of work and home led to the emergence of a new system of gender relations, in which the home was defined as an exclusively feminine domain. Women became, according to the new mentality of the period, the moral guardians of the sanctuary of the home. The home was often described as a haven, a shelter where men could find psychological and spiritual comfort in response to the pressures of the external world – a corrupted world dominated by speculation, competitiveness and immorality. Woman's moral and sexual purity guaranteed the purity of the domestic sphere. In turn, the safe domestic environment protected women's purity against the pollution of the public sphere.

The new model of the domestic woman found expression in the concept of the 'ángel del hogar', an ideal which represented a key aspect of nineteenth-century culture in Western European societies.[5] The 'ángel del

---

3 Michel Foucault, *The History of Sexuality* (London, Penguin, 1990).

4 Jagoe, *Ambiguous Angels*, 13–41, and 'La misión de la mujer', in Catherine Jagoe, Alda Blanco and Cristina Enríquez de Salamanca, *La mujer en los discursos de género: textos y contextos en el siglo XIX* (Barcelona, Icaria, 1998), 21–53; and Bridget Aldaraca, *El ángel del hogar: Galdós y la ideología de la domesticidad en España* (Madrid, Visor, 1992), 43–66. See also, in this respect, Lynda Nead, *Myths of Sexuality: Representations of Women in Victorian Britain* (Oxford, Basil Blackwell, 1990), 32–39.

5 For the significance of the concept of the 'ángel del hogar' in contemporary discourses on gender see Aldaraca, *El ángel del hogar*, 43–66; and Jagoe, *Ambiguous Angels*, 13–41, and 'La misión de la mujer', 21–53.

hogar' was defined in the literature of the period as a chaste, submissive, patient and suffering being. Most importantly, she was described as completely devoted to her home and family and, therefore, bound to the domestic sphere, where she was granted unprecedented spiritual and psychological power. The role of women as guarantors of order within the home was fundamental in a world where industrialization and urban overcrowding were perceived by sections of the bourgeoisie as having a potentially disintegrating effect on the family – the domestic unit and the maintenance of domestic order being considered the basis of social stability.[6] In addition, domestic order was seen as contributing to industrial progress and national prosperity. For example, improved morals engineered by stable domestic arrangements (involving an increase in the number of marriages) would lead to a larger population and, therefore, to economic growth.[7]

In this ideological context, domesticity, marriage and motherhood were constructed by the bourgeoisie as the norm of behaviour; any digression from this norm, usually represented by the sexual waywardness of the undeserving working-class woman, was categorized as abnormal, unnatural or deviant, thereby initiating a process of reform.[8] But if marriage and the family were to constitute the basis of a stable society, then for this stability to be maintained the domestic ideology of the middle classes would need to be extended to all social groups.[9] The question immediately

6 This point is made by Galdós in a humorous passage in which Feijoo advises Fortunata, 'Lo primero que tienes que hacer es sostener el *orden público*, quiero decir, la paz del matrimonio' (II, 144).

7 Nead, *Myths of Sexuality*, 33–35. It has to be taken into account, however, that although morality was believed to lead to a growth in population and, therefore, to colonial expansion and an increase in manpower, it was also thought that it could result in a decrease in economic productivity, as it can affect the mobility and flexibility of the working population.

8 Nead, *Myths of Sexuality*, 32–39. This does not imply, Nead argues, that there was a single and unified code of respectable morality against which all the other deviant categories were set and defined. Indeed, definitions of sexuality within middle-class discourses were often inconsistent and contradictory, mainly because of the problems posed by the uncertain nature of female sexuality. This lack of coherence resulted in the bourgeois categorization of respectable and unrespectable in terms of class, as a way of creating a sense of a unified and coherent class identity. In the specific case of Spain, Jagoe (*Ambiguous Angels*, 8, 19) has observed that, in the climate of political instability of the second half of the century, the allegiance to an ideal of womanhood served to create class solidarity by uniting the disparate groups within the middle classes against the aristocratic values of the old regime.

9 The extension of the ideology of domesticity to social classes other than the middle classes did not include, however, the 'colonization' of the aristocracy. By propounding the ideal of true womanhood the middle classes were, in fact, trying to boost their moral superiority by being different to the immoral aristocracy.

arises here of how this attempt to make a respectable norm of behaviour universal fits in with the need to maintain the boundaries between the classes. It is important to remember that industrialization and urbanization had not only delivered power to the bourgeoisie but had also generated a sense of anxiety and unease with regard to relations between the classes. In establishing family and domestic values as a universal model of behaviour – promoting them as shared – the middle classes were, in effect, seeking to ease those anxieties and neutralize the effects of class conflict.[10] But, although working-class women had to be taught to fulfil their feminine role in the private sphere, they were also expected to do this without transgressing class boundaries. The middle classes were aware of the dangers that the assimilation of bourgeois values by the working classes would entail. Hence, they tended to adopt a condescending attitude to their social inferiors of both sexes, exhorting them to practise the virtues of resignation and patience. It could be said that the middle classes had a vested interest in 'feminizing' (making passive) both working-class women and men. At the same time, the middle classes were trying to inculcate in their social inferiors the conviction that displaying aspirations to prosper socially was a challenge to God's will and could lead only to ruin.[11]

Although middle-class efforts to make a more respectable working class were often met with greater success when directed towards the upper layers of the poorer classes, in that people in those strata were more likely to comply with bourgeois ideals, other working-class groups also became a target of the bourgeois project of moralization. Working-class prostitutes attracted special attention in this regard. Prostitution had reached threatening proportions in Spain in the last third of the century. During this period hygienists, moralists, criminologists, anthropologists, legislators and novelists approached the problem from varying perspectives, the proliferation of literature on prostitution reflecting the very real social problem it had become. This phenomenon had particular importance in Madrid, where, as a result of the city's growth in the second half of the century, prostitution reached much higher levels than elsewhere in Spain. Madrid was, in fact, the first Spanish city where the 'reglamentación' of prostitution was implemented. Similarly, it was also in Madrid that the largest number of studies on this issue appeared.[12] The problem of

10 Nead, *Myths of Sexuality*, 36.

11 As noted by Geraldine Scanlon in *La polémica feminista en la España contemporánea 1868–1974*, 2nd edn (Madrid, Akal, 1986), 93.

12 Matilde Cuevas de la Cruz, 'Aproximación a la consideración social de la prostitución madrileña', in Luis E. Otero Carvajal and Angel Bahamonde Magro (eds), *Madrid en la sociedad del siglo XIX* (Madrid, Comunidad de Madrid, Consejería de Cultura, 1986), II, 164.

prostitution directly affected the bourgeois family, since recourse to prostitutes by middle-class males represented the threat of physical and moral contagion for the bourgeoisie and, thus, a blurring of sexual categories.

Cuevas has noted that during the nineteenth century in Spain there was a transformation in the perception of prostitution.[13] The Penal Codes of 1848 and 1870 introduced important reforms to the 1822 Code. This reform of the penal code, Cuevas argues, reflected the triumph and legitimization of the double moral standards among the bourgeoisie and the dominant ideology of the time. Moral principles, assigning different rules of sexual behaviour to men and women, were the same as those propounded by Christian doctrine, although now they had become deprived of their original sense due to the 'mercantilización' of life. As Cuevas puts it, 'La virginidad, exigida a la mujer, significa ahora un *ahorro* de sentimientos y actos amorosos para su buena *inversión* (el matrimonio)'.[14] A man, however, would be able to 'contravene the laws of fidelity' as long as he acted with discretion and his respectability was not endangered. Prostitution and the prostitute – the object with which the middle-class man satisfied his instincts – represented the opposite pole to the respectable bourgeois marriage, in which conjugal love was idealized and romanticized and sexual relations were regarded as a mechanism for the reproduction of the bourgeois family.

The acceptance of prostitution as a necessary evil brought about the need to keep it under continual surveillance and control through its regulation. In Spain, the regulation of prostitution took shape in the 'Reglamento' of 1865 implemented in Madrid, an initiative that served as a model for various 'reglamentos' that subsequently came into force in other Spanish cities.[15] The need to regulate prostitution was reinforced by the current of thought on hygiene, which regarded prostitution as a focus of infection and diseases (both physical and moral) and, therefore, highly harmful to society. The legal regulation of prostitution was but one part of a wider network of disciplinary mechanisms, including reformatory institutions for the regeneration of prostitutes, as well as other philanthropic activities outside the institutions, such as home visiting. The restoration to society of prostitutes constituted a major objective of philanthropic activity, particularly in the second half of the nineteenth century. In the British context it has been argued that the evangelical

---

13 Cuevas de la Cruz, 'Aproximación a la consideración social de la prostitución madrileña', 164–73.

14 Ibid., 165.

15 For a study of the origins of this 'Reglamento', see Jean-Louis Guereña, 'Los orígenes de la reglamentación de la prostitución en la España contemporánea. De la propuesta de Cabarrús (1792) al Reglamento de Madrid (1847)', *Dynamis*, 15 (1995), 401–41.

revival led to the creation of a great number of charitable societies between 1850 and 1860, many of which were devoted to the rescue of prostitutes. The same could be said of Spain where, as noted in the previous chapter, the Catholic revival of the Restoration had as its characteristic instrument the philanthropic association run by women from the wealthier classes.

Donzelot views nineteenth-century philanthropy as playing a vital role in the emergence of what he calls 'the social', a new sector or domain that was a function of 'domination, pacification and social integration', but was at the same time detached from any direct political role. Philanthropy, as he puts it, 'is not to be understood as a naively apolitical term signifying a private intervention in the sphere of so-called social problems, but must be considered as a deliberately depoliticizing strategy for establishing public services and facilities at a sensitive point midway between private initiative and the state'.[16] According to Donzelot, philanthropy was an instrument for social control, a strategy for disciplining the lower orders by promoting the family as a major concern.

Within the new domain of 'the social', middle-class women played a key role in the regulation and surveillance of irregular sexualities. But if it is true that philanthropy opened up a new sphere for women's work and an opportunity to function beyond the enclosed and limited domestic world, it is also true that this liberation only benefited middle-class women. Moreover, middle-class female emancipation entailed the subjection of the women of the working classes, since these were exposed to the supervision and regulation of the philanthropist. In this sense, philanthropy can be seen as a double-edged sword, for it acted both as an instrument for the emancipation of middle-class women and as a mechanism for the control of the lower classes. As Nead comments, 'Philanthropy highlights the relationships between class and sexual politics and the way in which issues of class and gender are continually interwoven'.[17]

The participation of women in the field of philanthropy gave rise to a number of debates centred on the propriety of middle-class women's work in the reclamation of prostitutes.[18] Although the main argument

---

16 Jacques Donzelot, *The Policing of Families: Welfare Versus the State* (London, Hutchinson, 1980), 55.

17 Nead, *Myths of Sexuality*, 197.

18 In contemporary Spain opinions were divided with regard to the role of women in the field of philanthropy, although, as a contributor to *La Voz de la Caridad* observed, there was a general agreement that, 'en materias de caridad no puede disputarse a la mujer una mayor aptitud natural, un entusiasmo más puro y una abnegación más sublime, porque es preciso confesar que [...] la mujer vale más que el hombre bajo el punto de vista de la ternura y de los sentimientos compasivos' (15 July 1883), 131–32.

deployed by supporters of women's work in this field was that philanthropy represented a natural and justifiable extension of women's domestic role into the public sphere, the philanthropist also tended to emphasize the sentiment that between herself and the prostitute there was a common understanding, based on the fact that they were both women. Thus, the prostitute would be more willing to accept the approach of another woman. As a contemporary commentator stated,

> It has been felt that no efforts on behalf of the fallen were likely to be so successful as those which were made by their own sex. They are able better to enter into their feelings, to sympathise with them, to receive from them their tale of sorrow, and to advise them for their present and eternal welfare.[19]

Femininity provided a common bond that could defuse the question of social difference and bring the social classes back together. However, the attempt to neutralize the effects of class distinction did not entail its complete elimination. Quite the opposite, for as one nineteenth-century philanthropist insisted, 'cordial friendships [between the philanthropist and the working-class woman] could be formed without losing positions on either side'.[20] In essence, the wayward lower-class woman could be brought back to the norm of respectability in order to avoid social disintegration; but during this process of 'normalization', and despite the alleged common bond of femininity, the positions of both philanthropist and prostitute were clearly marked out. As Nead notes,

> The philanthropic act also set up a vital difference within the category of the 'feminine'. The missioner functioned as the norm against which the prostitute was deviant and this was, of course, a hierarchical relationship since the missioner was intended to assist and advise her deviant sister.[21]

Even when the reclamation process was over, 'rescue did not mean an easy exchange of a fallen identity for a respectable one'.[22] Moreover, since submission and deference (aimed at producing an orderly and disciplined working class) were among the 'virtues' that the middle classes were trying to impose on their social inferiors, it would be unrealistic to imagine that there was much common ground on which to establish an equality between the two.

19 A. O. Charles, *The Female Mission to the Fallen* (London, 1860), 4.
20 L. E. O'Rorke, *The Life and Friendships of Catherine Marsh* (1917), quoted by Anne Summers, 'A Home from Home – Women's Philanthropic Work in the Nineteenth Century', in Sandra Burman (ed.), *Fit Work for Women* (London, Croom Helm, 1979), 43.
21 Nead, *Myths of Sexuality*, 200.
22 Ibid., 49–50.

Hence, the task of neutralizing the effect of class difference proved a difficult one. 'Cordial friendships' were not always easily maintained and, as some historians have observed, women workers had to be constantly urged to be respectful and courteous to the poor, and not to dictate to them.[23] Since authoritarianism can produce self-assertive and even rebellious reactions from the working classes, rather than the expected submission and obedience, it would be naive to regard philanthropy merely as an instrument of social control. In this respect, philanthropy did not succeed in solving the problem of the lack of communication between the classes. Furthermore, recognition should be given to the argument, to be developed below, that values traditionally considered as the preserve of the bourgeoisie – in this case of bourgeois women – also existed in working-class cultures, without any imposition from above.

Filth, Drains and Foul Odours in *Fortunata y Jacinta* and *Nazarín*: The Discourse on Public Hygiene

One discourse that gained unprecedented emphasis as a result of the pressures of urban and industrial expansion was the discourse on public health. This intersected with, and reinforced, the discourse on domesticity (and the related discourse of the reformer-philanthropist). In stressing the link between urban growth on the one hand, and immorality and disorder on the other, Mort has pointed out that 'Urbanization had produced a cultural miasma; for public health reformers dirt stood as the grand metaphor for all forms of urban disorder'.[24] The working classes in general and prostitutes in particular came to be associated with filth, contagion and immorality, a link that was strengthened by the outbreaks of cholera in nineteenth-century Spain (the last took place in 1885, the year before the first part of *Fortunata y Jacinta* was published). These outbreaks brought filth, poor sanitation and disease into even closer association with the working classes, whose unhygienic and immoral habits – neglect of cleanliness and idleness – were believed to have generated the epidemics. Ill-health was widely seen as the consequence of the working classes' innate moral failings. It was therefore proposed that, in order to improve their own condition and achieve respectable independence, the

---

23 Summers, 'A Home from Home', 43; and Jane Lewis, 'Women and Late-Nineteenth-Century Social Work', in Carol Smart (ed.), *Regulating Womanhood: Historical Essays on Marriage, Motherhood and Sexuality* (London, Routledge, 1992), 92. As seen in Chapter 1, in *El visitador del pobre* Concepción Arenal repeatedly advised home visitors to be humble when dealing with the poor.

24 Frank Mort, *Dangerous Sexualities: Medico-Moral Politics in England since 1830* (London, Routledge & Kegan Paul, 1987), 40.

poor had to be educated into physical health and cleanliness. The domestic space of the masses needed to be medicalized and monitored. Imposition of habits of cleanliness would help strengthen moral character, enabling the working classes to combat what was perceived as innate moral weakness, the assumption being, as Corbin has pointed out, that 'a crowd with a liking for cleanliness soon has a liking for order and discipline'.[25] Such views led to a programme of sanitary reform and public health control, the central aim of which was the surveillance and regulation of the poor – 'a programme which was simultaneously medical and moral; directed both to the reform of the environment and the training of the mind'.[26] An integral part of this project was the regulation of sexual immorality. It was a programme constructed around a series of polarities or oppositions – largely established, in the same way as the discourse on domesticity, in terms of class – which were essential to its regulatory aims. As Mort has observed,

> In the discourse of the urban poor, reformers constructed the sexual through the class-related polarities which were central to their programme: physical health/non health, virtue/vice, cleanliness/filth, morality/depravity, civilization/animality. The binary oppositions were organized in such a way that each polarity functioned to reinforce the other. Bourgeois cleanliness was impossible without the image of proletarian filth, middle class propriety could not be defined without the corresponding representations of working class animality, and so on.[27]

25 Alain Corbin, *The Foul and the Fragrant: Odor and the French Social Imagination* (Leamington Spa, Berg Publishers, 1986), 157. In Spain, the introduction to a Royal Decree of 1853 by which public baths for the poor had been established in Madrid read, 'La limpieza [...] produce en la casa del pobre el orden, la regularidad y hasta la economía; realza su dignidad y le inspira sentimientos de moralidad y decoro, mientras que la falta de aseo trae consigo el vicio y la degradación', quoted by Esteban Rodríguez Ocaña, 'Paz, trabajo, higiene. Los enunciados acerca de la higiene industrial en la España del siglo XIX', in Rafael Huertas and Ricardo Campos (eds), *Medicina social y clase obrera en España (siglos XIX y XX)* (Madrid, Fundación de Investigaciones Marxistas, 1992), II, 390–91. Galdós's interest in hygiene is reflected in the various books on the issue that he had in his private library. Among these were *Conclusiones relativas a la profilaxis y los medios de atenuar los efectos del cólera morbo epidémico* (Madrid, Rafael G. Rubio, 1890); Jean Batiste Fonssagrives, *Higiene y saneamiento de las poblaciones*, 4 vols (Madrid, El Cosmos, 1885) (the pages are only cut on the first volume); Dr López de la Vega, *La higiene del hogar* (Madrid, Impr. La Guirnalda, 1878); A. Riant, *Hygiéne du cabinet de travail* (Paris, J.B. Billière et F., 1883); Leon Richer, *Le livre des femmes* (Paris, Typ. N. Blanpain, 1873); and Manuel de Tolosa Latour, *Discursos leídos en la Real Academia de Medicina....* (Tema: concepto y fines de la Higiene Popular) (Madrid, Tip. de la Vda. e Hijos de M. Tello, 1900).

26 Mort, *Dangerous Sexualities*, 20.

27 Mort, *Dangerous Sexualities*, 41.

The legal regulation of prostitution was one of the main therapeutic strategies adopted by public health reformers against what was regarded as a social pathology.[28]

Another manifestation of the need to control prostitution was, as mentioned above, the creation of reformatory institutions for fallen women. The Convent of Las Micaelas in *Fortunata y Jacinta* is one such institution.[29] Following a Foucauldean approach, it can be argued that the convent, and the regime instituted in it, sought to categorize deviant femininity, to separate it from respectable femininity, and ultimately, to restore it to the norm of behaviour through a process of surveillance and indoctrination. The nuns in Las Micaelas set out to fight against physical and moral filth through the implementation of a surveillance programme of work based on cleanliness, a programme aimed at the restoration of the

28 During the last third of the century venereal diseases had come to be regarded less in terms of individual sin, that is, less as a sign of the moral degeneration of the individual than as an attack on society, or as a social danger. This shift in perception led to the intervention in social matters of public health experts who, in the name of their science, and counting on the support of the law, claimed to have both the duty and the right to safeguard society's interests: namely, the physical and moral health of the nation. See Ramón Castejón Bolea, 'Enfermedades venéreas en la España del último tercio del siglo XIX. Una aproximación a los fundamentos morales de la higiene pública', *Dynamis*, 11 (1991), 243. Stressing the link between the physical and the moral threat posed by prostitution, Rafael Eslava stated, 'El contagio inmoral de la prostitución, y el contagio infectante de las enfermedades venéreas, son dos fenómenos patológicos correlativos que exigen medidas comunes de preservación y saneamiento. No es posible desligar la profilaxis médica de la profilaxis social' (*La prostitución en Madrid, Apuntes para un estudio sociológico* [Madrid, Vicente Rico, 1900], 190).

29 The fictional Convent of Las Micaelas was in fact based on a real institution of the same name. Scanlon (*La polémica feminista*, 113–14) has observed that in 1880 there was a total of ten institutions for the reclamation of prostitutes in the main Spanish cities, of which Las Micaelas was the best known. It is ironic that these institutions were accused of increasing prostitution. As the inmates were being exploited and used as cheap labour, Scanlon notes, this forced into prostitution many female home workers who were unable to compete with the cheaper prices for goods that the institutions charged. María Dolores Pérez Baltasar (*Mujeres marginadas. Las casas de recogidas en Madrid* [Madrid, Gráficas Lormo, 1984, 107–19]) has noted that the real institution of Las Micaelas was founded in 1845 by María Micaela Desmaisières, who gave it the name of 'Señoras Adoratrices', although it became popularly known as Las Micaelas by reference either to the name of its founder or to one of the two groups which she established within her 'Colegio': the 'Micaelas' and the 'Filomenas'. The educational methods of rehabilitation used by María Micaela were more liberal than was suggested by unfounded rumours which circulated about this institution and its rules. Galdós's fictional convent therefore seems to reflect a more stereo-typical kind of controlling institution than the real version. As Pérez Baltasar notes, in Madrid there were other reformatories for fallen women whose educational techniques were less liberal than those employed in Las Adoratrices.

prostitute to the norm of domesticity and femininity. Before going on to analyse the various mechanisms of control and the ways in which this control is imposed on and/or deflected by the lower classes, it is first necessary to examine the specific images that, during this period, emerged around the figure of the prostitute. It should be noted that this system of images constructed by the various discourses on public health was in itself an instrument of power and control – according to the thesis that discourses generate a body of knowledge that gives those who produce it the power to deploy a series of disciplinary strategies.

The dominant images of prostitution associated the prostitute with filth in the streets, with decomposing animal and vegetable waste, and with drains. These were believed, at a time when the miasmatic theory of disease diffusion still carried considerable weight, to be the source of the miasma, or smells, that polluted the atmosphere and generated disease.[30] The prostitute was seen as an agent of putrefaction, literally and figuratively: she was perceived, as Corbin notes, as 'a putrid woman', whose body smelled bad.[31] The most prominent image of prostitution produced in the period linked the prostitute with drains and sewers, that is, with the action of draining away filth rather than with filth itself.[32] This image also has its roots in pre-Pasteurian beliefs, mythologies indeed, connected with the diffusion of disease. At a time when the germ theory of disease still had to be demonstrated, not only filth but also damp were believed to be among the possible causes of disease. Washing with too much water was believed to be dangerous, as it was associated with dampness and putrid stagnation.[33] It is important to note here that the cleaning regime implemented in Las Micaelas is mainly based on the elimination of dirt through polishing, scrubbing and brushing, rather than washing.

If water inspired distrust, its movement – the circulation of water – was considered salubrious, since it was believed that things that were in

30 Nead, *Myths of Sexuality*, 121; and Alain Corbin, 'Commercial Sexuality in Nineteenth Century France: A System of Images and Regulations', in Catherine Gallagher and Thomas Laqueur (eds), *The Making of the Modern Body: Sexuality and Society in the Nineteenth Century* (Berkeley and Los Angeles, University of California Press, 1987), 209–19. As Corbin notes (*The Foul and the Fragrant*, 145), the association of filth with deviant social groups, particularly prostitutes, appeared as early as the eighteenth century. Their presence was believed to diminish when rubbish disappeared from the streets. He notes the observations of Chauvet, a social commentator, who described Florence as a place where rubbish was hidden away behind screens, where streets were paved and 'strewn with odoriferous flowers and leaves' and where, therefore, there was no prostitute in sight.

31 Corbin, 'Commercial Sexuality', 210.

32 Ibid., 211.

33 Corbin, *The Foul and the Fragrant*, 32–33, 91–92.

circulation could not become corrupted: hence the importance attached to the elimination of filth through drainage. Drains could decrease the dangers of putrid stagnation.[34] In thse same way that drains and sewers were used to eliminate waste and filth in an attempt to prevent infection, the prostitute also became visualized as a 'human sewer' that society could use to drain away its excess of seminal fluid, its excess of male desire.[35]

The association of prostitutes with drains had already been drawn by Saint Augustine, the early Church's main authority on sexuality and marriage. At that time, the existence of prostitution was already accepted as a necessary evil. As Saint Augustine put it, 'Suppress prostitution and capricious lusts will overthrow society'. The prostitute's function as a drain was to siphon off the sexual effluent that prevented men from rising to the level of their God.[36] The Spanish public health expert Angel Pulido observed in 1876 that Saint Augustine compared prostitution with 'esas cloacas construidas en los más suntuosos palacios para recoger los productos corrompidos y asegurar la salubridad del aire'. Using another simile connected with the sanitation of the social body, Pulido described prostitution as 'una llaga depuradora del organismo social; rebelde a toda cicatrización, pero que debe ser incesantemente combatida para que no se extienda y ponga en grave peligro la totalidad de aquél'.[37] In the first half of the nineteenth century, Alexandre Parent-Duchâtelet, the public health expert and champion of regulation in mid-century France, admitted the

---

34 Corbin, *The Foul and the Fragrant*, 32–33, 91–92.

35 Corbin, 'Commercial Sexuality', 211; and Charles Bernheimer, *Figures of Ill Repute: Representing Prostitution in Nineteenth-Century France* (Cambridge, MA, Harvard University Press, 1989), 15–16. As Corbin observes, from an organicist point of view, the notion that air and fluids should be kept in a permanent state of movement was the result of the impact of William Harvey's discoveries in relation to the importance of the circulation of blood in the body. The attention given by Alexandre Parent-Duchâtelet, the leading public health expert on drains and prostitution in mid-nineteenth century France, to the efficient functioning of the drainage system and its ventilation reflect his and other doctors' belief that infection resulted mainly from the absence of movement in water and in the air.

36 Alain Corbin, *Alexandre Parent-Duchâtelet: La Prostitution à Paris au XIX Siècle* (Paris, Seuil, 1981), 10; and Nickie Roberts, *Whores in History: Prostitution in Western Society* (London, Harper Collins, 1992), 61.

37 Angel Pulido, *Bosquejos médico-sociales para la mujer* (Madrid, Imp. Víctor Saiz, 1876), 116. For an analysis of the cloacal imagery of infection, filth and decay in relation to the female body, and prostitution in particular – as well as other threatening aspects of nineteenth-century urban life, such as the presence of public refuse and stench, the regular recurrence of epidemics, the squalor of the poor, mendicity, madness and criminality – see Noël Valis, 'On Monstrous Birth: Leopoldo Alas' *La Regenta*', in Brian Nelson (ed.), *Naturalism in the European Novel: New Critical Perspectives* (New York, Berg, 1992), 191–209.

need for prostitution within this Augustinian perspective, reinforced by the laws of thermodynamics: desire, like steam, was seen as a force that carried with it the risk of explosion, which rendered necessary a safety valve.[38] For Parent, sewers and prostitution constituted two linked aspects of public health. Significantly, Parent wrote his studies on public health and on prostitution not successively, but simultaneously. He tried to justify his commitment to the study of prostitution by arguing that this scabrous aspect of human life that others had tried to avoid represented in effect another kind of sewer. Thus, he wrote,

> If, without scandalizing anyone, I was able to enter the sewers, handle putrid matter, spend part of my time in the refuse pits, and live as it were in the midst of the most abject and disgusting products of human congregations, why should I blush to tackle a sewer of another kind (more unspeakably foul, I admit, than all the others) in the well-grounded hope of effecting some good by examining all the facets it may offer?[39]

Both sewers and prostitution are an important part of Spanish public health treatises in the nineteenth century, which bear witness to the connection between the two established in the imagination of people who lived during this period. The hygienist Juan Giné y Partagás compared the cleaning of 'cloacas' and 'alcantarillas' carried out by the council with the cleaning up of prostitution.[40] Similarly, the *Revista de la Sociedad Española de Higiene* (1883) includes an article on the Madrid drainage system closely followed by another on prostitution.

The prostitute, from a pre-Pasteurian perspective, was perceived, like rubbish and sewers, as a source of miasma. It is significant that Parent, who was assured in his conviction – against the opinion of most contemporary hygienists – of the innocuousness of rubbish and foul odours, found an important exception to this view, believing that the proximity of putrescence and sewers aggravated venereal disease, hastening its progress considerably. Although Parent could not find an explanation for

38 Corbin, *Alexandre Parent-Duchâtelet*, 13. As Corbin (*Time, Desire and Horror: Towards a History of the Senses* [Cambridge, Polity Press, 1995], 90) has written, 'Rehabilitation [...] met its implacable limit in the system itself; it would never do for all the prostitutes to repent overnight since the passions would then swamp the world. It was essential to keep in existence, but fenced off, a fraction of the animality which the common people were criticized for incarnating, but the disappearance of which risked disturbing the whole social body.'

39 Quoted by Bernheimer, *Figures of Ill Repute*, 15.

40 See Juan Giné y Partágas's introduction to Prudencio Sereñana y Partagás, *La prostitución en la ciudad de Barcelona, estudiada como enfermedad social y considerada como origen de otras enfermedades dinámicas, orgánicas y morales de la población barcelonesa* (Barcelona, Imp. de los sucesores de Ramírez y Cñía, 1882), v.

this exception to his general rule of the innocuousness of putrescence, Corbin has observed that 'the moral bases of such a conviction are evident: in the author's mind, the virulence of the illness transmitted by female sewers, by the vaginal filth of fallen women, is naturally linked to the mire and to excremental effluvia'.[41]

Prostitutes and sewers, both channels for the disposal of human waste, were 'necessary evils' that needed to be constantly regulated and super-vised – that is, contained and sanitized – in order to limit the threat of infection. Parent dreamt of making the brothel, together with the hospital and the asylum, into one of the mechanisms for the medicalization of the social body. He conceived the 'maison de tolérance' as a place of 'normal' and 'healthy' sexuality, free of turpitude and voluptuousness. He believed that, if submitted to a severe medical surveillance, it could become 'the sanitized drain through which the seminal surplus would flow away'. The 'seminal drain', subjected to the light of power, was conceived as the antithesis of the house of clandestine debauchery.[42] The salubrity of these two sectors of public hygiene was essential in order to assure the good functioning of the social organism and the maintenance of social harmony. As Parent wrote,

> Prostitutes are as inevitable in an agglomeration of men as sewers, cesspits, and garbage dumps; civil authority should conduct itself in the same manner in regard to the one as to the other: its duty is to survey them, to attenuate by every possible means the detriments inherent to them, and for that purpose to hide them, to relegate them to the most obscure corners, in a word, to render their presence as inconspicuous as possible.[43]

The nineteenth-century programme of regulation of prostitution involved, as the above quotation shows, placing the prostitute under the gaze of power at the same time as keeping her invisible from those elements of the population considered healthy through strategies of con-finement and seclusion. In Spain, one of the aims of the 'Reglamento' of 1865 was to preserve public decorum by forbidding prostitutes to appear in public places 'en horas de afluencia' or to stand at the door or at the balconies of the brothel.[44] Similarly, the hygienist Francisco Javier Santero, writing in 1885, advised that 'casas de prostitución' should be situated in secluded areas, and had to be 'señaladas con un distintivo especial'. He also recommended that prostitutes should not go out into

41 As Bernheimer (*Figures of Ill Repute*, 15–16) notes. According to Parent, rubbish needed to be evacuated and recycled, but one did not have to let the obsessive fear of insalubrity hamper industrial progress; see Corbin, *Alexandre Parent-Duchâtelet*, 15.
42 Corbin, *Alexandre Parent-Duchâtelet*, 38, and 'Commercial Sexuality', 215–16.
43 Quoted by Bernheimer, *Figures of Ill Repute*, 16.
44 Scanlon, *La polémica feminista*, 109–10.

the streets to 'excite' passers-by.[45] In order to prevent infection, the prostitute, a 'visible' cause of miasma, needed to be contained and kept out of public sight in the same way as rubbish. In this ideological context, clandestine prostitution constituted a real danger, since it escaped the control of the authorities, defying containment, supervision, and the 'sanitizing' action of public hygiene. It is not surprising, therefore, that clandestine prostitutes were considered – not only by Parent but also by most hygienists later in the century, in France as much as in Spain – as the most syphilitic. However, this was impossible to know with certainty, given the lack of police records on an issue that escaped their control.[46]

The anxieties aroused by syphilis paralleled the fears inspired by the retention and accumulation of excrement and rubbish due to the lack of efficient and sanitized drainage. Further, the proliferation of discussion on unregistered prostitutes, especially during the second half of the century, reveals, as Corbin has shown, an anxiety about 'the social circulation of vice': that is, about the risk of the spread of erotic behaviour through the social body as a whole. This sparked fears concerning the integrity of bourgeois women. Clandestinity thus involved not only a risk of syphilis, or physical contagion, but also a risk of moral contagion – or, in other words, an erosion of moral categories.[47] In Spain, the view that clandestinity constituted a moral threat to marriage and the family was also expressed by many contemporary hygienists. These defended the regulation of prostitution on the grounds that its absolute prohibition would encourage clandestine prostitution, which in turn would lead to the spread of syphilis to the bourgeois home. Prudencio Sereñana y Partagás, for example, believed that lack of regulation '[llevaría] el virus venéreo hasta lo más sagrado de la familia [el tálamo conyugal]'.[48] From a different perspective, the prohibitionists argued that the regulation of prostitution would increase the number of clandestine prostitutes (and

---

45 Francisco Javier Santero, *Elementos de higiene privada y pública* (Madrid, El Cosmos, 1885), II, 488.

46 In Spain in 1872 it was calculated that clandestine prostitution in Madrid was seven times higher than regulated prostitution. Although this was probably overestimated, it gives some indication of the extent of the problem; see Cuevas de la Cruz, 'Aproximación a la consideración social de la prostitución madrileña', 170–71. The obsession with unregulated prostitutes illustrates fears not only of syphilis, but also of the unknown: of that which escaped scrutiny and control.

47 Alain Corbin, *Women for Hire: Prostitution and Sexuality in France after 1850* (Cambridge, MA, Harvard University Press, 1990), 22, 24. This collapse of sexual categories was accentuated by the fact that, as Corbin has noted (22), towards the end of the century, the dividing line between adultery, freedom of morals, debauchery, vice and prostitution became increasingly blurred.

48 See Sereñana y Partagás, *La prostitución en la ciudad de Barcelona*, 13.

therefore the number of cases of syphilis), as many women would refuse to be registered. Moreover, it was believed that the inefficiency of sanitary control would similarly lead to the spread of syphilis. The increase of debauchery and illegal births, and the decrease in marriages, were other arguments used against regulation. The prohibitionist Antonio Prats y Bosch declared, 'no es sólo la Medicina la que está demandando la pronta desaparición de las enfermedades sifilíticas: lo exige también la moral, guardadora de la paz de las familias'.[49] Thus, although hygienists of the time agreed on the need to fight the spread of syphilis, they were divided between those who favoured the regulation of prostitution and those who defended its abolition. The abolitionists' impact on the discourse on public hygiene and in the political sphere was, however, relatively limited.[50]

The ravages of syphilis were considered by contemporary hygienists on both sides of the divide as more devastating than those caused by the most deadly epidemics.[51] Gelabert, writing in 1886, observed that the ravages caused by syphilis alone were greater than those caused by all the other infectious diseases put together.[52] In the introduction to Sereñana's book, Giné y Partagás compares prostitution with 'una cloaca sin arrastre', an image that emphasizes the threat of syphilis posed by prostitution

49 Antonio Prats y Bosch, *La prostitución y la sífilis: Ensayo acerca de las causas de la propagación de las enfermedades sifilíticas y los medios de oponerse a ellas* (Barcelona, Luis Tasso, 1861), 9. Among those who favoured the extinction of prostitution was Juan M. Bofill, who compared the 'casas de mancebía' with an 'arroyo' into which all the 'cloacas del vicio' flow. Interestingly, here he is referring not just to the prostitutes but also to their clients and even the sanitary inspectors and policemen who come together there; see *Discurso pronunciado el día 7 de mayo de 1890 contra la existencia y reglamentación de las casas de mancebía* (Figueras, Imprenta de A. Garbi Matas, 8), 1890. The main argument put forward by the prohibitionists was that physical and moral hygiene could not be separated. Concepción Arenal (*El pauperismo* [Madrid, Librería de Victoriano Suárez, 1897], I, 405–27) expressed the view that physical infection could not be successfully attacked when immorality was at the same time being encouraged. She argued against the opinion that prostitution was a necessary evil, stating that vice and corruption (or 'podredumbre moral', as she puts it) could not be sanitized, or that it was not possible to 'regulate disorder'.

50 As discussed by Castejón Bolea, 'Enfermedades venéreas', 246–47.

51 See, for instance, Pulido, *Bosquejos médico-sociales para la mujer*, 135; and Juan Giné y Partagás, *Curso elemental de higiene privada y pública* (Barcelona, Imprenta de Narciso Ramírez y Cñía, 1872), III, 335.

52 E. Gelabert, *De la prostitución, en sus relaciones con la Higiene, en el doble concepto de la profilaxis de la sífilis y de la reglamentación...* as discussed by Castejón Bolea, 'Enfermedades venéreas', 243–44. Castejón Bolea (240, 244–45) has pointed out that the moral connotations attached during this period to venereal diseases (commonly perceived as resulting from a transgression of a sexual norm) and the social fears and anxieties about the spread of syphilis led to an exaggeration of the impact of such diseases.

rather than its function as a 'sanitized drain'.[53] Similarly, Philippe Hauser, writing in 1884 in the influential *Revista de España*,[54] regarded syphilis as 'uno de los agentes debilitantes y degenerativos de la raza humana'.[55] Like other hygienists he was haunted by the spectre of hereditary syphilis. Syphilis, he believed, invaded all social classes without distinction, whether through direct transmission or through inheritance. As Rodríguez Ocaña has pointed out, Hauser's arguments take into consideration the national economy, as all loss through either disease or death was regarded as detrimental to economic activity.[56] J. Viñeta-Bellasierra expressed a similar view in a speech of 1886, significantly entitled *La sífilis como hecho social punible y como una de las causas de degeneración de la raza humana*, in which he stated, 'La sociedad debe estar compuesta de individuos fuertes, vigorosos y mejorarse sin cesar'.[57]

It might be argued that in *Fortunata y Jacinta*, although there is no direct reference to the problem of syphilis, the fact that Mauricia and Fortunata are occasional and, therefore, clandestine prostitutes echoes contemporary concerns about clandestine prostitution. The Convent of Las Micaelas, with the rising wall hiding the interior of the convent from the world outside, reflects anxieties about the visibility of prostitution and the need to hide it away from the public eye, a fear related to pre-valent contemporary views on miasmas and infection, including venereal diseases. Further, the associations established in the novel between prostitution and other perceived agents of putrefaction, such as rubbish, sewers, decomposing flesh and the foul smell emitted by them, are an indication of the threat posed by syphilis.

In one scene, which ironically takes place in the reforming institu-tion of Las Micaelas, Fortunata and, particularly, Mauricia are associated with immorality and filth. While the two women are washing clothes, they are interrupted by a nun in the middle of a conversation in which Mauricia is tempting her friend to take Juanito away from Jacinta. The supervisory gaze of the nun forces them to stop talking and carry on

53 See Sereñana y Partagás, *La prostitución en la ciudad de Barcelona*, v.
54 Worth noting here are Galdós's connections with this journal, which he edited in the early 1870s. Some of his novels (such as *La sombra*, *El audaz* and *Doña Perfecta*) were published serially in the journal, as noted by W. H. Shoemaker, *The Novelistic Art of Galdós* (Valencia, Albatrós Hispanófila, 1980), II.
55 Philippe Hauser, 'El siglo XIX considerado bajo el punto de vista médico-social', *Revista de España*, 101 (1884), 214–15.
56 Esteban Rodríguez Ocaña, *La constitución de la medicina social como disciplina en España (1882–1923)* (Madrid, Ministerio de Sanidad y Consumo, 1987), 24.
57 J. Viñeta-Bellasierra, *La sífilis como hecho social punible y como una de las causas de la degeneración de la raza humana* (Barcelona, Est. tip. Edit. La Academia, 1886), 59, note 22.

with their work. At this moment the narrator observes,

> Mauricia dio salida al agua sucia, y Fortunata abrió el grifo para que se
> llenara la artesa con el agua limpia del depósito de palastro. Creeríase que
> aquello simbolizaba la necesidad de llevar pensamientos claros al diálogo un
> tanto impuro de las dos amigas. (I, 632)

Here, the association is made not so much with the dirty water as with
the process of draining it away. However, this whole scene is being observed by the supervising nun who, as the narrator points out, does not
leave Mauricia and Fortunata alone and wants to see how they rinse the
clothes. The association between prostitution and drains is made from
the perspective of a representative of establishment views, and therefore,
presented as a bourgeois ideological construction.

In a scene towards the end of the novel, when Fortunata is back in
Severiana's house waiting for the birth of her second child, she contem-
plates from her window the sweepers draining away the muddy water
that had collected in the square after the snow has melted:

> El suelo [...] era [...] charca cenagosa, en la cual chapoteaban los barrenderos
> y mangueros municipales, disolviendo la nieve con los chorros de agua y
> revolviéndola con el fango para echarlo todo a la alcantarilla. Divertido era
> este espectáculo, sobre todo cuando restallaban los airosos surtidores de las
> mangas de riego, y los chicos se lanzaban a la faena, armados con tremendas
> escobas. (II, 410)

Here, Fortunata is presented in connection with stagnant water, also
regarded, in the same way as the prostitute, as a focus of miasmas. The
dangers of stagnant water were emphasized by contemporary Spanish
texts on public health,[58] which referred repeatedly to the effects, due to

---

58 See, for instance, Santero, *Elementos de higiene privada y pública*, II, 190–91, 259; and
El Siglo Médico (1865), 739. It was believed that irrigation of the streets, considered
necessary in order to drain rubbish away and to purify the atmosphere, should not
be excessive and needed always to be accompanied by sweeping up. As López de la
Vega put it, 'Una cosa es regar y otra encharcar' (*La higiene del hogar*, 63). This
commentator considered stagnant water as 'el primero y más mortal enemigo de la
salud pública', as emanations from it could have noxious effects (20, 33). This concern
was also voiced by Fonssagrives (*Higiene y sanamiento de las poblaciones*, I, 94–96).
(Galdós possessed the books by López de la Vega and Fonssagrives in his private
library, as cited in note 25.) These beliefs are representative of the distrust generated
by water and the importance given to movement and fluidity. In *Fortunata y Jacinta*
contemporary anxieties about stagnant water are expressed by Moreno-Isla in a
passage in which he complains about the street cleaners saturating the streets and
pavements. As he exclaims, 'Ya están regando esos brutos y tengo que pasarme a la
otra acera para que no me atice una ducha este salvaje con su manga de riego. "Eso
es, bestias, encharcad bien para que haya fango y paludismo..."' (II, 332).

heat and the lack of movement, of the decomposition of the organic substances it contained and the threat posed by the miasmatic emanations resulting from this decomposition. Pulido made an association between the dangers arising from stagnant muddy water and those presented by prostitution when he described syphilis as a 'monstruo misterioso que se desenvuelve y conserva en el seno de la prostitución, como el miasma en el agua cenagosa, y como el veneno en la cabeza de la víbora'.[59] In the above image Fortunata is linked not only to the miasmatic stagnant water but also – as in the scene in the convent – to the action of draining it away,[60] which highlights both the threat posed by prostitution and its function as an instrument of public sanitation.

In spite of the associations generated by this image, the scene is presented as 'divertida', and follows a description of Fortunata looking at the square covered in snow earlier in the morning, a spectacle described by the narrator as 'precioso'; this prevents the above associations from working effectively. The spectacle of the pretty white snow turning into mud that needs to be sluiced away may be symbolic of Fortunata having been turned into 'fango' or filth by Juanito,[61] although in this instance Galdós seems to be stressing the positive aspect of clearing away the mud rather than highlighting the negative connotations of the stagnant muddy water. Furthermore, this scene, in which Fortunata can contemplate the view of the square, represents a prospect of visual freedom which is contraposed to the scene in 'Las Micaelas por dentro', when Fortunata's view of the river is gradually erased by the rising wall of the church. Here, the rising wall makes the outside world invisible to the women, this 'visual confinement' reinforcing their physical isolation from the 'respectable' world outside the convent, from which they have been segregated. On the contrary, in the scene where Fortunata is looking at the square, the physical and, most importantly, visual barriers – which represent the categorization of deviant and respectable femininity – have disappeared.

Another prostitute associated with drains is Andara in *Nazarín*. Here, the association is made explicitly, as Andara tries to hide in a drain when running away from the authorities after her violent fight with another prostitute. This association, however, is offset by her amusing account of the event: 'Yo iba preguntando a qué santo me encomendaría, y buscaba un agujero donde meterme, aunque fueran los de la alcantarilla. ¡Pero no cabía, por mucho que me estirara; no cabía, Señor!...' (40).

---

59 Pulido, *Bosquejos médico-sociales para la mujer*, 134.
60 It should be remembered that drains were believed to lessen the danger of putrid stagnation.

In another scene in *Fortunata y Jacinta*, Fortunata, immediately prior to her last encounter with Juanito, has a dream in which she is associated with a cart carrying unhygienic cuts of meat dripping blood in the street (II, 256).[62] It has been noted that in nineteenth-century hygienists' discourse, the association between the prostitute and dead flesh became a leitmotif.[63] Like sewers, the dissection of cadavers and the slaughtering, dismembering and flaying of animals were all considered different aspects of urban pathology.[64] Significantly, as Corbin has observed, working-class houses of prostitution were named 'slaughterhouses' ('maisons d'abattage').[65] It is also noteworthy that Madrid's slaughterhouse was in Calle de Toledo, the location of Fortunata's dream and of the working-class tenement building visited by Guillermina and Jacinta at the beginning of the novel.

The regulations governing dead flesh and those that applied to prostitution were not dissimilar. In accordance with contemporary fears about miasmas, the main concern was to conceal them from public gaze. Parent proposed that dead animals be carried in covered carriages. (In France, an ordinance of 1803 had established that cadavers would have to be carried to the dissection theatres in closed carriages.) In the same way, transportation of prostitutes between the four enclosed spaces through which they had to circulate (brothel, hospital, prison and, if necessary, the rehabilitation institution) should also be carried out in covered carriages. He also planned that the main entrance to the knacker's yard be situated at the back of the building, in order to hide it from public view. The 'maisons de tolérance', similarly, should have double doors and the windows should be rigorously locked, among other precautionary measures, to keep them as inconspicuous as possible. The important thing was to hide death (the slaughter of animals) as much as immoral sex, to keep both under tight supervision and control.[66]

---

61 As Maxi thinks to himself, 'El la arrojó a la basura… yo la recogí y la limpié…' (I, 707). In another scene, Maxi repeats this idea when he tells Fortunata, 'yo te saqué de las barreduras de la calle, y tú me cubres a mí de fango' (I, 700).

62 Corbin (*The Foul and the Fragrant*, 31) has pointed out that blood was considered the most putrescent of animal remains. Blood trickled out in the open air, coated the paving stones and decomposed in the gaps, creating a dangerous focus of miasmas.

63 Corbin, 'Commercial Sexuality', 211.

64 It should be noted in this respect that Parent-Duchâtelet was constantly moving from the discourse on prostitution to that revolving around sewers, the dissection of animals and slaughterhouses, an oscillation which reflects the author's – and other nineteenth-century hygienists' – mental association between what were considered different sectors of public hygiene.

65 Corbin, 'Commercial Sexuality', 211–12.

66 Ibid., 214–15. See also Corbin, *Alexandre Parent-Duchâtelet*, 40–41.

The dream sequence in which Fortunata is seen in connection with putrescence is immediately followed by another in which Juanito approaches Fortunata and tells her that he is ruined. In this scene Fortunata's domestic qualities are emphasized in a passage in which she tries to offer Juanito comfort for his misfortunes: 'Alma mía, yo trabajaré para ti; yo tengo costumbre; tú no; sé planchar, sé repasar, sé servir... tú no tienes que trabajar...' (II, 258). Here, the previous association of prostitution with putrid flesh is undermined by the text's subversion of the ideological polarity between the prostitute and the respectable domestic woman.[67] However, this scene is presented in an ambiguous way because, from a Freudian perspective – where dreams become self-projections – Fortunata's dream can also be interpreted as a projection of her self-image as an independent woman: by working outside the private sphere of the home, Fortunata sees herself as independent of the breadwinner. From this perspective, Fortunata is shown to be subverting the contemporary domestic discourse, or, indeed, never to have internalized it.

One important aspect of filth that is often linked to prostitution is the foul smell of the prostitute herself. In *Fortunata y Jacinta* the priest Nicolás associates Fortunata with bad odour and pollution when, after Maxi is beaten up by Juanito, he tells her to leave doña Lupe's house:

> Esto se acabó. Ni yo tengo que hacer nada con usted, ni usted tiene nada que hacer en esta casa. Cuenta concluida. Al arroyo, hija; divertirse; usted sale de aquí, y cuando se vaya, zahumaremos, sí, zahumaremos... (I, 719)[68]

Although Nicolás, through the use of this image, draws a parallel between moral and physical filth, a few lines later the narrator dismisses his middleclass perception of Fortunata as 'polluting' when he mocks the priest by making a humorous reference to his own bad smell:

> Nicolás repetía una figura de que estaba satisfecho: 'Zahumar, zahumar y zahumar'. Y a propósito de espliego, a él, físicamente, tampoco le vendría mal... esto sin ofender a nadie. (I, 719)

Ironically, Nicolás, who took upon himself the responsibility of Fortunata's 'moral cleansing' is presented as physically filthy and foul-smelling. The narrator notes humorously that Fortunata, who was crying because of Nicolás's recriminations, had to surreptitiously make use of the handkerchief to protect her nose from the unpleasant smell that the priest's clothes gave off:

---

67 With the triumph of the ideology of domesticity, deviant femininity was defined in relation to domestic values. The prostitute's sexual disorder was partly regarded as an indication of her inability to maintain domestic order. See Nead, *Myths of Sexuality*, 4.

68 In this quotation the use of the word 'arroyo' by Nicolás reflects the contrast that he establishes between the safety of the bourgeois hearth and the danger of the streets.

Cierto es que Fortunata lloraba; pero algunas veces la causa de la aproximación del pañuelo a la cara era la necesidad en que la joven se veía de res-
guardar su olfato del olor desagradable que las ropas negras y muy usadas
del clérigo despedían. (I, 717)

Andara, in *Nazarín*, provides another example of the coupling of
prostitution with unpleasant smells. This character is first presented in
the company of other women whose dirty condition (masked by cosmetics), stench and foul language tell him and his reporter friend that they
are prostitutes:

entraron alborotando cuatro mujeres con careta, entendiéndose por ello no
el antifaz de cartón o trapo, prenda de Carnaval, sino la mano de pintura que
se habían dado aquellas indinas con blanquete, chapas de carmín en los
carrillos, los labios como ensangrentados y otros asquerosos afeites [...]
Despedían las tales de sus manos y ropas un perfume barato, que daba el
quién vive a nuestras narices, y por esto y por su lenguaje al punto com-
prendimos que nos hallábamos en medio de lo más abyecto y zarrapastroso
de la especie humana. (13)

Foul language, or 'verbal filth', is another aspect of filth that appears
frequently in connection with prostitution during this period. The narrator refers once more to the women's filthy language in the episode
where they are seen insulting Nazarín, after he accuses the aunt of one of
them of robbing him:

hubimos de intervenir para poner un freno a sus inmundas bocas. No hubo
insolencia que no vomitaran sobre el sacerdote árabe y manchego, ni
vocablo malsonante que no le dispararan a quemarropa... (17)

When the narrator and his friend finally manage to send the four prostitutes away from Nazarín's house, the association between bad smell and
verbal filth is again established when the narrator states, 'por la escalera
abajo iban soltando veneno y perfume' (18).

With regard to the use of perfumes and cosmetics, some social historians have observed that from the late eighteenth century, with the progress
in bodily hygiene, and especially increased washing, their use declined.
They now began to be regarded as unhygienic and unhealthy.[69] In pre-
modern times, bathing was considered more as a sensual activity than as
a means of cleaning oneself. It was believed that water corrupted the
body physically and morally, since it made it soft and moist, or, in other

---

69 Corbin, *The Foul and the Fragrant*, 66–85 and 176–99 in particular; and Constance
    Classen, David Howes and Anthony Synnott, *Aroma: The Cultural History of Smell*
    (London, Routledge, 1994), 70–84.

words, feminine,[70] and open to external miasmas. Historically, some had considered dirt to be a symbol of holiness.[71] During previous centuries, perfumes had played an important role in personal hygiene. They were attributed protective qualities because they were believed to serve not only to mask unpleasant odours but also to dispel them.[72] In addition, they were held to be therapeutic, their fragrance being thought to stimulate mind and body.

These practicalities aside, Europeans also drew great aesthetic pleasure from the use of perfumes. However, there were many who did not approve of them. For some religious groups, such as the Puritans, perfume evoked sentiments concerning sensual lust and vanity. In their view, perfume was an artifice designed to disguise humanity's proclivity to sin. This outlook, which had an impact on popular attitudes towards perfume in the nineteenth and twentieth centuries, can be traced back to the early Christians, who, in their reaction against perceived pagan sensuality, not only regarded the use of perfume as decadent but even ceased washing themselves, taking pride in their honest sweat and dirt, which they considered as producing the natural scents granted by God.[73] In *Fortunata y Jacinta*, such beliefs are echoed in a scene in which Fortunata interprets Nicolás's dirt and foul smell as a sign of holiness. Ironically, this scene takes place when Nicolás visits Fortunata for the first time, in order to carry out his 'purifying' mission. In a humorous passage the narrator draws attention to the priest's scruffy, soiled clothes and his dirty hands ('negras y poco familiarizadas con el jabón') (I, 559), and describes the effect that they have on Fortunata:

> El ropaje negro del cura revelaba desaseo, y este detalle bien observado por Fortunata la ilusionó otra vez respecto a la santidad del sujeto, porque en su ignorancia suponía la limpieza reñida con la virtud. Poco después, notando que su futuro hermano político olía, y no a ámbar, se confirmó en aquella idea. (I, 559)

This passage is used by the narrator to ridicule the association between filth and foul smell on the one hand, and moral corruption on the other.

---

70 Georges Vigarello (*Concepts of Cleanliness: Changing Attitudes in France since the Middle Ages* [Cambridge, Cambridge University Press, 1988], 117) has shown that the moral connotations of softness were set in opposition to virtue, in the same way that physical weakness was opposed to moral force.

71 Classen, Howes and Synnott, *Aroma*, 70.

72 Vigarello (*Concepts of Cleanliness*, 138) has observed that perfume was believed to act against unhealthy air and noxious miasmatic emanations by attacking and transforming the very essence of unpleasant odours.

73 Classen, Howes and Synnott, *Aroma*, 51.

With the change in standards of personal cleanliness, which gathered pace in the nineteenth century, dirt ceased to be endowed with any protective qualities. Perfumes, like dirt and cosmetics, were now believed to clog the pores and weaken the body through their heavy vapours, preventing perspiration and other corrupt internal fluids from escaping.[74] Moreover, because washing was more common, they were needed less to mask odours. In fact, while washing with water was becoming increasingly acceptable, indiscreet, offensive perfumes began to be distrusted because they aroused suspicions about a person's cleanliness.

Perfumes were replaced by the sweeter, more delicate fragrance of flowers. Similarly, paints (red and white) and powders were abandoned. What became important was to tear off any artificial mask − of paint, powder or scent − to open the pores and air the skin. The thick vapours of impregnated flesh and heavy scents were relegated to the courtesan's boudoir and the brothel salon.[75] Some considered perfumes to be almost as unhealthy as foul smells. The British sanitary reformer Edwin Chadwick, for instance, believed that 'all smell is disease'.[76] Unaffected cleanliness, represented by the subtle scent of flowers, was advocated in preference to the physical, as well as moral, filth of artificial masks. Sobriety in the use of perfumes and cosmetics has to be understood in the context of the new feminine ideal, which placed modesty above all other feminine virtues.[77] Up to the end of the nineteenth century, the advice on hygiene given by doctors in respect of smell was to use sweet, delicate, natural perfumes and to avoid strong, 'animalistic' scents, such as musk, civet and ambergris, which now became associated with putrid and excremental odours.[78]

74 Vigarello (*Concepts of Cleanliness*, 41–89, 137–41) notes that this transformation in the conception of cleanliness at the end of the eighteenth century was connected with a pursuit of nature and a rejection of artifice. Cleanliness became more a matter of keeping the body in good physical condition than of aesthetics or external appearances. This does not mean, however, as Vigarello has emphasized, that there was an immediate revolution in habits of washing, since at the end of the eighteenth century bathing still aroused mistrust, hygiene treatises being unclear about the frequency of baths. Cleaning the skin still simply entailed, for many, washing the linen, as linen was considered to absorb sweat and impurities. Cleaning the body was seen more as a matter of rubbing than of washing, an attitude reminiscent of the fears inspired by the use of water for washing in general, as noted earlier.

75 Corbin, *The Foul and the Fragrant*, 85.

76 Classen, Howes and Synnott, *Aroma*, 82–83.

77 Corbin, *The Foul and the Fragrant*, 185; and Aldaraca, *El ángel del hogar*, 43–63.

78 In connection with this, Corbin (*The Foul and the Fragrant*, 74) has written, 'the excremental odor of the emunctories situated near the genitals − as is the case with the musk deer's abdomen − would explain the sense of shame and, in the final analysis, the feelings of modesty that the genitals aroused'.

Before the mid-eighteenth century excrement was attributed thera-peutic qualities; it was therefore not regarded as abnormal to use it in aromatic preparations. From that time onwards, however, the new beliefs about the dangers of putrefaction led to a change in attitudes towards excrement and, in general, towards all the animal substances – which were reminiscent of excrement – that had been used in perfumery up to that date. Doctors and moralists stressed the connection between the noxious smell of these perfumes and the smell of excrement. Heavy scents were held to conceal pernicious poisons.[79] The rejection of animal perfumes also represented a denial of sexual odours (towards the end of the nine-teenth century musk was confirmed to be more reminiscent of sexual secretions than any other perfume) at a time when women's sexuality was perceived as a threat and was often denied by the medical profession.[80]

Corbin has argued that the sudden awareness of an increasingly differentiated society led to a refinement of the analysis of smell.[81] The rising middle classes needed to find an olfactory identity that could set it apart from both the aristocracy and the working classes. Thus, whereas the perceived moral corruption of the working classes was associated with excrement, filth and stench, and that of the aristocracy with heavy, musky perfumes, the olfactory sign of the middle classes would be the absence of intrusive smell – in effect, a differentiated terrain of neutrality.[82] Corbin notes that this negative perception of perfume was connected with the rise and spread of the bourgeois mentality in a further sense. Perfume vanished and evaporated, and, unlike rubbish, could not be recovered or

---

79 Corbin, *The Foul and the Fragrant*, 67–68. As Corbin notes, at the beginning of the nineteenth century, the French physician M. J. B. Orfila (whom Galdós mentions in *Fortunata y Jacinta* [I, 463]) was influential in the relegation of perfumes to the status of partial poisons.

80 Ibid., 67–68. In *The Foul and the Fragrant*, 184, Corbin observes that psychiatric discourse also contributed to the discrediting of disturbing animal perfumes. He has shown that around mid-century, accompanying the advances in psychiatry, the strong and 'intoxicating' odours of these perfumes were considered harmful to the nerves and productive of psychiatric disorders. 'Hysteria, hypochondria, and melan-cholia are its most usual effects', wrote one doctor as early as 1826. In the wake of Pasteur's discoveries, medical discourse against the use of strong, 'immoral' perfumes intensified. The search for 'base sensations' was said to increase nervous irritability and to encourage 'feminism' and debauchery. The moralizing aim of such psychi-atric tactics was now more obvious than when the attack on perfumes primarily constituted a warning against miasmatic infection. Here, too, medical discourse was used to validate already existing ideas about femininity, women's sexuality and women's role in society.

81 Corbin, *The Foul and the Fragrant*, 143.

82 Classen, Howes and Synnott, *Aroma*, 83.

recycled: it thus became a symbol of loss and waste. Money spent on perfume was seen as being squandered, literally evaporating. This process represented the antithesis of accumulation and saving. Perfume was wasteful and frivolous and, therefore, immoral. As Corbin writes, 'for the bourgeois, there was something intolerable in this disappearance of the treasured products of his labor. Perfume, evocative of softness, disorder and a taste for pleasure, was the antithesis of work.'[83]

In *Fortunata y Jacinta*, Nicolás warns Fortunata that perfumes are prohibited in the convent: 'Ya sabe usted que ni perfumes ni joyas ni ringorrangos de ninguna clase entran en aquella casa. Todo el bagaje mundano se arroja a la puerta' (I, 594). The imposition of this rule implies an association of working-class prostitutes with smells connected with immorality. This association is deflated in a later scene, in which the narrator describes the visit paid to the convent by the frivolous middle- and upper-class lady benefactors. It is significant that here, the 'perfume mundano' (with its pejorative connotations of luxury and frivolity) worn by the lady visitors, together with their elegant attire, is presented in connection with the sins that some of them are said to have committed. Ironically, the whole scene contrasts with the exaggerated cleanliness, mocked by Galdós, that the convent presented for the purpose of the visit:

> Marquesas y duquesas [...] y otras que no tenían título pero sí mucho dinero, desfilaron por aquellas salas y pasillos, en los cuales la dirección fanática de Sor Natividad y las manos rudas de las recogidas habían hecho tales prodigios de limpieza que [...] se podía comer en el suelo sin necesidad de manteles [...] Las señoras entraban y salían, dejando en el ambiente de la casa un perfume mundano que algunas narices de reclusas aspiraban con avidez. Despertaban curiosidad en los grupos de muchachas los vestidos y sombreros de toda aquella muchedumbre elegante, libre, en la cual había algunas, justo es decirlo, que habían pecado mucho más, pero muchísimo más que la peor de las que allí estaban encerradas. (I, 624–25)

It was thought that the threat posed by animal perfumes could be defused by the delicate fragrance of flowers – which had become a symbol of chastity and innocence – and the scented oils and waters extracted from them. Thus, a system of floral images emerged that linked the natural and sweet perfume of flowers with the figure of the young girl. Floral odours 'echoed the traditionally mysterious collusion between woman and flower'.[84] The perfume of flowers constituted an antithesis not only to the disturbing excremental odours of animal perfumes but also

---

83 Corbin, *The Foul and the Fragrant*, 69.
84 Ibid., 183.

to the putrid odours of the working classes – and particularly prostitutes – so often associated with excrement.[85]

In *Nazarín*, *Chanfaina* links the smell of the perfume worn by Andara with excrement when, after discovering her hiding place, she exclaims, '¿Por qué en vez de traerte acá este *pachulí* que trasciende a demonios no te trajiste toda la perfumería de los estercoleros de Madrid, grandísima puerca?' (53).[86] Andara's foul smell is highlighted from the moment she is first introduced in the novel, when she takes refuge in Nazarín's house after the fight she is involved in. Here, the narrator notes that her clothes are 'impregnadas de una pestilencia con falsos honores de perfume' (37). Significantly, Andara's hiding place is given away by the strong smell of her perfume escaping from Nazarín's window, which is described by *Chanfaina* as 'un olor... así como de esa perfumería condenada que gastan las mujeronas' (48). This episode, which strengthens Andara's association with bad smell, is a reflection of the influential role that olfactory perceptions played during this period and of the moral values attached to them. Here, however, the force of this association is lessened by the humorous conversation between *Chanfaina* and Nazarín, when she tells him that not only can she smell cheap perfume but also wine: 'Y también me da olor a vinazo... ¿Se nos está su reverencia echando a perder?... Porque el de la misa no será' (48). And when Nazarín assures her that he cannot smell anything, she replies in another comic passage, 'Pues yo digo que trasciende... Pero no hay que disputar, porque no tendrán la misma *trascendencia* sus narices y las mías' (48). Andara also uses this humorous term when she reassures *Chanfaina* that she will work hard in the cleaning of Nazarín's house, so that her smell does not give him away: 'yo trabajaré aquí hasta que no quede la menor *trascendencia* del olor que gasto' (54). The humorous tone of the passage discussed above, particularly the malapropism 'trascendencia', serves to devalue the importance given by contemporary bourgeois discourse to smells and the moral values attached to them.

It is significant that Andara thinks that fire is the only efficient way to get rid of the stench that invades Nazarín's house. Thus, after setting

85 Corbin (*The Foul and the Fragrant*, 143–44) comments on the persistent bourgeois anxiety aroused by excrement. In the wake of the cholera epidemic of 1832 in France, the dangers of the proximity of excrement were stressed more than ever, as the epidemic had been found to originate in that group of the population that was perceived as wallowing in its own filth. Organic waste (particularly excrement) was associated with animality, and both with the masses. The fetid animal crouching in dung in its den constituted the stereotypical image of the masses.

86 Constance Classen (*Worlds of Sense, Exploring the Senses in History and across Cultures* [London, Routledge, 1993], 92–93) notes that the 'spicy' smell of patchouli tended to be associated with prostitutes and seductresses.

the house on fire she says with satisfaction, '¡que busquen ahora el olor…, mal ajo!' (55). Andara regards *Chanfaina*'s advice and instructions about washing the whole place with water as utterly useless. Once she knows for certain that her 'ensayo de fumigación' has succeeded, she exclaims, '¡Qué burra es esa Chanfaina! ¡Crees que lavando se quita el aire malo! No, ¡contro!, eso no va con agua…¡El aire malo se lava con fuego, sí, ¡mal ajo!, con fuego!' (56). Here, the narrator is reflecting an ancient Hippocratic belief in the disinfecting qualities of fire. Fire had been used for centuries to purify the atmosphere. Aromatic fumigations and gunpowder (explosions were believed to clear the air) were often used for this purpose. Scientists did not attribute the same disinfectant power to water because it was more difficult to prevent it from becoming stagnant. Moreover, humidity was considered more dangerous than dryness.[87] Fire was thought to be particularly useful as a measure against the spread of epidemics.[88] The stench emitted by Andara is so strong that it needs to be eliminated with fire, thus becoming associated with the fetidity of epidemics and with the miasma in the atmosphere, that is, with infection and disease. This episode, however, is presented in quite a humorous way by the narrator – Andara's bad language itself is rather comical. In another humorous passage, when Andara is contemplating the smoke rising from Nazarín's house, the narrator comments,

> creeríase que la humareda hablaba y que decía al par de ella: "¡Que aplique la *Camella* sus narices de perra pachona!… Anda, ¿no queríais tufo, señores caifases de la *incuria*? Pues ya no huele más que a cuerno quemado…, ¡contro!, y el guapo que ahora quiera descubrir el olor…, que meta las uñas en el rescoldo…, y verá… que le *ajuma*…" (56)

Galdós's use of humour in this passage may be directed at Andara's un-educated, traditional suspicion of water. If this were the case, we should perhaps also read irony into the fact that the cleaning programme of Las Micaelas was based on polishing and rubbing rather than washing.

The pestilential smell of Andara's perfume is juxtaposed in the text with the scent of flowers. When Andara asks Nazarín if he likes the scent of her perfume, he replies, 'A mí no. Sólo me agrada el olor de las flores' (48). Andara tells Nazarín that she likes flowers also but they are too expensive to buy. She continues telling him how some time ago she had a

---

87 Corbin, *The Foul and the Fragrant*, 97–98, 103.

88 Corbin (*The Foul and the Fragrant*, 103) has noted, for example, that in the early eighteenth century, during the Great Plague, Marseilles' authorities ordered blazes to be lit in the city for three consecutive days. He also observes the old habit, once epidemics had run their course, of burning the huts, cabins and shanties that had been built outside the town to provide refuge to the infirm who had been expelled.

friend who used to bring her flowers. However, here there is an ironic twist. As Andara admits to Nazarín, these flowers were covered in dirt, as her friend was a street sweeper and used to collect them from the streets (48–49). In this image, filth and flowers, representing two antithetical poles in the olfactory scale of feminine value, are fused.[89] By destroying binary oppositions, the text undermines the bourgeois attempt to classify women into antithetical categories of moral worth.[90] On the other hand, the narrator may be implying here that Andara, as a prostitute, cannot tell the difference between flowers and rubbish, in which case he would be echoing rather than subverting contemporary ideas on filth and smells. To add to this ambivalence, Andara is not presented as a disturbing character. This whole episode in which she takes refuge in Nazarín's house is, in fact, described in quite a comical way. Similarly, Andara's bad language, unlike Mauricia's language in *Fortunata y Jacinta*, is humorous rather than threatening. This weakens the association established in *Nazarín* between prostitution and filth.

It is also appropriate that a feminine character like Nazarín[91] should appear in connection with flowers, since the flower symbolized all that was considered essentially feminine. It has been argued that scents served

89 Although from the end of the eighteenth century women were classed as the 'perfumed' sex – as opposed to men, who were expected either to reject olfactory artifice or stick to a limited range of fragrances regarded as 'masculine' – the category of the 'feminine' was itself divided into several olfactory sub-categories. The two poles of this scale were prostitutes, considered as 'bad odours', and maidens, whose innocence and docility was associated with the natural fragrance of flowers. There were also other categories between these two extremes, such as that represented by mothers and wives, associated with the smells of cooking, and the category of 'femmes fatales', whose heavy and spicy scents symbolized their licentious attractiveness; see Classen, Howes and Synnott, *Aroma*, 162. In this regard, it is ironic that in *Fortunata y Jacinta*, in a visit Juanito pays to Fortunata during one of their affairs, he complains about Fortunata's smell of 'canela y petróleo' (II, 78), since these are odours associated with domesticity. Similarly he is often seen scolding Fortunata for not being more refined and 'sophisticated'; in short, more of a seductress, like other kept women he knows. Juanito, in his patriarchal mind, somehow needs to have clear the division between the respectable bourgeois wife and the fallen woman. Fortunata's proclivity to domesticity blurs this polarity, threatening to bring confusion into his mind.

90 Jagoe (*Ambiguous Angels*, especially 102–19) makes the point that in *Fortunata y Jacinta* Galdós undermines the patriarchal habit of classifying women into the antithetical categories of 'angel in the house' and 'fallen woman'. It can be argued that olfactory perceptions play an important role in this destruction of binary dualities.

91 In this regard, see Jo Labanyi, 'Representing the Unrepresentable: Monsters, Mystics and Feminine Men in Galdós's *Nazarín*', *Journal of Hispanic Research*, 1 (1992–93), 225–38.

not only to establish class differences during this period but also gender distinctions. Although up to the end of the eighteenth century the same perfumes had been used by both men and women, around this time women shifted to more delicate floral fragrances, whereas many men abandoned the use of scents altogether or changed to sharper scents, such as pine and cedar, which were considered an acceptable alternative. By the end of the nineteenth century, floral scents had come to be typed as exclusively feminine. The flower garden had become a feminine domain, whereas men were associated with the woods.[92] This insistence on the olfactory difference between men and women needs to be viewed in the cultural and social context of a period in which men and women were perceived as being different in all ways. By associating Nazarín with the smell of flowers, Galdós implicitly subverts this olfactory classification of the sexes, thus casting doubt on contemporary cultural stereotypes of masculinity and femininity. Olfactory perceptions are used by the narrator to undermine binary dualities, not only between masculinity and femininity but also within the feminine category.

In *Fortunata y Jacinta*, bourgeois associations of odours with social class and gender stereotypes are again disrupted. In the episode when Guillermina tries to 'purify' Mauricia just before her death, she undertakes once more the fight against filth – interrupted after Mauricia's expulsion from Las Micaelas – in all its modes, physical, moral and verbal. In this episode, Guillermina is seen taking particular interest in tidying and cleaning (in particular Mauricia's room) in preparation for the arrival of the viaticum. Guillermina was hoping that Severiana would have found some natural flowers to decorate the room, but all Severiana had were artificial ones. Finally, she decides to use pine and holm oak

92 Classen, Howes and Synnott, *Aroma*, 83–84. As these commentators have shown, not only did scents become feminized during the nineteenth century but also the whole sense of smell. From the Enlightenment onwards the importance attached to the sense of smell as a means of acquiring knowledge began to decline. Sight gradually replaced smell as the sense par excellence of science and knowledge, thus becoming increasingly associated with men – representatives of the world of science, politics and commerce – and, therefore, with power and control. Smell, on the other hand, was perceived as the sense of intuition, sentiment and domesticity, thus becoming associated with women. It is significant, however, that smell was also considered the sense of 'savages' and animals which, like women, were exploited and denigrated by contemporary Western culture. This is another example of the contradictions inherent to the discursive construction of the ideal of femininity and gender ideology in the nineteenth century. As Aldaraca has argued (*El ángel del hogar*, 43–66), behind bourgeois male discourses that idealized women's domestic role and posited male and female as different but complementary lay the essential belief in – if not disdain towards – women's inferiority and the desire to 'survey' and regulate them.

branches and attach the cloth flowers to them (II, 182, 186). Mauricia is thus associated with what at the time was typified as the masculine scents of the woods, rather than with the natural smell of flowers. In fact these flowers are odourless. The linking of Mauricia with masculine odours overturns established stereotypes, blurring the categories between the feminine and the masculine. Also, the fact that Guillermina cannot find natural flowers may be related to the ultimate failure of her and the bourgeoisie to purify Mauricia, bringing her back to what was considered to be the accepted feminine role.

Furthermore, the text subverts the coupling of floral scents with feminine stereotypes by linking Fortunata to the fragrance of flowers. Since Fortunata appears in the eyes of the bourgeoisie as a fallen woman, her association with flowers makes her stereotypically feminine:

> A Fortunata le gustaban mucho las flores [...] [T]enía los balcones llenos de macetas y se pasaba buena parte de la mañana cuidándolas [...] No la hacía gracia ninguna flor que no tuviese fragancia, y particularmente las camelias le eran antipáticas. (II, 93)[93]

Interestingly, camellias are the flowers with which Andara is associated. The fact that they are not fragrant underlines the ambivalence shown by the narrator in respect of this association. Contemporary preference for camellias – Feijoo was surprised by Fortunata's dislike of these showy and fashionable flowers (II, 93) – may be connected to the sensory shift from smell to sight that took place from the eighteenth century, and the value accorded by some to this aspect of flowers rather than their fragrance.[94] Fortunata's love for flowers – the narrator points out her liking for fragrant flowers such as roses and carnations (II, 93) – is another sign of her natural domestic virtues, which were supposedly confined to the bourgeoisie and believed to exist in the working class only as a result of instruction or coercion from outside. In an article published in the Buenos Aires newspaper *La Nación*, entitled 'La rosa y la camelia', Galdós praises the rose for its fragrance, which he considers symbolic of virtue, purity, modesty and decency ('pudor'), regretting the contemporary predilection,

---

93 The narrator also comments on Fortunata's fondness for Feijoo's eau de Cologne (II, 96), a scent – acceptable to both men and women – which had gained primacy over the strong odours of animal perfumes. See Corbin, *The Foul and the Fragrant*, 280, note 40.

94 See note 92. The link between camellias and prostitution was also established in Alexandre Dumas's *La dame aux camélias*, the story of a fallen woman who is purified by death from tuberculosis. In *Nazarín*, Andara refers to another fallen woman nicknamed la *Camella*, after Dumas's heroine, as Andara notes (*Nazarín*, 45). It is interesting that Andara consistently calls camellias 'camellas': the animal reference here introduces a comical note, in spite of its linking prostitution to animality.

particularly among upper-class women, for the odourless and also artificial camellia (it was then grown only in glasshouses). It is significant that, in this article, Galdós associates roses with femininity, domesticity and motherhood, whereas the camellias are presented in connection with prostitution, barrenness and the inability to raise children.[95]

The Panoptic Strategy in the Convent of Las Micaelas

The perception of prostitution as a threat to public health and to respectable morality led to the deployment of a series of strategies of control. The regulatory project implied that prostitution was tolerated and could, therefore, remain within society but under its control. Along with the legal regulation of prostitution, philanthropic activities, whether within or beyond the walls of the enclosed institution, formed part of this network of mechanisms aimed at the control of what was regarded as a source of physical and moral infection: that is, as filth. In *Fortunata y Jacinta*, the image of Mauricia la Dura sitting on a pile of manure in the vegetable garden of the Convent of Las Micaelas (I, 649) is significant from the point of view of these associations. This image symbolizes the link between organic and moral decay, a common association drawn during this period.

Within this ideological framework, the Convent of Las Micaelas can be seen as representing the possibility of recycling those sectors of society perceived as waste, rendering them, ultimately, useful to society. As Nead has observed, during this period filth and waste were not only considered a public health hazard but also part of a system of retrieval, conversion and exchange. In the same way that waste could be retrieved and converted into productive capital it was also possible to reclaim the

---

95 *La Nación* (10 March 1866 and 13 March 1866), in W. H. Shoemaker (ed.), *Los artículos de Galdós en 'La Nación'* (Madrid, Insula, 1972), 293–95 and 301–03. As Galdós wrote, '[La camelia] [n]o tiene como la rosa el tallo erizado de espinas defensoras de su honestidad: no tiene aquellas crueles armas del recato que hieren a todos los que atacan su pudor. La flor de las estufas tiene un talle accesible, en la tersa varilla que le sirve de sustentáculo no hay ni una escabrosidad ligera que aleje la mano profana [...] La camelia no rechaza ninguna mano: es flor que se entrega a todo el mundo. Tampoco vemos agrupados en torno a ella esas tiernas florecillas que son como hijuelos de la flor desarrollada [...] En la camelia no vemos nada de esto; ella no deja sucesión: el floricultor que la creó se encarga de crear otra más tarde [...] Pudiéramos decir [...] que la camelia no *tiene hijos* (author's emphasis); o mejor, que la camelia no sabe criarlos, o no ha nacido para tenerlos [...] [La camelia] es un cuerpo hermoso pero sin aroma: *es la flor prostituida; la flor sin pudor, la flor sin familia*' (my emphasis) (303).

prostitute and make her useful by bringing her back into the accepted economic and sexual orders. In this sense, rubbish and the prostitute can both be considered to be outside *and* inside the respectable economic system, moving across economic categories.[96] From this perspective it is not surprising to find institutions for the moralization of prostitutes coexisting with a system of government that regarded the toleration of prostitution as beneficial to society.

This section will explore how the elements of panopticism work within the institutionalized milieu of the convent, concentrating on how the disciplinary mechanisms of control were deployed and resisted. Tsuchiya has already observed the parallel between Las Micaelas and Bentham's panopticon. However, her study, taking as a point of departure Foucault's theory that power does not emanate from a single central site but from a multiplicity of local centres, focuses on the spread of the disciplinary mechanisms through the entire social body, the family in particular; rather than on a detailed analysis of the functioning of the panoptic scheme within the enclosed institution of Las Micaelas. After analysing the Convent of Las Micaelas as a panoptic institution, with specific reference to the characters of Mauricia and Fortunata, I will trace these two characters' later trajectories in the novel. This will include analysis of how control strategies work at a more private, personal level in the home. The functioning of control and resistance beyond the enclosed institution will show how the Las Micaelas episode fits with the novel's overall denunciation of bourgeois attempts at imposing 'hygienic' and domestic values on working-class prostitutes.

Before looking at the various strategies of control deployed in the novel, it is first necessary to examine in detail, by reference to Bentham's original essay *Panopticon, or the Inspection-House* (1791), how the disciplinary elements of his panopticon scheme work. This will be supported by discussion of Foucault's analysis of the panopticon and his theories concerning discipline, power and control. Foucault argues that in the early nineteenth century, mental coercion replaced physical punishment as the major characteristic of penal repression. The new techniques of power submitted individuals to a regimented programme of surveillance and regulations aimed at their improvement and their eventual restoration to the accepted norm of behaviour.

Foucault portrays Bentham's panopticon scheme as a model for this new mode of disciplinary power. Crucially, he is eager to demonstrate how the surveillance and disciplinary elements of Bentham's plan could be transferred to the wider social domain. Foucault illustrates how the

96 Nead, *Myths of Sexuality*, 121.

disciplinary aspects of panopticism operate in the context of a plague-stricken town, whose inhabitants have been subjected to quarantine regulations and the whole series of control measures that these entail – spatial partitioning, constant inspection, and the regulation of movement, or 'fixing' of individuals. The aim of these measures was to prevent not only contagion but also any chances of rebellious, criminal or disorderly behaviour that the threat of death could generate. As Foucault observed,

> This enclosed, segmented space, observed at every point, in which the individuals are inserted in a fixed place, in which the slightest movements are supervised, in which all events are recorded, [...], in which each individual is constantly located, examined and distributed [...] – all this constitutes a compact model of the disciplinary mechanism.[97]

For supervision and control to operate at their maximum efficiency, says Foucault, the labelling of people in broad categories such as 'mad/sane', 'dangerous/harmless', 'normal/abnormal' is not sufficient, since the category classed as 'abnormal' or 'deviant' constitutes a 'dangerous mixture' in itself. Hence, further classifications become necessary. The social management of the plague[98] served as a model for disciplinary projects based on the construction of multiple segregations, which counteracted the confusion and disorder created by the 'mixing together' of 'deviant' citizens. As Foucault writes, 'Discipline fixes, it arrests or regulates movements; it clears up confusion; [...] it establishes calculated distributions'.[99] Through this process of classification, irregularities can be tracked down and dealt with immediately.

Bentham's panopticon prison is the architectural projection of this strategy. It was designed as a circular building with a central tower from which a view could be commanded of the prisoners' cells, distributed around the periphery of the building. Each cell constituted a 'spatial unit', in which each prisoner was 'perfectly individualized and constantly visible'.[100] The placing of prisoners in their own individual spaces ensured that no communication between them was possible. The panopticon's aim was to individualize, thereby reducing collectivity and interpersonal exchanges, as an antidote to the perception of the lower classes as the

---

97 Michel Foucault, *Discipline and Punish: The Birth of the Prison* (London, Penguin, 1991), 197.

98 The use by Foucault of the model of the plague is significant to this discussion, given the association established between prostitution, filth and infection, and the 1885 cholera epidemic in Madrid.

99 Foucault, *Discipline and Punish*, 219.

100 Ibid., 200.

threatening 'masses'.[101] Supervision was the pivotal aspect of this disciplinary project. The main feature of the panopticon's architecture was that although prisoners could be constantly observed in their cells, screening devices ensured that they could never see the centrally sited superintendent. It was thus impossible for inmates to know whether at any given moment they were being watched. This placed the responsibility of discipline on the inmates themselves, guaranteeing order through a system of subtle coercion. This kind of subtle coercion had a preventive purpose, in that Bentham believed that the prospect of punishment would lead to abstention from misbehaviour. Thus, although the body might not necessarily be subjected to physical punishment, the individual in Bentham's panopticon was under constant pressure from supervision.

In Bentham's scheme the prison population was highly segmented. Divisions were established according to the type of offence committed, and between young and old, male and female, the violent and the quiet and, most interestingly, between 'decent' and 'dissolute' females.[102] Once this main classification had been constructed, Bentham went on to propose a system of 'mitigated seclusion' according to which the prisoners would be allowed to form small groups of two, three or, at the maximum, four during the hours of work, having to separate again during the hours of rest. Each group would have to be under constant surveillance to avoid 'all means of intoxication'.[103] Bentham placed great emphasis on the way these groups were to be formed. Factors such as age and character would be taken into consideration. Furthermore, in this system of regulation by selection, each group would be 'assorted' by the inspector in such a way that prisoners 'may be checks upon one another [...] with

101 Galdós was clearly aware of the new developments in prison architecture and organization. In an article of 31 January 1884 for the Buenos Aires newspaper *La Prensa* he wrote about the replacement of the old prison of El Saladero in Madrid by a new cellular prison, the Cárcel Modelo, built that same year and later to appear in his novel *Nazarín*. This prison was built in the radial form of the panopticon – hence its nickname 'el Abanico', as it is referred to in *Nazarín* (169). It had a central 'rotonda' from which prisoners in their individual cells could be constantly observed. After deploring the architectural defects, living conditions and organization of El Saladero, including the 'mixing together' of prisoners who had committed wildly differing kinds of offence, Galdós praises the new prison as a paradigm of the efficiency, practicality and greater humanity of the new scientific system of prison administration. See W. H. Shoemaker (ed.), *Las cartas desconocidas de Galdós en 'La Prensa' de Buenos Aires* (Madrid, Cultura Hispánica, 1973), 46–47.
102 See the panopticon plan printed at the opening of John Bowring (ed.), *The Collected Works of Jeremy Bentham* (Edinburgh, 1843), IV.
103 Jeremy Bentham, *The Panopticon; or, the Inspection-House* (1791), quoted in Bowring (ed.), *The Collected Works*, IV, 39–172.

regard to any forbidden enterprise'. Discipline would be ensured to a large degree by reciprocal surveillance, or self-policing. This was, according to Bentham, 'a capital part of [...] [the inspector's] business'.[104]

The key feature of panoptic supervision was the coupling of surveillance with the notion of improvement. The panopticon exercised a 'reformatory' power. Its role was not simply to protect society from those who threatened it, but also, most importantly, to morally rehabilitate the offender, so as to render him or her useful, especially in economic terms, to society. But for an individual to be improved it was necessary to obtain his or her submission. In this sense, the training of individuals to accept docility and obedience through repetitive work became a major objective of the plan.

The great advantage of the panopticon project, Bentham argued, was its application to any sort of institution in which a particular form of behaviour had to be imposed. As Bentham wrote,

> It will be found applicable [...] without exception, to all establishments whatsoever, in which [...] a number of persons are meant to be kept under inspection. No matter how different, or even opposite the purpose: whether it be that of punishing the incorrigible, guarding the insane, reforming the vicious, confining the suspected, employing the idle, maintaining the helpless, curing the sick, instructing the willing in any branch of industry, or training the rising race in the path of education.[105]

Furthermore, the disciplinary techniques and methods of surveillance could work beyond the walls of institutions, propagating themselves though the whole of the social body. In this propagation, according to Foucault, lay the main distinction between the older, limited systems of surveillance and control and those ushered in by the science and reasoning of the Enlightenment.[106]

The Convent of Las Micaelas is but one example in a long tradition of providing institutions for the regeneration of prostitutes conceived and organized according to the principles of the panopticon scheme.[107] This

---

104 Bentham, *The Panopticon*, 76.
105 Ibid., 40–41.
106 Foucault, *Discipline and Punish*, 209–10.
107 Stanley Nash ('Prostitution and Charity: The Magdalen Hospital, a Case Study', *Journal of Social History*, 17 [1984], 617–28) has observed that the Magdalen charity, the first institution set up in England, in 1758, for the reform of penitent prostitutes, anticipated the technology of social engineering used in nineteenth-century state-run prisons and other similar institutions. Nash argues that the Magdalen – a private enterprise – constitutes an example of an early stage in the evolution of modern techniques of state authority. The description of the disciplinary programme implemented in the Magdalen bears a striking resemblance to the one established in

reforming institution offers an illustration of, on the one hand, the segregation or categorization of respectable femininity, which remains outside the walls of the convent, and on the other, deviant femininity, which is contained within them.[108] The wall of the new church, which is being built at the time of Fortunata's admittance into the convent, can be seen as a symbol of the need to keep both groups apart. The fact that the narrator describes the wall in the process of being built may be connected with his desire to draw the reader's attention to this segregational policy. The physical boundary established by the wall is reinforced by the rituals of the institution. When entering Las Micaelas, the women enter another world, one governed by a whole set of different rules which symbolize their social exclusion from the outside world. The wall establishes a physical, as well as a visual, division between the two worlds.[109] The narrator describes how the wall gets higher and higher every day, and underlines the visual aspect of this separation: 'Cada día, la creciente masa de ladrillos tapaba una línea de paisaje. Parecía que los albañiles, al poner cada hilada, no construían, sino que borraban.' (I, 619) Whereas the boundaries that mark off the normal from the deviant become more visible and obvious, the outside world becomes invisible to the women. This 'visual confinement' emphasizes both the physical enclosure to which the women are submitted and their isolation from the respectable world outside the convent. In the same way, the interior of the convent is hidden to people on the outside. Maxi observes how the growing mass of bricks prevents him from seeing what is happening inside. In this respect, Cohen has pointed out that

> The segregated and insulated nineteenth century institutions made the actual business of deviancy control invisible, but its boundaries visible. That is to say, what went on inside these places was supposed to be unknown. Institutions like prisons gradually became wrapped with an impenetrable veil of

---

Las Micaelas. The Magdalen – and similarly Las Micaelas – resembled to a large degree the prison penitentiary envisaged by John Howard, the champion of prison reform in Britain, in the 1770s. (It is noteworthy that *La Voz de la Caridad* includes several articles on Howard and his reform plans.) It is significant that an institution for the reclamation of prostitutes, such as the Magdalen, should have pre-dated the panoptic formula that was to be refined, from the 1780s onwards, by many theorists of penology, and which was also used by Bentham in the planning of his model prison.

108 Although some bourgeois women, such as Doña Manolita, are also confined in Las Micaelas because of 'sexual sins' (I, 621–22), the main aim of this institution was the control of *working-class* women, as these were seen to represent the real threat.

109 Tsuchiya ('"Las Micaelas por fuera y por dentro"...', 61–62) has also observed the physical and visual barrier that the half-constructed wall creates between the outside and inside worlds.

secrecy. Segregation came to mean insulation and invisibility. This was the transition which Foucault charted – from the visible, public spectacle (torture, execution, humiliation) to the more discreet form of penitentiary discipline.[110]

The narrator establishes a comparison between the growing row of bricks and a veil used for covering naked flesh: 'cada hilada de ladrillos iba tapando discretamente aquella interesante parte de la interioridad monjil, como la ropa que se extiende para velar las carnes descubiertas' (I, 601). Prostitution needs to be kept away from the public eye, in the same way that naked flesh is veiled. However, the humorous reference to the interior of the convent as 'aquella interesante parte de la interioridad monjil' suggests the author's desire to ridicule contemporary attempts at 'insulation' and to make the control of deviancy 'invisible'.

The invisibility of the convent's interior clearly suggests middle-class anxieties about the 'visibility' of prostitution and the threat posed by the mixing of the respectable and non-respectable classes. William Acton, a mid-century authority on prostitution, expressed this fear of the visibility of vice and the resulting collapse of sexual categories:

> Vice does not hide itself, it throngs our streets, intrudes into our parks and theatres, and other places or resorts, bringing to the foolish temptation and knowledge of sin to the innocent; it invades the very sanctuary of home, destroying conjugal happiness [...][111]

The rising wall, which acts as a barrier for hiding vice, can also be seen, as argued earlier, as symbolic of fears about miasmas and infection: just as rubbish needed to be contained and concealed in refuse dumps to prevent infection,[112] so the prostitute, another 'visible' cause of miasma from a pre-Pasteurian perspective, needed to be kept out of sight.[113]

Once deviant femininity is categorized and isolated, a whole programme of supervision and discipline is put in operation. But for surveillance to be effective, it becomes necessary to establish a system of further divisions and classifications. When describing the inside of Las Micaelas, one of the first things that the narrator points out is the division of the 'recogidas' into two groups: 'Las Filomenas' and 'Las Josefinas'.[114] The

---

110 Stanley Cohen, *Visions of Social Control: Crime, Punishment and Classification* (Cambridge, Polity Press, 1985), 57.

111 William Acton, *Prostitution Considered in Its Moral, Social and Sanitary Aspects in London and Other Large Cities; with Proposals for the Mitigation of Its Attendant Evils*, 2nd edn (London, 1870), quoted by Nead, *Myths of Sexuality*, 115.

112 Corbin ('Commercial Sexuality', 214) talks about the obsession with the problem of refuse dumps during the first part of the nineteenth century.

113 Nead, *Myths of Sexuality*, 121.

first group was formed by 'fallen' women, whereas the second was made up of young girls who had been taken to the convent by their parents (or often by their stepmothers) in order to be educated. These groups needed to be kept separate so as to prevent the flow of bad influences, or 'intoxication', as Bentham puts it. Galdós emphasizes that there is no communication whatsoever between the two groups of women. They live in different sections of the building and their timetables for eating and recreation are different. The deviant group needs to be kept apart to ensure that no contact is established and that there are no 'leakages' into the more 'respectable group' of young girls. This ensures that the two different categories do not break down.

Once this main binary division has been established, further separations will be needed within each of the above groups so that effective surveillance can be exercised. Galdós points out the severity employed by the nuns to prevent small groups from forming during the hours of labour. This is necessary to ensure discipline and efficiency at work, which could otherwise be disturbed by the women engaging in conversation and forming alliances. When groups form at other times, the nuns not only take great care to ensure that the right relationships are established, but also use the better behaved women as 'checks' on those they consider 'suspicious':

> Mucho rigor y vigilancia desplegaban las madres en lo tocante a las relaciones entre las llamadas arrepentidas, ya fuesen *Filomenas* o *Josefinas*. Eran centinelas sagaces de las amistades que se pudieran entablar y de las parejas que formara la simpatía. A las prójimas antiguas y ya conocidas y probadas por su sumisión, se las mandaba acompañar a las nuevas y sospechosas. Había algunas a quienes no se permitía hablar con sus compañeras, sino en el corro principal en las horas de recreo. (I, 606)

This system of classification and surveillance is similar, it might be observed, to that proposed by Bentham in his *Panopticon*.

Furthermore, as noted earlier, surveillance goes hand in hand with the notion of reformation. The women in Las Micaelas are subjected to a programme of physical and moral discipline aimed at their rehabilitation as normal members of society. Life in the convent is dominated by all

---

114 Pérez Baltasar (*Mujeres marginadas*, 114) notes that Galdós's classification of the women as 'Filomenas' and 'Josefinas' differs from the one established in real life by the founder of the institution, who gave these two groups the names of 'Micaelas' and 'Filomenas'. These groups were strictly separated from each other, although not all the time. In *Fortunata y Jacinta* Galdós observes that there was no communication whatsoever between the two groups of women (I, 627). The fact that a classification was established in the real institution is significant for the purposes of this discussion.

sorts of timetables, schedules and regulations. Discipline extends to all areas of everyday life. The narrator describes, rather humorously however, the strict rules of surveillance and discipline imposed by the nuns:

> A las cinco de la mañana ya entraba Sor Antonia en los dormitorios tocando una campana que les desgarraba los oídos a las pobres durmientes. El madrugar era uno de los mejores medios de disciplina y educación empleados por las madres, y el velar a altas horas de la noche una mala costumbre que combatían con ahínco, como cosa igualmente nociva para el alma y para el cuerpo. Por esto, la monja que estaba de guardia pasaba revista a los dormitorios a diferentes horas de la noche, y como sorprendiese murmullos de secreto, imponía severísimos castigos. (I, 605)

The image of the nun walking into the women's dormitory sounding a shrill, piercing bell, and the humorous and empathetic description of the women as 'las pobres durmientes', counteract the seriousness of the nuns' attempts to implement a regimented system of discipline. The narrator does not seem to be taking this 'disciplinary regime' very seriously. Indeed, he goes on to show that this system of surveillance is flouted. Thus, in spite of the nuns' efforts to avoid any kind of 'intoxication' between the women in the convent, this control mechanism is undermined by the great influence that Mauricia has on Fortunata, both in the convent and in the rest of the novel, an influence which, ironically, has more of an effect on her future behaviour than bourgeois indoctrination. It is also ironic that, in spite of all the surveillance exercised by the nuns, Mauricia will manage to 'steal' Sor Marcela's brandy bottle and become literally 'intoxicated'. Here, the use of irony enables the author to criticize, even ridicule, the nuns' disciplinary tactics and, therefore, to subvert contemporary ideas on control.

The major instrument of discipline employed in Las Micaelas is work.[115] According to bourgeois thinking, work enforced habits of self-discipline and perseverance and taught submission to order, since it set a pattern of behaviour and implied an adjustment to certain routines and rhythms. Work was believed to make people more docile and easily 'trained', more adaptable to the rules of behaviour imposed on them. Ultimately, work made people productive. As such, it became associated with virtue, whereas idleness was perceived as the source of all vices, as it implies non-productive time in which evil could flourish. In this context, Samuel Smiles observed that, 'national progress is the sum of

---

115 Fernando Alvarez-Uría (*Miserables y locos: Medicina mental y orden social en la España del siglo XIX* [Barcelona, Tusquets, 1983], 169) observes that both prisons and asylums – two major manifestations of bourgeois power in the nineteenth century with respect to deviancy – founded their 'imperio del orden' on work.

individual industry, energy and uprightness, as national decay is of individual idleness, selfishness and vice'.[116] The self-disciplinary habits generated by repetitive work helped individuals to improve themselves, to become self-sufficient and independent. Individual improvement, or 'self-help', would in turn result in national and social progress.

The inculcation of virtuous habits associated with work was particularly important in connection with prostitutes, since these were usually typed as 'naturally' idle and lazy by the majority of public health experts of the period, idleness and aversion to work being cited as the main causes leading to prostitution. The criminologists Constancio Bernaldo de Quirós and José M. Llanas Aguilaneido stated that, 'Todos los autores que han estudiado a las mujeres dedicadas a este triste oficio, afirman que los hábitos psicológicos habituales en ellas son la pereza, el ocio, el horror a toda clase de trabajo metódico y continuado, la apatía más completa'.[117] The fact that the working classes could become self-sufficient, however, can also be regarded as being a threat to the bourgeoisie. Nevertheless, since the main outlet that women had in the labour market was domestic service, it can be argued that this constituted a compromise, in the sense that servants could be regarded as self-reliant and, at the same time, dependent on their bourgeois masters.

But what was the relevance of the work ethic to women in a society where they were relegated to the domestic sphere? The programme of work implemented in Las Micaelas was based on domestic training, as was also the case with other institutions such as women's asylums.[118] It provided a strategy for the regulation of sexuality, in the sense that it was designed to educate the prostitutes into accepted feminine roles and, in particular, to train them in the skills and routines of domestic service. The range of household routines imposed by the nuns entailed the practice of those virtues advocated by the bourgeoisie – including order, discipline, cleanliness and punctuality – all of which could be transferred to the female sphere of the domestic environment. Through the undertaking of these domestic duties the prostitute could recover her lost femininity and be restored, after leaving the institution, to the family unit and traditional domestic life. This is a reflection of the contradictions inherent in bourgeois discourse, as it implies that there was a

116 Samuel Smiles, *Self-help* (1859), quoted in John M. Golby (ed.), *Culture and Society in Britain 1850–1890: A Source Book of Contemporary Writings* (Oxford, Oxford University Press, 1987), 107.

117 Constancio Bernaldo de Quirós and José M. Llanas Aguilaneido, *La mala vida en Madrid* (Madrid, B. Rodríguez Serra, 1901), 59.

118 Elaine Showalter, *The Female Malady: Women, Madness and English Culture, 1830–1980* (London, Virago Press, 1987), 82–84.

stage when the prostitute was 'good' before becoming 'fallen', thus undermining the idea of the 'innate' immorality often attributed to the poor in general, and to prostitutes in particular, by contemporary social commentators who often ignored the economic conditions in which they lived.[119] Also, it is ironic that the convent is designed to train the women in domestic service, as Galdós notes (I, 568), when a large proportion of women who fell into prostitution were domestic servants who had been seduced by their masters.[120] Further, the undertaking of domestic duties by lower-class women allowed bourgeois women to be freed from work which, ironically, meant that they were made idle, as several hygienists of the period noted.

The tasks that the women have to carry out in Las Micaelas are very much the same as those that they were expected to undertake in contemporary asylums: cleaning, laundry and needlework. As in asylums of the time, the nuns in Las Micaelas employ a regime of work – very often hard and unnecessary work – in order to keep the women's minds free from 'temptations'. It was believed that work had the virtue of occupying the mind, thereby diverting it from any potentially disruptive and disquieting thoughts.[121] In *Madness and Civilization* Foucault argues that

> Work possesses a constraining power superior to all forms of physical coercion, in that the regularity of the hours, the requirements of attention, the obligation to produce a result detach the sufferer from a liberty of mind that would be fatal and engage him in a system of responsibilities.[122]

Similarly, in his description of the daily regime in Las Micaelas, Galdós points out that

> Los trabajos eran diversos y en ocasiones rudos. Ponían las maestras especial cuidado en desbastar aquellas naturalezas enviciadas o fogosas, mortificando las carnes y ennobleciendo los espíritus con el cansancio. (I, 605)

---

119 These commentators attributed the causes of prostitution mainly to the prostitutes' inherent idleness, their lack of moral sense and religious beliefs, and their love for luxury. There were some, however, who saw lack of available work, and the resulting deprivation suffered by these women, as the main cause of prostitution. This opinion was expressed, for example, by R. Vega Armentero in 'La prostitución', *Semanario de las Familias*, 2, No. 50 (10 December 1883), 432–33; and Concepción Arenal, *La Voz de la Caridad* (15 August 1877), 164–67 in particular.

120 As Eslava (*La Prostitución en Madrid*, 78–79) notes.

121 Alvarez-Uría, *Miserables y locos*, 167; Michel Foucault, *Madness and Civilization: A History of Insanity in the Age of Reason* (London, Routledge, 1992), 248; and Showalter, *The Female Malady*, 82–84. This view was also voiced by contemporary Spanish hygienists, among them López de la Vega, *La higiene del hogar*, 234–35.

122 Foucault, *Madness and Civilization*, 247.

Laundry work in particular was believed to have important therapeutic benefits, as the aggressiveness and intensity of physical labour involved in this activity could serve as an outlet for nervous energy, thereby preventing the women patients from becoming violent.[123] In Las Micaelas, the symbolism of cleaning linen,[124] especially bed linen, is significant from the perspective of the restoration of prostitutes to the accepted feminine norm. Most of the work undertaken by the women in the convent was based on cleaning. Cleanliness as an instrument of discipline was aimed both at its physical and moral functions, the natural relation between the physical and the moral condition being emphasized.[125] It is significant that the narrator draws a parallel between the nuns' 'polishing' of the 'reclusas' and the cleaning tasks carried out by the women, which also mainly revolve around polishing. Ironically, the polishing activities forced upon the women are depicted as the most futile.[126]

In the chapter 'Las Micaelas por fuera', the narrator, when describing the buildings occupied by the new religious orders, comments on the bad taste of the architecture. However, this is immediately contrasted with the clean atmosphere that one could breathe in them. The new architectural style might have been 'deplorable' and 'cursi' but, as the narrator points out humorously, 'despide olor de aseo, y tiene el decoro de los sitios en que anda mucho la *santidad* de la escoba, del agua y el jabón' (I, 592; my emphasis). Functional cleanliness overrides any concern for architectural form. When describing the Convent of Las Micaelas in particular, the narrator contrasts once again, in an ironic tone, 'la

---

123 Showalter, *The Female Malady*, 82–83.

124 Corbin (*Time, Desire and Horror*, 27, 25) has observed how nuns used linen as an instrument for the rehabilitation of fallen women, a link being established between repentance and the restoration of the whiteness of the fabric. Caring for linen had become a tactic for 'orderly cleanliness', for the education of both body and soul. He also notes, significantly, that the Immaculate Virgin was the patroness of linen workers.

125 In *The Panopticon* Jeremy Bentham observed that 'moral purity and physical are spoken in the same language'. Cleanliness, he wrote, is an 'antidote against sloth, and keeps alive the idea of decent restraint and the habit of circumspection' (Bowring [ed.], *The Collected Works*, IV, 158). The link established between physical cleanliness and morality made the former a core objective of reforming institutions.

126 The programme of moral regeneration set up in the convent reflects the unrealistic and impractical solutions offered by some contemporary commentators to the problem of prostitution. Others, such as Angel Pulido, admitted that prostitutes needed to be provided with 'medios honrosos de subsistencia', without which any moralizing initiative was doomed to failure. Thus he exclaims, '¡Quién se acuerda de la virtud cuando ahoga la miseria!' (*Bosquejos médico-sociales para la mujer*, 151, 153). In *Fortunata y Jacinta*, the practical Feijoo makes a similar observation to Fortunata when she insists that she wants to be 'honrada' (II, 98).

pulcritud y la inocencia artística de las *excelentes* señoras que componían la comunidad' (I, 593; my emphasis). In portraying the inside of Las Micaelas the narrator notes that '[l]as paredes estaban estucadas [...] porque este es un género de decoración barato [...] y sumamente favorable a la limpieza' (I, 593). The use of plaster is significant, as it was considered to be an effective agent against infection. As walls were thought to be repositories of ancient filth, in the sense that humidity helped miasmatic substances to become adhered to them, plaster was recommended as a building material. Plaster made walls waterproof, thus preventing the absorption of humidity and the subsequent miasmatic impregnation of the walls.[127]

The narrator portrays this zeal for cleanliness on which the regeneration of the women is based as exaggerated, even fanatical:

> Sor Natividad [...] [era] tan celosa por el aseo del convento que lo tenía siempre como tacita de plata, y en viendo una mota, un poco de polvo o cualquier suciedad, ya estaba desatinada y fuera de sí, poniendo el grito en el Cielo como si se tratara de una gran calamidad caída sobre el mundo, otro *pecado original* o cosa así. Apostol fanático de la limpieza, a la que seguía sus doctrinas la agasajaba y mimaba mucho, arrojando tremendos anatemas sobre las que prevaricaban, aunque sólo fuera *venialmente*, en aquella moral cerrada del aseo [...] – Si no tenéis alma, ni un adarme de gracia de Dios – les decía, y *no os habéis de condenar por malas sino por puercas*. (I, 606–07; my emphasis)

Although through this extract an association is established between lack of physical cleanliness and sin, between filth and immorality, these associations cannot be taken seriously, for several reasons. First, the character through whom the associations are drawn is portrayed as fanatical; hence, her perspective cannot be trusted. Second, the humorous tone adopted by the narrator immediately invites the reader to dismiss such associations. Finally, the information is presented from the point of view of a bourgeois character (the narrator points out Sor Natividad's high-class origins [I, 585]), which allows the author to distance himself from it.

The most prominent images of prostitution and filth are presented by the narrator towards the end of the chapter, when it becomes clear that the disturbing and disruptive Mauricia, the character through whom these associations are established, is beyond the control of the nuns. In the first of these images the drunken Mauricia, after claiming to have seen the Virgin, takes refuge on a pile of compost in the convent's vegetable

---

127 Santero, *Elementos de higiene privada y pública*, I, 536 and II, 140, 392; and Corbin, *The Foul and the Fragrant*, 25, 91.

garden (I, 641).[128] For the bourgeoisie organic waste represented animality, sin and death.[129] Mauricia's drunken state reinforces not only the immorality, but also the animality and savagery that were often associated with the working classes. In 'Las Micaelas por dentro' Mauricia is frequently described as a 'fiera' ready to attack (on several occasions in the novel Fortunata is herself referred to as 'fiera'). Often Mauricia has to be tied up and even locked up in a cage, like an animal in the zoo. Her foul language and harsh manners reinforce her savagery and animality. Also, in keeping with contemporary thought, Mauricia's unruly behaviour is often linked with lunacy. The image of Mauricia sitting on the manure represents all the moral failings that the bourgeoisie bestowed upon the undisciplined working classes. Immorality, filth, drunkenness, animality and madness are set in stark contrast to cleanliness, temperance, civilization, domesticity and passivity. Mauricia is seen here as constituting the opposite pole to the resigned, submissive and asexual wife that the discourses on domesticity and hygiene were trying to manufacture.

However, the above image is presented in the novel as a bourgeois ideological construction and, therefore, as biased and unreliable. Again it is Sor Natividad, a representative of dominant conservative views, who observes that Mauricia's place is with the rubbish. Thus, when she finds out that Mauricia has taken refuge on top of the dung heap, she exclaims, 'Ya... , en la basura [...]; es su sitio' (I, 649). Furthermore, this image is contradictory and ambiguous, since manure is also symbolic of growth ('compost' being technically the opposite of '*de*composition') and can, therefore, represent the dual properties of fertility and decay. Critics have observed that the use of such ambiguities by Galdós allows him to

---

128 As Corbin notes (*The Foul and the Fragrant*, 154–56), the kitchen garden was seen as representing a rural element within an urban environment. This commentator has observed the dual and complex symbolism of the countryside during the eighteenth and nineteenth centuries, when the idyllic vision attached to it was being replaced by one more negative, as filth and rubbish began to invade its image. The peasant now tended to be identified with the dung-man and associated with manure and foul odours. With advances in public hygiene, the town was slowly being cleared of its refuse. The town had become the place of the imputrescible, symbolized by money, whereas the countryside stood for poverty and putrid excrement. In the same way as the countryside, the image of the kitchen garden had began to take on pejorative connotations: the air coming from kitchen gardens, stinking of manure, was believed to conceal many dangers of miasma.

129 Alain Corbin, 'Backstage', in Michelle Perrot (ed.), *From the Fires of Revolution to the Great War* (Cambridge, MA, Belknap Press, 1990) (vol. IV of *A History of Private Life*, ed. Philippe Ariès and Georges Duby), 477.

undermine the mainly bourgeois perspective of the narrator.[130] The ironic use of such an ambiguous image here lessens the value of the association of prostitution and drunkenness with filth and immorality. This image also works at a different ironic level in that it is one of physical and moral degeneration situated within the realm of civilization represented by the convent. Mauricia's regression to immorality and animality thus serves to expose the failures of the panoptic strategy implemented in Las Micaelas. This irony contributes to the dissociation of the author from the bourgeois attempt to impose an orderly and 'civilized' way of life on those social groups that are considered a threat to social stability. In this way, Galdós disengages himself from the associations established by his bourgeois characters and, sometimes, by the bourgeois narrator himself, thereby resisting complicity with a system of control based on the categorization and labelling of sexuality.

The image of Mauricia sitting on the manure heap also symbolizes her rebellion against the controlling power of the bourgeoisie. While sitting on the manure, Mauricia is shown throwing filth at one of the 'reclusas' when the latter orders her, on behalf of the nuns, to come down from the dung heap and join the other women. This act, like her constant use of foul language, becomes symbolic of her rejection of discipline and, in particular, of bourgeois hygienic discourse. Corbin has noted the reluctance of the masses to accept the reformers' discourse on public health and their 'loyalty', in effect, to filth. He observes, for example, how throwing excrement was a feature of the Shrovetide Carnival. Another aspect of this loyalty to filth, he argues, was reflected in their persistent use of foul language.[131] By 'throwing filth and its verbal equivalent', as Corbin puts it, Mauricia is reacting against a capitalist society which, after having condemned the working classes to live in filth, blames them for their own condition, categorizing them as innately 'unhygienic' and thus in need of discipline and control. Social historians have shown how some disciplinary practices generated self-assertive and even rebellious reactions from the working classes, rather than the expected passive surrender. In this respect Foucault has observed that wherever there is power, there is also resistance, coming from, or existing within, the system of power relations.[132] Later Fortunata will, of course, also reaffirm her own system of values as a reaction to the controlling influence and coercion from the bourgeoisie.

130 See, for example, James Whiston, 'Language and Situation in Part I of *Fortunata y Jacinta*', *Anales Galdosianos*, VII (1972), 79; and Geoffrey Ribbans, *Pérez Galdós: Fortunata y Jacinta* (London, Grant and Cutler, 1977), 39–40.

131 Corbin, *The Foul and the Fragrant*, 214–15.

132 Foucault, *The History of Sexuality*, 95–96.

After Mauricia's second attack in Las Micaelas, it becomes obvious that she is beyond the control of the nuns, and even of Guillermina. The disciplinary project implemented in the convent has failed to normalize her behaviour. When all corrective practices fail, she has to be removed from the reformatory. The wild and unreformable Mauricia is thrown into the streets (a symbol of danger in contrast to the security of the home), like a bull released into the bull ring to go to its death:

> Se le franquearon todas las puertas, abriéndolas de par en par y resguardándose tras las hojas de ellas, como se abren las puertas del toril para que salga la fiera a la plaza. (I, 655)

At the moment of her expulsion from the convent, she becomes once more associated with rubbish, in a scene where she is followed by a group of street sweepers (I, 656). Significantly, the term 'residuum' was used in nineteenth-century social and moral commentaries to refer to both organic and human refuse: the residuum was not only the lowest layer of society and the effluent of civilized society, but was also considered a major social threat because it was deemed to be outside society and thus beyond the control mechanisms of the bourgeoisie. Mauricia, reluctant to conform to social rules, constitutes 'residual' rather than 'recyclable' matter, and thus needs to be expelled from the convent and subsequently eliminated or 'excreted' from the 'social organism' through her death. Interestingly, the image discussed above, which links Mauricia to sweepings of the street, was the very image employed by the mid-nineteenth-century social surveyor Henry Mayhew when describing vagrants, whom he associates not only with street sweepings, but also with manure. Like prostitutes, vagrants were perceived as a 'pestilence', both physical[133] and moral. Mayhew described vagrants as

> A vast heap of social refuse – the mere human street-sweepings – the great living mixen – that is destined, as soon as the spring returns, to be strewn far and near over the land, and serve as manure to the future crime-crop of the country.[134]

Prostitution can, indeed, be seen as a kind of vagrancy. According to the portrait that Parent-Duchâtelet painted of the prostitute – a portrait that was often reproduced in the literature on prostitution during the rest of the century and influenced many novelists – she represents

---

133 As Gertrude Himmelfarb points out (*The Idea of Poverty: England in the Early Industrial Age* [London, Faber & Faber, 1984], 340), they were carriers of tramp-fever, a disease similar to typhoid and cholera.

134 Henry Mayhew, *London Labour and the London Poor* (1851–62), quoted by Himmelfarb, *The Idea of Poverty*, 340.

movement, instability, 'turbulence' and agitation. Hence the need for confinement.[135] In Spain, Bernaldo de Quirós and Llanas Aguilaneido observed the striking resemblance between prostitutes and vagrants.[136] They stressed the prostitute's need for change and movement, and her aversion to both family life and any kind of methodical work. In *Fortunata y Jacinta* Mauricia is often seen wandering the streets. She is, in fact, a 'corredora de prendas'.[137] In the novel it is not clear where she lives after leaving the convent. Like vagrants, she does not seem to be 'fixed' in any particular place. When she is finally thrown out of the convent, she exclaims, '¡Ay, mi querida calle de mi alma!' (I, 655).[138] After Mauricia is expelled from Las Micaelas, her respectable sister Severiana tells Jacinta about the need to 'contain' Mauricia, echoing the contemporary need for 'fixing' the dangerous groups of the population:

135 Corbin, *Women for Hire*, 7, 19. In *Time, Desire and Horror*, 86, Corbin notes that Balzac described prostitutes as 'essentially mobile' and, in that respect, animalistic. Stability was, therefore, the first step for the re-education of the prostitute. Hence the need, in *Fortunata y Jacinta*, to 'fix' Mauricia.

136 Bernaldo de Quirós and Llanas Aguilaneido, *La mala vida en Madrid*, 59–60. In France, Oscar Commenge (*La prostitution clandestine à Paris* [Paris, Schleicher Frères Editeurs, 1897], 11) observed the increasing numbers of young women drifting through the streets of Paris with no fixed abode, and expressed his fears and anxieties about this particular sector of the population which was reluctant to submit to a regulated life and to a fixed residence.

137 Jo Labanyi (*Gender and Modernization in the Spanish Realist Novel* [Oxford, Oxford University Press, 2000], 180–81) notes that the verb 'correr' is used in the novel to signify both financial and sexual expenditure. Significantly, Mauricia is never explicitly called a prostitute in the novel. The only indirect reference is during Mauricia and Fortunata's first encounter in Las Micaelas, in which Mauricia tells Fortunata that they have already met once before in 'casa de la Paca' (I, 607). Fortunata's clarification that she had only been there twice out of financial need (I, 610) makes the reader assume that they are talking about a 'casa de citas' or a clandestine brothel. It can thus be argued that it was Mauricia's association with the street, verbal filth and alcoholic intoxication that provided sufficient grounds to construct her as a prostitute in society's eyes. Of course, there is also the fact that Mauricia is an unmarried mother.

138 Doña Lupe's young maid Papitos represents another example of the association drawn between the streets, vagrancy and moral corruption. Papitos is picked up, or 'rescued', from the danger of the streets by doña Lupe: 'La recogí de un basurero de Cuatro Caminos, hambrienta, cubierta de andrajos. Salía a pedir y por eso tenía todos los malos hábitos de la vagancia' (I, 545). Papitos is associated with vagrancy and, therefore, she is seen as an incipient or potential prostitute: it is significant, in this respect, that doña Lupe found her in a rubbish dump. On one occasion in the novel, when Mauricia is found seriously injured near doña Lupe's house and Papitos insists that she wants to go by herself to the 'botica' to see how Mauricia is cured, doña Lupe does not allow her to go (II, 164). Of course, she also tries to impose her regime

yo quería hablar a la señorita para ver si doña Guillermina tenía proporción de meterla en cualquier parte donde la *sujetaran*. En las Micaelas no puede ser, a cuento de que allí la tuvieron que echar por escandalosa... Pero bien la podrían poner, si a mano viene, en un hospicio, o casa de orates, al menos para que no diera malos ejemplos. (II, 67–68; my emphasis)

It is significant that Severiana thinks that Mauricia should be secluded in a workhouse-like institution or in a lunatic asylum, thereby echoing the equation established by some contemporaries between the different marginal groups – whether prostitutes, beggars or lunatics – an equation founded on the perception of these sectors of the population as destructive and irrational, as well as on the need to 'fix' them and subject them to discipline. The threat posed by Mauricia's reluctance to be 'fixed' and disciplined is voiced, once again, by Maxi when he tells doña Lupe and Fortunata that, after her stay with the Protestant pastor and his wife, Mauricia has been taken back to her sister's house, but that 'allá tampoco la pueden sujetar' (II, 167).[139]

Ironically, it is her respectable job as 'corredora de prendas' that sends Mauricia into the streets and into contact with the dangers of public space. Mauricia is depicted in the novel, when she is not under the effects of alcohol, as a hard-working woman. The narrator notes that doña Lupe, for whom Mauricia used to work, 'echaba muy de menos [a Mauricia], porque aunque era muy alborotada y disoluta, cumplía siempre bien' (I, 543). Also, when she is found drunk and injured in the street, just before her death, doña Lupe exclaims, '¡Pobre mujer! ¡Tener ese vicio! De veras lo siento, no hay otra como ella para correr alhajas' (II, 164).

The narrator highlights once more Mauricia's qualities and abilities as a worker when, after Maxi's account of Mauricia's stay with the pastor and his wife, he states, 'doña Lupe compadeció a la Dura, deplorando que

---

of surveillance on Fortunata, although the latter will resist. Doña Lupe's 'recycling' of Papitos – her training of Papitos as a housemaid – can be seen as paralleling the nuns' recycling of the women in Las Micaelas in order to turn them into domestic servants. Labanyi (*Gender and Modernization*, 124–25, 191–95, 198 and 200 in particular) discusses the role played by certain bourgeois and petit-bourgeois characters in *Fortunata y Jacinta*, as well as in other novels, in recycling human 'refuse'.

139 Fortunata is also often seen by Guillermina in similar terms. During her second 'interview' with Fortunata, Guillermina tells her, 'veo que usted no tiene atadero' (II, 250). Towards the end of the novel, when Guillermina finds out that Fortunata has gone out, leaving the child with the young maid, she thinks to herself, 'a esta no la sujeta nadie' (II, 482). Guillermina believes that Fortunata is going to return to prostitution, and considers her unfit to fulfil her role as a mother. She links her to the streets when she exclaims, '¡Marcharse a paseo! Qué ganas de calle tenía' (II, 483). She makes this association once more when Fortunata comes back and she scolds her, 'callejera, cabra montés. Esta visto: no sirve usted para madre...' (II, 487).

con vicio tan inmundo malograse las cualidades de inteligente corredora que poseía' (II, 167). Mauricia is also shown to work hard in the convent, at least before the symptoms of her attacks begin to show. The emphasis placed by the narrator on Mauricia's capacity for hard work dismisses the association made by contemporary social and moral commentators between prostitution on the one hand, and idleness and aversion to work on the other. This also exposes the weaknesses of the dominant ideology thesis, since this ideology does not leave any room for the possibility that certain values traditionally considered to be bourgeois, such as respectability, cleanliness and hard work, already existed in the working classes without having been imposed from above. Both Mauricia and Fortunata are depicted as hard-working women in the novel and, when secluded in the convent, they are shown to enjoy the cleaning tasks imposed by the nuns. The reform programme instituted in the convent may, from this perspective, be seen as redundant. There is no reason to believe that these virtues were imposed from outside. As one historian has pointed out in respect of cleanliness and other so-called bourgeois values,

> Cleanliness [...] was not necessarily simply a bourgeois habit imposed upon, or taught to, the working classes. It was also a habit which some working-class groups were perfectly capable of discovering for themselves and valuing in its own right as one of the attributes of decent and respectable living. There is plenty of evidence that the working classes wished to be respectable not because some middle-class pundit told them to be so, but because they liked it and disapproved of shiftless and sluttish ways. Similarly, the working classes did not need to be told by the middle class that family life was important, that honest toil was better than loafing, or that saving for a rainy day was sensible.[140]

These values were thus not 'alien imports', absorbed by a passive and helpless working class. Working-class culture was not purely defensive and static and it would be wrong to assume that the working classes were naive and, therefore, incapable of developing their own independent culture.

In fact, Fortunata is not portrayed in the novel as a tabula rasa, despite the assertion by the narrator, Juanito and Guillermina that she is 'unhewn stone' that needs to be 'shaped' by society. The narrator refers to her inclination towards work on several occasions, both in the Las Micaelas episode and in the rest of the novel. It is noteworthy that before entering the 'reforming' institution she is already shown doing housework and enjoying it, particularly cleaning, as the narrator notes:

140 F. M. L. Thompson, 'Social Control in Victorian Britain', *Economic History Review*, XXXIV (May 1981), 196.

> [Fortunata] [g]ustaba mucho de los trabajos domésticos, y no se cansaba nunca. Sus músculos eran de acero, y su sangre fogosa se avenía mal con la quietud. Como pudiera, más se cuidaba de prolongar los trabajos que de abreviarlos. Planchar y lavar le agradaba en extremo, y entregábase a estas faenas con delicia y ardor, desarrollando sin cansarse la fuerza de sus puños. (I, 493)

Maxi and Feijoo also admire her capacity for hard work.[141] So does doña Lupe, who comments to Maxi, '¡Qué trabajadora es tu mujer! Siempre que vengo aquí me la encuentro planchando o lavando. Francamente; no creí...' (I, 698). Doña Lupe's observation is significant, as it suggests that she did not expect Fortunata – as a member of the working classes and, particularly, as a 'fallen woman' – to be a hard-working woman. Fortunata's proclivity towards domesticity and family life, her wish to become a devoted wife and mother, are also frequently emphasized. The narrator makes Fortunata admit that she would have been happy being the wife of a bricklayer or of an 'obrero honrado' (I, 686; II, 205).[142] Moreover, as Maxi proudly points out to doña Lupe, Fortunata is thrifty (I, 537), thrift being regarded in the period as an essential quality in a housewife.[143] Similarly, the novel shows that Fortunata has an autonomous sense of sexual morality ('honradez'), independent of any imposition from above. Fortunata is shown to possess these qualities *before* she is submitted to the bourgeoisie's 'educational' programme. Thus, Galdós's setting up of a panoptic institution in the novel allows him to denounce and, to an extent,

141 Maxi associates hard work with 'honradez' when he comments, 'Tiene la honradez en la médula de los huesos [...] Le gusta tanto trabajar, que cuando tiene hecha una cosa la desbarata y la vuelve a hacer por no estar ociosa' (I, 490).

142 As mentioned earlier (note 89) Juanito does not comprehend, and even dislikes, Fortunata's proclivity to domesticity because it blurs the dividing line that he has constructed in his mind between the respectable wife and the prostitute – or seductress. When he wants to break his relations with her for the second time he thinks to himself, 'La pobrecilla no aprende, no adelanta un solo paso en el arte de agradar; no tiene instintos de seducción, desconoce las gaterías que embelesan. Nació para hacer la felicidad de un apacible albañil, y no ve nada más allá de su nariz bonita. ¿Pues no le ha dado ahora por hacerme camisas?¡Buenas estarían!...' (II, 76). Although bourgeois discourses constructed an image of women as essentially domestic, and women were expected to engage themselves in domestic tasks, this did not apply in practice to bourgeois women, who were mostly idle. Bourgeois ideas on domesticity were thus mainly an instrument for the control of working-class women. In *Fortunata y Jacinta* it is ironic that Jacinta, the representative in the novel of the bourgeois wife, would never be expected to sew Juanito's shirts. In this sense, Fortunata is presented as different from other mistresses, but also from Jacinta.

143 The narrator observes Fortunata's skill in domestic management: 'Fortunata tenía una despensa admirablemente provista, y en ropa y trapos gastaba muy poco [...] No era glotona; pero sí inteligente en víveres y en todo lo que concierne a la bien provista plaza de Madrid' (II, 104).

ridicule the bourgeois attempt to impose hygienic and domestic values on a social group, in this case working-class prostitutes, considered a threat to respectable femininity and public health and, therefore, to the stability of the society of the day.

Fighting Filth beyond the Walls of Las Micaelas

Mauricia's expulsion from the convent represents the inability of the bourgeoisie to reform her. Bourgeois society, after having used Mauricia for its own reforming purposes, has to dispose of her, unable to deal with her disruptive and ungovernable behaviour. As a 'residual deviant', she needs to be segregated from the group of deserving or hopeful women. However, some time later, when Mauricia is approaching her death, and is, consequently, more malleable and easily influenced, the bourgeoisie goes back to her in a last attempt to restore her to the norm, an attempt that eventually failed with her incarceration in the convent.

The episode of Mauricia's death illustrates how philanthropy and control work at the private level of the home. This episode can be seen as an extension of the cleansing project undertaken in Las Micaelas. The images of physical and moral filth abound here, with the narrator drawing constant parallels between the two. Guillermina is aware that Mauricia's sickness, and the fact that she is nearing death, offers her the ideal chance to gain control over her.[144] As Prochaska has noted in this respect,

> Christianity, born with a death, fed on the dying. This was part of the power of the philanthropist's faith. In the cholera wards and the countless sick beds, it gave an answer, however melancholy, to the problem of evil, and death [...] The death-bed scene, with its ritual women visitors, reminiscent of that most famous scene at the foot of the Cross, is one of the most enduring images of that century's life and literature.[145]

In *Fortunata y Jacinta* the narrator makes clear that Mauricia's repentance – or at least what appears to be repentance – is, to a large extent,

144 In view of Mauricia's imminent death, Guillermina encourages Severiana to take her out of hospital so that she can be looked after at home (II, 174). The system of 'hospitalidad domiciliaria' was favoured by most doctors from the beginning of the nineteenth century, and was believed to be the most efficient way of assisting the sick poor, see Fernando Alvarez-Uría, 'Los visitadores del pobre: Caridad, economía social y asistencia en la España del siglo XIX', in *De la beneficencia al bienestar social: Cuatro siglos de acción social* (Madrid, Siglo Veintiuno, 1993), 117–46, 126 (footnote 12). It was also the most intrusive and interventionist way of dispensing charity, as the episode of Mauricia's death shows.

145 Frank Prochaska, *Women and Philanthropy in Nineteenth-Century England* (Oxford, Clarendon Press, 1980), 160.

motivated by the proximity of death. As doña Lupe relates to Fortunata,

> La infeliz tarasca viciosa, con [...] las ternezas de Doña Guillermina, y más
> aún, con la proximidad de la muerte, estaba que parecía otra, curada de sus
> maldades y arrepentida *en toda la extensión de la palabra,* diciendo que se
> quería morir lo más católicamente posible, y pidiendo perdón a todos con
> unos ayes y una religiosidad tan fervientes que partían el corazón. (II, 171)

Mauricia's reform is shown in the novel as Guillermina's personal
philanthropic enterprise. Guillermina's encounter with the Protestant
pastor and his wife shows that she is determined to have monopoly control
over her reclamation. When Mauricia has a mental convulsion and leaves
the Protestants' house, the narrator comments that Guillermina 'le echa un
cordel al pescuezo y se la lleva' (II, 167). In a British context, Prochaska
has observed the rivalries between the different and numerous charities
that emerged around the middle of the nineteenth century which,
curiously, 'competed for the custom of the poor'. In this sense, he argues,
philanthropic enterprise could be considered a feature of laissez-faire
capitalism.[146] In the novel, Guillermina can also be seen as competing for
Mauricia's custom.[147] Later, after Mauricia has been found injured and
taken to hospital, Guillermina will persuade Severiana to take her out of
hospital and bring her into her house, where she will be able to
undertake her 'private' philanthropic project. Guillermina's obsession
with cleaning Severiana's house, particularly Mauricia's room, and the
entrance to the building are symbolic of her attempts to purify Mauricia
and bring her back to the realm of the Catholic religion before her death.
Guillermina also insists that the entrance to the building should be
properly swept, and forbids the children to throw rubbish there. The
elimination of physical filth, as much as that of moral and verbal filth –
notably Guillermina's attempts to cleanse Mauricia's foul language – is,
once more, an essential part of Mauricia's reform. It is noteworthy, in
connection with the association of prostitution with foul odours, that
after Severiana has finished cleaning the house she burns lavender in order
to get rid of the bad smell, as the narrator notes (II, 205). Guillermina's
sermon to the neighbourhood children is interrupted by the arrival of
the priest Nones, to whom she declares, 'Tengo que estar en todo. Si yo
no tratara de enseñar a esta gente la buena crianza, vendría usted luego
con el Santísimo y tendría que entrar pisando lodo, y cuanta inmundicia

---

146 Prochaska, *Women and Philanthropy*, 106.

147 Since the Protestant and Catholic notions of philanthropy became very close after the
rise of industrial capitalism, Guillermina's intransigent attitude towards the Protestant pastor and his wife would seem to be out of place and a cause of ridicule by
Galdós.

hay' (II, 183–84). Her exaggerated zeal for cleanliness is undermined by Nones when he replies, '¿Y qué importa?' As Guillermina's words to Nones show, she is establishing a hierarchy in which she places herself in an elevated moral position with regard to the working-class neighbourhood.

The viaticum episode not only serves Guillermina's plans for indoctrinating Mauricia, but is also used by her as an edifying spectacle for the whole working-class community. Guillermina involves all the neighbours in her cleaning project. She makes the women sweep the corridor, take candles and flowers to Severiana's house and bring indoors the 'pingajos' that are hanging outside their houses. Finally, she orders them to take care of their physical appearance: 'Es preciso que estéis todas muy decentes', she advises (II, 185); although she also makes clear that cleanliness must not be mistaken for luxury, 'No se quiere lujo, sino decencia' (II, 186). Moments before the arrival of the viaticum, Guillermina inspects the neighbourhood to make sure that everything is in order:

> Guillermina recorría toda la *carrera*, desde la puerta del cuarto de Severiana hasta la de la calle, dando órdenes, inspeccionando el público y mandando que se pusieran en última fila las individualidades de uno y otro sexo que no tenían buen ver. (II, 187)

Here, the narrator, through the humorous use of 'individualidades', mocks Guillermina's decision to place the less respectable-looking people at the back of the crowd. The narrator, continuing in a humorous tone, goes on to observe that Guillermina ordered that a piano, which had been placed opposite the entrance to the house, be removed, as she considers that it 'estorbaba *la edificación del vecindario*, por el apetito que algunos sentían de ponerse a bailar' (II, 188; my emphasis).

Guillermina's obsession with cleaning and tidying are paralleled by her zeal to purify Mauricia and make her repent her sins. The instillation of a sense of guilt is part of what Foucault qualified as 'subtle' or more sophisticated instruments of control, in that the individual is subjected to constant mental coercion. Foucault observed that the self-acknowledgment of one's guilt was used in lunatic asylums as an instrument of self-control. The madman was made to feel 'morally responsible for everything (within him) that may disturb morality and society, and must hold no one but himself responsible for the punishment he receives'.[148] Thus, fear of punishment was considered to act as an efficient instrument of subtle coercion in the management of patients. Similarly, Prochaska has shown that a major aim of the philanthropist's indoctrination programme was to instil in the recipient a sense of guilt and shame. In this way the

---

148 Foucault, *Madness and Civilization*, 246–47.

philanthropist could gain the prostitute's humility, which would in turn prepare the ground for her repentance and reformation. Nothing was more disturbing to the women visitors, Prochaska notes, than the sinner's unwillingness to confess her sins. By making her recognize her sins, the philanthropist was, in fact, placing herself on a higher moral plane than the prostitute, in spite of the assumption that philanthropy was trying to create a kind of sisterhood between the philanthropist and the prostitute.[149] Since the main aim of philanthropy was to improve or reform the character of those controlled, this necessarily implied the existence of a moral code of behaviour that positioned the philanthropist higher in the hierarchy than the prostitute.

In the novel, the narrator does not leave any doubts regarding the inferior moral position in which the philanthropist places Mauricia. Similarly, when describing the relationship between Guillermina and Fortunata – it has to be stressed that in Guillermina's eyes Fortunata is a fallen woman – the narrator makes clear that, for the philanthropist, the existence of a moral hierarchy is beyond question. When Guillermina first meets Fortunata in Severiana's house on the occasion of Mauricia's death, she overtly declares her moral superiority when she says, '¡Si esto parece comedia! ¡Encontrarse aquí, en un acto de caridad, dos personas tan… no se me ofenda si digo tan opuestas por sus antecedentes, por su manera de ser…! Y no quiero rebajar a nadie' (II, 229). In fact, Guillermina is openly humiliating and belittling Fortunata. Similarly, the narrator points out Fortunata's feeling of inferiority in relation to Guillermina: 'Fortunata no sabía qué decir, ni qué cara poner, ni para donde mirar; tanto la asustaba y sobrecogía la presencia de la respetable dama' (II, 228). This suggests that any idea of a relationship based on terms of equality was far from real.

The maintenance of an equal relationship was also made impossible by a necessary degree of interference on the part of the philanthropist since, as noted in Chapter 1, it was difficult to strike a compromise between benevolence and altruism on the one hand, and authoritarianism and the desire for control on the other. Galdós's presentation of Guillermina as a double-edged character – she is described as human and caring at times, but as domineering and acting out of self-interest at others – is a reflection of the difficulty experienced by the philanthropist in maintaining this balance. This undermines the idea of philanthropy as a successful mechanism of control, since discipline could often lead to assertiveness and rebellious behaviour. Indeed, in *Fortunata y Jacinta*, neither Mauricia nor Fortunata are shown as passive and submissive

149 Prochaska, *Women and Philanthropy*, 155–57.

characters, not even at the moment of their deaths, when the philanthropist can exercise her power with less constraint.

Indeed, in the episode of Mauricia's death, in spite of the efforts to
control her behaviour, Mauricia's repentance and, therefore, her inter-
nalization of bourgeois hygienic discourse and submission to discipline is
presented ambiguously through the chapter. On the occasion of
Fortunata's first visit to Mauricia after she has been taken sick to
Severiana's house, Mauricia seems to admit her guilt without hesitation:
'Sí..., bien mala he sido, bien remala...' (II, 175). Also, she tries to
convince Fortunata that she should repent her sins:

> 'Oye tú, arrepiéntete... pero con tiempo, con tiempo. No lo dejes para última
> hora, porque... eso no vale. Tú tampoco eres trigo limpio, y el día que hagas
> sábado en tu conciencia, vas a necesitar mucha agua y jabón, mucha escoba
> y mucho estropajo...' (II, 175)

Here, Mauricia seems to have internalized bourgeois ideas connecting
physical and moral cleanliness. Later in the episode Mauricia insists once
again to her friend that she must repent everything: 'Arrepiéntete de
todo, chica, pero de todo... Somos muy malas... tú no sabes bien lo malas
que somos' (II, 187). However, the narrator comments, significantly, that
Mauricia 'estaba como bajo la presión de un gran temor', thereby
undermining the genuineness of Mauricia's repentance and presenting it
rather as prompted by fear. Similarly, when Mauricia receives her
daughter's visit and exclaims, '¡Ay, qué mala he sido!', the narrator notes
that she said it 'sin efusión, como quien cumple un trámite' (II, 193).
Although she overtly admits that she has repented of her sins, urging
Fortunata to do the same, Mauricia repeats and maintains to the very end
the idea that Fortunata's love for Juanito is not a sin. Mauricia defends
her right to have an idea of her own, '¿No puede una tener una idea?...'
(II, 199). These words are echoed later in the novel by Fortunata.
Mauricia, like Fortunata just before her death, is convinced of the
validity of her idea as a means of attaining salvation, even if it does not
conform to bourgeois canons:

> Y por la santidad que tengo entre mí, te digo que si el marido de la señorita
> se quiere volver contigo y le recibes, no pecas, no pecas... [...] Cuando me
> muera [...] el Santísimo me dirá que tengo razón... (II, 199)

Another aspect of the cleaning programme undertaken by Guillermina
is the cleansing of Mauricia's language. Galdós observes, humorously,
how Mauricia has been submitted to bourgeois attempts to control her
vocabulary:

> [Mauricia] iba a soltar un terno; pero se contuvo, porque le estaba absoluta-
> mente prohibido pronunciar palabras feas, siendo esto para ella un gran
> martirio, a causa de la poca variedad de términos de su habitual lenguaje.
> (II, 179)

Mauricia is shown to be under constant fear of pronouncing bad words.
Her effort to avoid swearing is shown to be the result of external coercion rather than a genuine act of repentance:

> A las preguntas que le hizo [Fortunata], respondía con la mayor concisión,
> porque el temor de decir alguna palabra fea enfrenaba sus labios. Estaba
> reducida a usar tan sólo la tercera parte de los vocablos que emplear solía, y
> aún no se le quitaban los escrúpulos, sospechando que tuviesen algún eco
> infernal las voces más comunes. Lo que Fortunata le oyó claramente fue
> esto, –¡Ay, qué gusto salvarse!...' Pero al punto frunció Mauricia el ceño. Le
> había entrado la sospecha de que la palabra *gusto* fuese mala. (II, 187)

Once again, the use of humorous language in this passage allows Galdós
to ridicule Guillermina's endeavours to curb Mauricia's filthy language.

The uncertainty of her repentance is reinforced by the fact that
Mauricia's fear of using filthy language seems to fade as the episode of
her death progresses. The narrator states that the night after she received
Holy Communion, '[e]l temor de pronunciar palabras malas parecía haberse
desvanecido en ella, porque escupió de sus labios algunas que ardían' (II,
196–97). Ironically, it is shortly after having been administered the sacra-
ments that she begins to behave in a rebellious and disorderly way, her
violent fits becoming more frequent and her language more aggressive
and filthy. During the mental convulsions that she suffers in the convent
and when she is nearing death, Mauricia is identified with everything
that represents the antithesis of the hygienic and domestic values propounded by the nuns in Las Micaelas.[150] The narrator observes, significantly, that the encounter with her daughter had a much deeper effect on
her than the fact that she received Communion (II, 197), which might
give some indication as to what triggered off her repeated convulsions.
Doña Lupe, who spent the night at her bedside, was shocked by Mauricia's
uncontrollable behaviour during her fits and her disturbing language
during the night. As she reports to Fortunata the following morning,

> Juraría que todo el aguardiente que ha bebido en su vida se le subió a la
> cabeza esta noche. Ya se levantaba, ya se revolvía, echaba las piernazas
> fuera de la cama, y los brazos como aspas de molino... ¡Luego unas voces y
> unos berridos...! Ya sabes el diccionario que gasta... (II, 201)

---

150 As Tsuchiya has pointed out ('"Las Micaelas por fuera y por dentro"...', 65), during
her fits, Mauricia's body appears to transgress gender boundaries.

Doña Lupe seems to have been shocked not just by the sacrilegious aspects of Mauricia's rantings but also by their sexual connotations.[151] Mauricia has one last fit just before her death (II, 224), which can be seen as symbolizing her final rejection of discipline.

Mauricia's expulsion from the convent and her death later in the novel symbolize the need to discard from society those members of the population who are beyond bourgeois control. Through Mauricia's rebellion Galdós shows how bourgeois attempts at control were resisted by the working classes or, put another way, how the bourgeoisie did not always succeed in imposing its values on its social subordinates. Her expulsion from the convent and eventual death in no way detract from the value or efficacy of her rebellion.[152]

But what of Fortunata? In the section of the novel dealing with Las Micaelas she is depicted as generally responsive to the regime of discipline and control. But the fact that she shifts from passive to active character after her stay in Las Micaelas, ultimately becoming a figure capable of challenging bourgeois moral values, proves the precariousness of her reform. As the narrator comments, 'las ideas tan trabajosamente construidas en las Micaelas, se desquiciaron de repente' (I, 667). In fact, her stay in the reformatory serves chiefly to introduce her to the unreformable Mauricia, who will prove a lasting influence on her. Indeed, it could be

---

151 Lucille V. Braun ('The Novelistic Function of Mauricia la Dura in Galdós' *Fortunata y Jacinta'*, *Symposium*, 3 [Winter 1977], 286) has drawn attention to the sexual symbolism that lies below the surface in Mauricia's rantings in this episode.

152 This point is also made by Akiko Tsuchiya ('"Las Micaelas por fuera y por dentro"…', 63–68). In her analysis of *La desheredada*, Tsuchiya discusses how Isidora defies and resists attempts to be shaped and controlled by masculine bourgeois discourse on women's sexuality. At the end of the novel, Tsuchiya argues, Isidora consciously chooses the path of prostitution because, although this does not guarantee total freedom from social surveillance and control, by refusing to follow a respectable and orderly bourgeois life she asserts her independence and sexual freedom; see 'The Female Body under Surveillance: Galdós's *La desheredada*', in Jeanne P. Brownlow and John W. Kronik (eds), *Intertextual Pursuits: Literary Meditations in Modern Spanish Narrative* (Lewisburg, PA, Bucknell University Press, 1998). Similarly, Stephanie Sieburth ('Enlightenment, Mass Culture, and Madness: The Dialectic of Modernity in *La Desheredada*', in Linda M. Willem [ed.], *A Sesquicentennial Tribute to Galdós 1843–1893* [Newark, DE, Juan de la Cuesta Hispanic Monographs, 1993], 39–40) has interpreted Isidora's final choice of prostitution as her – and the author's – rebellion against bourgeois disciplinary strategies. As a prostitute, Isidora in effect becomes the owner of the means of production and thus independent of bourgeois control, an independence that she would have lost had she become a working woman or a bourgeois wife, these being her two remaining options. More than this, as a carrier of syphilis and a destroyer of bourgeois fortunes and inheritances, the prostitute represented a force beyond bourgeois control and thus a danger to its social dominance.

argued that the moral indoctrination that Fortunata receives in the convent generates in her a subversive reaction which leads her to develop an autonomous identity. Jagoe has shown how Fortunata subverts and redefines the meaning of middle-class values related to gender roles in order to suit her own needs.[153] The fact that she can develop her own idea of 'honradez' in an autonomous way is a sign that she has a value system independent of the morality of those attempting to coerce her culturally. We have seen how, in Las Micaelas, she was shown to possess the domestic values already, particularly the delight in physical labour and cleanliness, which the nuns tried to instil in her. With respect to sexual morality, Fortunata never fully understands or apprehends the meaning of bourgeois terms such as 'honradez', not even at the moment of her death, because she attaches a different meaning to them in keeping with her own value system; that is, a non-institutionalized conception of respectability, marriage and motherhood. What bourgeois indoctrination does in her case is to create confusion in her mind: thus her constant questioning of the bourgeois concept of 'honradez' and her obsession with it, this being the result, in effect, of a badly assimilated ideology. Bourgeois indoctrination eventually triggers *pre-existing* ideas and values, thereby stimulating and accelerating the process of autonomous development. As a number of social historians have shown, the working classes were not simply helpless and naive victims of bourgeois coercion. Similarly, Fortunata is not a mere receptacle of a 'colonizing' bourgeois ideology. This implies a certain degree of autonomy, which runs counter to the idea of successful bourgeois acculturation.

Furthermore, it has been argued that since elements of the working classes already displayed respectable values as part of their own culture, they were predisposed to bourgeois influence. However, this argument allows little room for the possibility that working-class people developed their own autonomous culture independently of bourgeois influence: that ingrained working-class values would not inevitably take on a bourgeois complexion but would remain, essentially, working class in character. Thus, even though in certain respects working-class values and ideas differed little from those promoted by the bourgeoisie, they had different meanings attached to them, that is, the working classes conceptualized them in different ways. It would, therefore, be wrong to assume that the same terminological labels were always used to signify the same cultural beliefs.[154]

---

153 Jagoe, *Ambiguous Angels*, 102–19, and 'The Subversive Angel', 79–91.

154 As argued by Nicholas Abercrombie, Stephen Hill and Bryan Turner, *The Dominant Ideology Thesis* (London, George Allen & Unwin, 1980), chapter 4 in particular; and Thompson, 'Social Control', 189–208.

By making Fortunata transgress the institutionalized limits of respectability, domesticity and motherhood, Galdós portrays this character as a rebel in respect of her class. He is suggesting that the working classes, in this case working-class women, are perfectly capable of developing their own values, including those stereotypically labelled 'middle class', independent of bourgeois influence. Fortunata emancipates herself from contemporary bourgeois perceptions of domesticity and gender roles, as Jagoe has shown,[155] and, therefore, from a controlling discourse that categorizes her, like other working-class women, as deviant. However, Galdós depicts his character as essentially domestic and feminine, even if this is within a non-institutionalized framework. It is significant that Fortunata realizes herself, at the end of the novel, through motherhood. Even if Fortunata goes beyond the institutionalized boundaries imposed by bourgeois morality, she conceives her domestic role as a loyal wife and, particularly, a mother in a very conventional way. Hence her insistence that Jacinta is not Juanito's real wife, because she cannot have children. It is significant that in her last affair with Juanito she is more interested in fulfilling her 'pícara idea' than in Juanito himself; that is, her idea of motherhood takes over from her passion for Juanito. Thus, although Fortunata is portrayed as rebellious and subversive in respect of her class, in terms of gender the author adopts a much more conservative position.[156]

---

155 Jagoe, *Ambiguous Angels*, especially 117–18.
156 As Jagoe has observed (*Ambiguous Angels*, 115), Fortunata's characterization – the author's subversion of the dichotomy represented by the 'angel in the house' and the prostitute – reinforces the notion that women of all classes are innately more moral than men. However, in her analysis of the novel she concludes that Fortunata is a victor in terms of gender, although not in terms of class.

Chapter 3

The Drink Problem

Concerns about the social effects of drink during the nineteenth century, especially in its closing decades, need to be examined against the backdrop of changing attitudes to poverty that occurred a result of the processes of industrialization, urbanization and population growth.[1] At a time when a threatening working class had began to emerge, drinking, particularly excessive drinking, came to be seen as a vice associated with the undeserving working classes and their undisciplined and ungovernable behaviour. The perception of drunkenness as a major threat to social stability led to its being described as the major cause of poverty and its attendant social evils, such as mendicity, criminality, insanity, prostitution, domestic disorder, absenteeism from work, unemployment and subversion. Moreover, drink came to be regarded, towards the end of the century, as the main factor driving the perceived degeneration of the race. This chapter first identifies and examines the 'controlling' discourses that were produced around the issue of drink at the time and how these are dramatized in *Fortunata y Jacinta*; and, secondly, focuses on the links drawn during this period between drink and the burning issue of the degeneration of the race, clearly echoed in *Angel Guerra*. The issue of working-class drinking in relation to gender – a notable feature of both *Fortunata y Jacinta* and *Angel Guerra* – is also discussed by examining the contrasting attitudes adopted towards male and female alcoholism.

Drink and Social Stability: Discourses of Power
in *Fortunata y Jacinta*

Although several studies have addressed working-class characters in *Fortunata y Jacinta*, these have tended to concentrate on the figure of Fortunata and her relationship with the bourgeois world. Little has been written in detail about other working-class characters in the novel,

---

1 It should be noted that, although full-scale industrialization did not take off in Spain until the turn of the nineteenth century, an incipient process of industrialization was set in motion from about 1840.

especially those situated at the bottom of the social scale – those with whom antisocial, debauched behaviour such as excessive drinking and drunkenness tends to be associated. The character in the novel who appears most closely associated with drunkenness, Mauricia la Dura, has generally been viewed from a moralistic standpoint; by some as a symbolic character rather than a complex and ambiguous one.[2] Although critics, within this moralistic framework, have made some mention of her alcoholism, they have not related it to contemporary attitudes to drink. Nor has the issue of drinking in the novel been related to the theoretical perspective of bourgeois strategies of discipline and control and, in particular, to Foucault's notion of control through discourses. After examining the historical context in which attitudes to drink developed, this section explores the discourses produced in late nineteenth-century Spain by the middle classes and by those social groups with vested interests either in rigidly maintaining the existing social order, such as the religious establishment, or in following the path of reform, such as the medical establishment in its attempt to gain access to social power. A socio-historical perspective contributes to an increased understanding of the meaning of drink in *Fortunata y Jacinta*, and of the attitudes to it adopted by Galdós's bourgeois characters, whose views here – as we have seen in previous chapters – are frequently subverted.

Concern with the issue of drink during the nineteenth century, especially in its closing decades, needs to be examined in the context of an emergent working class and the threat of social dislocation that this represented in an increasingly industrialized and urbanized world. Historians have observed that in the pre-industrial era all classes drank, sometimes excessively, but this did not constitute a social concern. Similarly, drunkenness had little social stigma attached to it. Drinking was a cultural tradition for both the upper and lower classes and, as such, it was deeply rooted in social events. However, an important change took place in the nineteenth century, when, as a consequence of the transformations brought about by industrialization, drinking began to be regarded

---

2 See, for instance, Gustavo Correa, *El simbolismo religioso en las novelas de Pérez Galdós* (Madrid, Gredos, 1962), 110–17; Ricardo Gullón, *Galdós, novelista moderno* (Madrid, Taurus, 1960), 185; James H. Hoddie, 'Fortunata y Jacinta and The Eroica', *Anales Galdosianos*, XIV (1979), 130; José F. Montesinos, *Galdós* (Madrid, Castalia, 1969), II, 217; and Francisco Romero Pérez, 'The Grandeur of Galdós' Mauricia *la Dura*', *Hispanic Journal*, 3, No. 1 (Autumn 1981), 107–14.

3 Lilian L. Shiman, *Crusade against Drink in Victorian England* (London, Macmillan Press, 1988), 1. In Spain, contemporary observers also remarked that the consumption of alcohol increased considerably as a consequence of industrialization, spreading with particular force among the working classes and reaching the status of a medico-

as a social problem.[3] The issue of poverty came to be regarded during this period within the larger context of the 'social question'. Faced with this emergent threat, the Church was forced to adapt its ideology to the new circumstances, propounding the idea that (undeserving) poverty was for the most part self-inflicted (people *choosing* to be poor by opting for an immoral way of life). As a mid-century religious publication stated, 'las miserias materiales nacen casi siempre de las miserias espirituales';[4] it was therefore God's will that 'los más prudentes, los más misericordiosos y los más íntegros fuesen también los más ricos'.[5] Later in the century Concepción Arenal similarly declared that 'La raíz primera y más profunda de la miseria física es espiritual'.[6]

These ideas represented a response by the religious establishment to the new social and economic demands of a time during which notions of self-help, individual worth and personal betterment had begun to displace old beliefs and attitudes towards poverty. Under the influence of the new political economy of the free market and of the individual as free agent, the proposition that poverty was for the most part self-inflicted gained in currency. According to the new ideological perspective, drink became a convenient scapegoat for a wide array of social evils associated with poverty since, superficially at least, it was an easily identifiable cause.[7] The drinking poor were increasingly seen as contributing voluntarily to the states of physical and moral degradation in which they lived, thereby attracting the label 'undeserving'. The causes of drunkenness were attributed to the perceived vice, immorality and irreligiousness of the working classes, whereas living and working conditions were often ignored, or seen as a secondary factor that accentuated what were frequently regarded as innate moral defects of the poor. These views were echoed by the various discourses on drink that emerged during this period.

---

social problem. See Ricardo Campos Marín, *Alcoholismo, medicina y sociedad en España (1876–1923)* (Madrid, Consejo Superior de Investigaciones Científicas, 1997); and Ricardo Campos Marín and Rafael Huertas, 'El alcoholismo como enfermedad social en la España de la Restauración: Problemas de definición', *Dynamis*, 11 (1991), 263–86.

4 *El orador sagrado* (1853), II, quoted by José Antonio Portero, *Púlpito e ideología en la España del siglo XIX* (Zaragoza, Libros Pórtico, 1978), 221.

5 A. M. Claret, 'Sermón sobre la limosna', in *Colección de pláticas dominicales* (1862), X, quoted by Portero, *Púlpito e ideología en la España del siglo XIX*, 221.

6 Concepción Arenal, *El pauperismo* (1897), quoted by Díaz Castañón in her introduction to Arenal, *Obras completas*, ed. Carmen Díaz Castañón (Madrid, Atlas [Biblioteca de Autores Españoles], 1993), lxviii.

7 This tendency was reinforced by the influence in Spain of French positivism, which tended to attribute the cause of any social problem to alcoholism. See Campos Marín and Huertas, 'El alcoholismo como enfermedad social', 271.

As discussed in this book's Introduction, Foucault identified discourses, and in particular scientific discourses, as key instruments of power and control. As industrialization progressed, it was the discourse on Catholicism that in Spain provided the basic framework for the articulation of morality in the new economic system. In the same way as the Catholic Church tried to legitimize the interests of dominant social groups,[8] the political establishment sought to draw on religion for its survival and for the maintenance of the status quo. Religion, and the moralizing zeal attached to it, were a prominent feature of bourgeois culture.[9] But, as Foucault observed, power is exercised through an interplay of discourses, different truths being situated in a discursive formation of 'truth'. In this sense, religious discourse was interrelated with other discourses produced during this period, such as those located around self-help or the benevolent work of the reformer-philanthropist. A further notable discourse – one that played an important role in defining 'deviant' and 'abnormal' behaviour – was that produced by medicine, whose contribution to the shaping of the discourse on prostitution we have already seen.

According to Foucault, experts occupy positions of considerable power, not only because they are in command of a scientific and, therefore, rational and 'objective' body of knowledge but, most importantly, because they can 'fabricate' this knowledge, thereby establishing what Foucault called 'regimes of truth', which dominate those who are excluded from that specialist knowledge and, consequently, from the exercise of power. A discourse, said Foucault, can be labelled a 'regime of truth' when the professional group that produces it, motivated by vested socio-political interests, uses its position of power to make it true and underwrite its scientific validity. The formation of medical discourse was a result of the professionalization of medical science.[10] Medical experts saw the need to justify the importance of their role in order to gain a higher

8 Emphasis should be placed on the adaptability of the Church's ideology to the new capitalist attitudes towards wealth and the work ethic, which differed significantly from traditional Catholic views. See Portero, *Púlpito e ideología en la España del siglo XIX*, especially 157–238.

9 Raymond Carr (*Modern Spain (1875–1980)* [Oxford, Oxford University Press, 1980], 6) has observed that the religious awakening that took place in Restoration Spain originated as a reaction against the instability of the First Republic and the threat of anarchy that it represented for some sectors within the bourgeoisie and aristocracy. Also to be noted in this respect is the panic produced by the events of the Paris Commune of 1871, which led to the banning of the First International in Spain.

10 Particularly noteworthy here is the gendered nature of this professionalization, as traditional women healers were excluded. The one role that women were allowed to play in this Foucauldean scheme was that of philanthropy, as in the case of Guillermina in *Fortunata y Jacinta*.

social status and establish their authority by defending the hegemonic morality.[11] Medical discourse contributed to the notion that the drunk worker was self-made, reinforcing the moral ideas produced by the new religious discourse and underpinning the desire of dominant social groups to moralize on the issue of drink. As Alvarez-Uría has written:

> estas campañas médicas lanzadas por el bien de los obreros los responsabilizan de sus males a la vez que sirven de coartada a los intereses de un capitalismo vampiresco y despiadado que la etiología medica respeta porque va en ello su prestigio y su poder.[12]

It has been suggested that during the nineteenth century there was a general failure to distinguish between alcoholism, drinking and drunkenness.[13] Drinking was considered to lead inevitably to drunkenness, whereas drunkenness and alcoholism were seen by most as synonymous. According to Brian Harrison, the word 'drunkenness' (the state of being drunk) has been used since the Middle Ages, whereas the term 'alcoholism' (the diseased condition produced by alcohol) appeared only about 1860. It was not until the 1860s and 1870s that American experiments showed that alcoholism was a disease rather than an individual moral failing.[14] Thus, it is not surprising to find that the Spanish mid-century health expert Joaquim Salarich, in his *Higiene del tejedor* (1858), does not mention the term 'alcoholism'. The terms 'borrachera', 'embriaguez' and 'crápula' (which, significantly, had two meanings: 'embriaguez' and 'libertinaje' or 'disipación') were used instead. His failure to distinguish between drunkenness and alcoholism is reflected by his definition of 'borrachera' as 'la inclinación *habitual* de tomar inconsideradamente bebidas espirituosas hasta perder la razón' (my emphasis).[15]

11 Lynda Nead, *Myths of Sexuality: Representations of Women in Victorian Britain* (Oxford, Basil Blackwell, 1990), 25, 141–50.

12 Alvarez-Uría, *Miserables y locos: Medicina mental y orden social en la España del siglo XIX* (Barcelona, Tusquets, 1983), 323.

13 Brian Harrison, *Drink and the Victorians: The Temperance Question in England 1815–1875* (London, Faber & Faber, 1971), 21–22.

14 The term 'alcoholism' was coined by the Swedish physician Magnus Huss in his book *Alcoholismus Chronicus* (1852), in which he identified alcoholism, for the first time, as a specific disease.

15 Joaquim Salarich, *Higiene del tejedor* (1858), ed. Antoni Jutglar, *Condiciones de vida y trabajo obrero en España a mediados del siglo XIX* (Barcelona, Anthropos, 1984), 193. His perception of drunkenness as a passion – significantly, one chapter of his book is entitled 'De las pasiones' – is also indicative of the moral overtones attached to the word. Nearly twenty years after Salarich, the hygienist Angel Pulido (*Bosquejos médico-sociales para la mujer* [Madrid, Imp. Victor Saiz, 1876], 231) defined drunkenness in similar terms as 'la pasión de consumir bebidas alcohólicas hasta extraviar la razón'.

Despite the fact that alcoholism was described as a disease, medical men incorporated into their discourse all the pre-existing social and moral prejudice towards drunkenness, which led to its trivialization as a medical matter.[16] Campos Marín and Huertas have highlighted, in this respect, the complex and problematic definition of alcoholism in Restoration Spain.[17] The fact that the discourse constructed around alcoholism focused on the voluntary ingestion of alcoholic drink,[18] and, therefore, on the inherent guilt of the drinker, made it difficult for contemporary observers to describe it as a disease in its own right. At best, alcoholism was considered a peculiar pathology, half-way between a vice and a disease. The concepts of 'vicio' (a moral concept) and 'enfermedad' (a medical concept) were used constantly and interchangeably by Restoration hygienists, psychiatrists and social commentators who addressed the issue of alcoholism.[19] The individual and, most importantly, social effects attached to alcoholism – such as physical deterioration, madness, criminality, each of these seen as root factors in the physical and moral degeneration of the race[20] – contributed to this perception.

Public health discourse during this period was thus saturated with moralizing commentary. According to Salarich, the main cause of drunken-

16 Ricardo Campos Marín, 'Casas para obreros. Un aspecto de la lucha antialcohólica en España durante la Restauración', *Dynamis*, 14 (1994), 113.

17 Campos Marín and Huertas, 'El alcoholismo como enfermedad social', 263–86; and Campos Marín, *Alcoholismo, medicina y sociedad en España*, 30–55.

18 A contemporary commentator wrote in this regard: 'Nunca debe olvidarse que el alcohólico lo es por su voluntad, por su libérrima voluntad, y que antes de serlo, hubo un largo período durante el cual pudo arrepentirse de su conducta y abandonar sus hábitos de intemperancia' (A. Piga and A. Marioni, *Las bebidas alcohólicas: El alcoholismo* [1904], quoted by Campos Marín and Huertas in 'El alcoholismo como enfermedad social', 268–69). The notion of the 'voluntarismo' of the drinker was also emphasized by a contributor to the journal *La Voz de la Caridad*, 15 July 1883, 136. For a more detailed discussion of the perception of alcoholism as a 'voluntary disease', see Campos Marín, *Alcoholismo, medicina y sociedad*, 81–88.

19 Campos Marín and Huertas, 'El alcoholismo como enfermedad social', 263–86. The hygienist Philippe Hauser ('El siglo XIX considerado bajo el punto de vista medico-social', *Revista de España*, 101 [1884], 211), for instance, describes alcoholism as an 'enfermedad social' and a 'vicio social' in the same breath.

20 Degeneration theory was formulated in 1857 by the French psychiatrist Bénédict Morel (*Traité des dégénérescences physiques, intellectuelles et morales de l'espèce humaine et causes qui produisent ces variétés maladives*), who described hereditary alcoholism as one of the main factors of degeneration. The idea that alcoholism could be inherited, carrying with it, from one generation to the next, the increasingly damaging seeds of other degenerative diseases, including madness, hysteria, criminality, tuberculosis, meningitis and epilepsy, had a major impact on the Spanish medical discourse produced during the Restoration.

ness was 'el olvido de los deberes morales y religiosos'.[21] Other social critics saw beyond this narrow view and emphasized the contribution of broader socio-economic factors (such as poor nourishment, which encouraged drinking as a source of calories as well as increasing the alcoholic effect of drink) to the drunkenness of the working classes[22] – an attitude also voiced by a number of workers' representatives giving evidence to the Comisión de Reformas.[23] However, for most Spanish writers on the issue, alcoholism was considered the main cause of the proletariat's impoverishment. Even when working and living conditions were taken into account, the working classes were still often regarded as dissolute per se, and therefore responsible for their own misfortunes.[24]

The perception of drunkenness as a major cause of poverty and other social problems was voiced by Salarich when he asserted,

> La borrachera hace al obrero perezoso, jugador, querelloso y turbulento; le degrada y embrutece; destruye sus buenas costumbres; escandaliza a la sociedad, y le impele al crimen. La borrachera es la causa principal de las riñas, de muchos delitos, y de casi todos los desórdenes que cometen los obreros.[25]

Santero, another hygienist writing just a year before the publication of the first part of *Fortunata y Jacinta*, also remarked, in a similar moralizing tone, that the effects of drunkenness

---

21 Salarich, *Higiene del tejedor*, 194.
22 See, for example, Constancio Bernaldo de Quirós and José M. Llanas Aguilaneido, *La mala vida en Madrid* (Madrid, B. Rodríguez Serra, 1901), 100–01. A similar view is expressed by Fernando García Arenal in *Datos para el estudio de la cuestión social*, ed. Ramón María Alvar González (Gijón, Silverio Cañada, 1980), 42–43. (Originally published in 1885 [Gijón, Imp. del Comercio].) In this book García Arenal publishes the evidence that he collected in Gijón for the Comisión de Reformas Sociales.
23 *Reformas Sociales* (Información oral practicada en virtud de la Real orden de 5 de diciembre de 1883. Madrid) (Madrid, Manuel Minuesa de los Ríos, 1890), I, 101, 221, 235.
24 According to Ricardo Campos Marín (*Socialismo marxista e higiene pública: La lucha antialcohólica en la II Internacional (1890–1914/19)* [Madrid, Fundación de Investigaciones Marxistas, 1992], 27), the influence of the social environment, or other external factors, in the etiology of alcoholism was used in an ambiguous way. The concept of 'enfermedad social' (which made reference to the fact that alcoholism was a result of the influence of structural factors, particularly social inequalities) was combined with that of 'patología social' (a concept that related to any disturbance of the social, political and economic order of society, and which regarded alcoholism and other social evils as a clear symptom of a society that was diseased). In this respect, see also note 27.
25 Salarich, *Higiene del tejedor*, 194–95. This opinion also reflects the contradictions inherent in the bourgeois perception of the working classes. On the one hand, the latter are conceived as having bad habits, which are innate, but on the other, they are also considered to have 'buenas costumbres' that can be destroyed by drinking.

trascienden al orden social, porque el borracho pierde pronto los hábitos de trabajo, se hace holgazán y camorrista. De las tabernas es de donde salen la mayor parte de los crímenes; en las tabernas es donde se conciertan las grandes conmociones sociales.[26]

In *Fortunata y Jacinta*, Guillermina voices such views when, in the episode of her and Jacinta's visit to the tenement building, she exclaims, '¡Cuánta perdición! una puerta sí y otra no, taberna. De aquí salen todos los crímenes' (I, 318). The link between drink on the one hand, and disorder, degradation and immorality on the other is also evident in connection with the working classes in the scene where Juanito tells Jacinta about the disorderly life in the Cava de San Miguel, where Fortunata used to live with her family. In his description he refers to the loud rows caused by Izquierdo's and Segunda's drinking: 'Todo el santo día estaban riñendo [...] ¡Y qué tienda, hija, qué desorden, qué escenas! Primero se emborrachaba él solo; después los dos a turno' (I, 210–11). For Juanito, his contact with the 'pueblo' is equivalent to contact with vice. Jacinta's perception of the working classes is not too dissimilar. Thus, to Juanito's accounts of the disorderly life of the Cava she replies, 'No sé cómo te divertía tanto salvajismo' (I, 211). As I hope to show, the treatment of drinking in *Fortunata y Jacinta* offers a good example of how bourgeois control through discourses worked and, similarly, of the ways in which the lower classes and the author himself responded to these attempts at control.

The tendency to associate drink with the working classes during this period was a projection of bourgeois fears and anxieties about social groups perceived as potentially ungovernable and liable to escape control. This is shown by the fact that, although all classes drank, it was only working-class drinking that was connected with disorder, violence and irrationality. These characteristics were associated with working-class behaviour generally, and with rioting and irrational, 'savage' insurrections in particular. It is significant that in the novel these associations – between the working classes and unrespectable behaviour – are viewed from Juanito's and Jacinta's bourgeois perspective, functioning as 'focal characters'. By presenting the above associations as bourgeois constructions

---

26 Francisco Javier Santero, *Elementos de higiene privada y pública* (Madrid, El Cosmos, 1885), II, 489. This view of the taverns was shared by most commentators of the period. Concepción Arenal (*El pauperismo* [Madrid, Librería de Victoriano Suárez, 1897], I, 314 and 318 in particular) referred to taverns as 'focos de infección física y moral'. Taverns, according to Arenal, were a main breeding ground for criminality and political revolution. Similarly, a writer for *La Voz de la Caridad* described taverns as 'guaridas del vicio' and 'antesalas del presidio' (15 September 1878), 200. For an account of the association of taverns with criminality and political subversion, see Campos Marín, *Alcoholismo, medicina y sociedad en España*, 147–67.

and, therefore, as biased and unreliable, the author can disengage himself from them.

The process of industrialization brought with it the concept of 'work discipline'. According to the new mentality, drinking was seen as increasing absenteeism and undermining workers' performance, thereby reducing productivity and creating economic and social instability. The belief that alcoholism was a main factor of degeneration, and the social effects this could have in terms of decreased productivity and unwanted, increased spending on hospitals, asylums and prisons, reinforced this view.[27] Drunkenness was no longer perceived as 'a personal state of excess sociability', but rather as an 'antisocial vice'.[28] Excessive drinking thus became a major obstacle to overall national efficiency.[29] In keeping with these ideas, hard work was extolled and set against the 'vices' of idleness and drink, the latter often being linked in bourgeois discourses in a vicious circle, in which idleness served as both the cause and the consequence of drinking.[30]

The connection between drink and work avoidance is made by some characters in *Fortunata y Jacinta*. When Juanito recalls his life of dissipation in the Cava, he admits to Jacinta, 'pronto llegó un día en que allí no se hacía más que beber, palmotear, tocar la guitarra [...] Era una orgía

27 Alcoholism and other social problems, such as prostitution, mendicity, criminality, insanity and political revolution, were considered by organicist sociologists (who regarded society as a physical organism and therefore open to disease) as 'social pathologies' or 'enfermedades del cuerpo social', which 'trascienden con su influencia al estado físico de los individuos al par que trastornan el organismo social' (Santero, *Elementos de higiene privada y pública*, II, 487). In 1895, the French degenerationist psychiatrist P. M. Legrain wrote, 'el alcohol debe ser considerado como causa de degeneración tanto para el individuo como para su especie, como un peligro para la sociedad, como una fuente de gastos presupuestarios inútiles' (quoted by Campos Marín in *Socialismo marxista*, 42, note 45).

28 Shiman, *Crusade against Drink in Victorian England*, 1.

29 Jose Harris (*Private Lives, Public Spirit: A Social History of Britain, 1870–1914* [Oxford, Oxford University Press, 1993], 233) has suggested that, during the course of the nineteenth century, attitudes to drink shifted from perceiving it as a main cause of personal sin and suffering to a view that held excessive drinking to be a major drawback in the quest for economic progress.

30 In *El visitador del pobre* (1860) Concepción Arenal remarked, 'El pobre vicioso no suele ser trabajador; la ociosidad y el vicio se eslabonan para formar una cadena que le retiene en la más miserable de las esclavitudes' (*Obras completas*, I, 42). Of note here is the importance attached by contemporary observers to the issue of working-class leisure, of which immoderate drinking was seen as the main source. Arenal (*El pauperismo*, I, 281–326), among many others, talks about the dangers of irrational leisure activities, which she regards as encouraging dissolution, and advocates the creation of 'moral' and rational pastimes for workers.

continua. En la tienda no se vendía; en ninguna de las dos casas se trabajaba' (I, 212). Similarly, the petit-bourgeois character doña Lupe regards drinking as a 'vicio' and a 'perdición', which has jeopardized Mauricia's abilities as 'corredora de prendas'. Thus, she comments, 'Aprecio mucho a Mauricia, que a no ser por el maldito vicio, sería una buena mujer, trabajadora, fiel...' (II, 178). Doña Lupe's comment, however, has a positive aspect, in the sense that, although she associates drink with work avoidance, she admits that Mauricia is a hard-working woman, thereby undermining not only the association of the working classes with idleness but also the idea that idleness leads to drinking.[31]

However, in a society where women were largely excluded from the public sphere, women's alcoholism was not usually seen from the point of view of the effects that it might have had on the labour market; except inasmuch as the role of women (especially working-class women) in the private sphere of the home was seen as having an important indirect influence on the economic and social stability of the country, by turning the home into a space for developing a healthy and moral life for male workers. Women's work outside the home was a major concern of the period. Working women were seen as being exposed to the same dangers and temptations as men, and thus as likely to commit the same abuses.[32] Since women were expected to fulfil the social mission of mothers and homemakers, female alcoholism was usually seen in connection with

31 These contemporary views, which linked the working classes to idleness, and which regarded idleness as leading to drinking, are once more implicitly subverted by Galdós in *Misericordia* through the character of the drunkard 'la Petra', Almudena's housemate. 'La Petra' is shown to be good at trading and to enjoy it. The narrator observes that 'la Petra' 'había venido al mundo para ser [...] *comercianta*' (151), and that 'no se sentía mujer honrada y cabal sino cuando se dedicaba al tráfico' (151). Benina also admires her thrifty instincts (151–52). As with Mauricia, drink is the cause of her lack of perseverance at work. As the narrator comments, '[La Petra] tenía tino de comercianta [...] [,] pero nada le valió su buena voluntad, porque hubo de cogerla de su cuenta la Diega, que en pocos días la enseñó a embriagarse, y otras cosas peores. A los tres meses, Petra no era conocida [...] [,] no tenía constancia para nada, y ningún acomodo le duró más de dos días. Sólo duraba en ella el gusto del aguardiente' (142). It is ironic that the cause of her 'perdición' is precisely her work, which takes her into the streets, as was also the case with Mauricia. The contemporary criminologists Bernaldo de Quirós and Llanas Aguilaneido (*La mala vida en Madrid*, 59–60) present Galdós's description of this character as an example of the idleness and 'carácter vagabundo' of the prostitute. Although the novel does not make it explicit that she is a prostitute, like Mauricia her connection with the streets and the fact that she is an alcoholic provide sufficient grounds for this association.

32 Campos Marín, *Alcoholismo, medicina y sociedad*, 161–67; see also his 'La instrumentalización de la mujer por la medicina social en España a principio de siglo: Su papel en la lucha antialcohólica', *Asclepio*, 42, No. 2 (1990), 169.

women's negligence of their domestic duties, and often with prostitution. Interestingly, Mauricia's job as a 'corredora de prendas' does not appear to be the cause of her alcoholism. In fact, as doña Lupe's words reflect, work seems to bring out the best in her. Her 'respectable' sister Severiana also considers her to be 'enmendada' when, shortly after leaving the convent, she starts working again.

The link between drink and idleness is drawn in the novel also through the character of the drinker José Izquierdo. This character is seen by Guillermina to typify working-class idleness and ignorance: 'Lo que es usted, bien lo sabemos: un holgazanote y un bruto...' (I, 369). For Guillermina, Izquierdo is representative of the undeserving poor, unwilling to improve himself. Interestingly, despite her recriminations, Guillermina never refers to Izquierdo as 'borracho' or makes any direct allusion to his drunkenness. This may reflect the taboo nature of the issue of intemperance for the bourgeoisie.

It is ironic that Guillermina finds Izquierdo a job posing for a portrait painter, where all he has to do is sit still. In this instance, Galdós may be ridiculing the bourgeois work ethic, which was essentially aimed at gaining the obedience, submission and disciplined behaviour of the working classes. The fact that Guillermina thinks that Izquierdo would be suited to the passive job of artist's model may reflect the contemporary bourgeoisie's tendency to feminize the working classes: docility, meekness and submission were qualities that women from all social classes were expected to display, but also virtues that needed to be instilled in working-class men as well as women. This ironic episode questions the idea that working-class people should be docile and malleable, implicitly discrediting the bourgeoisie's attempts at control. Guillermina's offer of a job to Izquierdo does not represent a serious attempt to reform him. Once the deal is closed, she is not shown establishing any further contact with Izquierdo. The next time that they are shown together is towards the end of the novel, in the scene where Guillermina is waiting outside Fortunata's house for her return and Izquierdo offers her a beer (II, 493). Shortly afterwards, he is seen in a drunken slumber when he is supposed to be guarding Fortunata and her child during the night (II, 515, 516). Here drinking, *not* temperance, is ironically associated with docility and passivity. This may be a reflection of the author's desire to dissociate temperance from docility and submission to discipline.

Spanish commentators have noted that the image of the drunken male worker was used for political reasons by some contemporary authors who associated drunkenness with unemployment and subversion.[33] Thus,

33 Campos Marín, 'La instrumentalización de la mujer', 164.

the figure of the idle drinker was not only connected with indiscipline and low productivity, but also had a political dimension, which, in addition, indicated the different threats posed by male and female alcoholism. In *Fortunata y Jacinta*, Izquierdo is seen by some characters as politically dangerous. This reflects contemporary fears linking drunkenness with political revolution. In the episode where Jacinta and her maid pay him a visit to arrange the purchase of 'Pitusín', Izquierdo is seen as a perverse and uncivilized man, a 'bandido' and a 'monstruo'. The women are terrified in his presence: '"Este bandido – pensó Jacinta –, nos va a retorcer el pescuezo sin dejarnos chistar"' (I, 355). The narrator points out humorously that when both women found themselves inside his house, 'les entró un miedo tan grande que a entrambas se les ocurrió salir a la ventanilla a pedir socorro' (I, 355). Rafaela, the maid, even thinks up a 'plan' to defend herself and Jacinta from the 'monster' in case they are attacked (I, 355).

Despite these associations, at times endorsed by the narrator, this whole episode is described rather humorously, deflating such associations in the reader's eyes. The reader has already been alerted in the previous chapter to the fact that Izquierdo's drunken political ranting is only a product of his imagination and that he is, in fact, harmless. Thus, the connection between drunkenness and revolution is introduced only to be almost instantly dismissed as false. As the narrator comments, 'Todo era falso. Hay que declarar que parte de su mala reputación la debía a sus fanfarronadas y a toda aquella humareda revolucionaria que tenía en la cabeza. La mayor parte de sus empresas políticas eran soñadas' (I, 346). Even Guillermina demonstrates the falsity of the fears that the drunken Izquierdo inspires in other people. Thus she scolds him, 'usted es un infelizote que no ha tenido parte en ningún crimen ni en la invención de la pólvora' (I, 370). The fact that it is only the naive Jacinta and her maid who are frightened of Izquierdo is used by the author to suggest that contemporary fears linking drunkenness and revolutionary threat were similarly naive and unfounded. Galdós reinforces the lack of validity of this association by having Izquierdo, during the Restoration, become a model for historical paintings (I, 348), whose purpose was to create a sense of nationalism through the representation of Spanish history.

In symbolizing all the negative qualities attributed to the working classes, drunkenness served as a reference point for drawing class differences and demarcating the boundaries between the respectable and the unrespectable. Galdós shows the embarrassment caused to some of the bourgeois characters by drunkenness. When Juanito gets drunk one night during his honeymoon, he is reluctant to admit the fact. Thus, when

Jacinta asks him, '¿Crees acaso que el vino...?', he answers swiftly, '¡Oh! no, hija mía, no me hagas ese disfavor' (I, 229). Adopting a similar attitude, Jacinta does not dare say the word 'borracho': 'La palabra horrible negábase a salir de su boca' (I, 233). Estupiñá's shame and remorse when recalling the viaticum episode (which took place when he was made drunk by his nephew and some friends) should also be noted in this respect. The narrator points out that 'el recuerdo de la degradación de aquella noche le entristecía siempre que repuntaba en su memoria' (I, 175). Here, the humorous way in which this episode is described serves to undercut the association between drunkenness and vice.

Nevertheless, in the novel, the coupling of intemperance with degradation and lack of respectability is not exclusively a bourgeois attitude. Ido del Sagrario is eager to make clear to other characters that it is meat that makes him 'drunk' and not alcohol (I, 298). Ido is representative of the effects of poverty and malnutrition on the working classes. The irony here is that he gets 'drunk' on something – meat – considered the basis of good nourishment. Thus, on one occasion when he arrives home 'under the influence' of the meat that he has eaten, his wife Nicanora exclaims, 'tú has comido, ¿verdad...?' (I, 350). Galdós seems in this instance to be using the irony of Ido getting 'drunk' on food to draw the reader's attention to the miserable condition of the poor. Similarly, Fortunata's remorse over her relationship with the drunkard Juárez el negro, to whom she is forced to turn after her first affair with Juanito, is emphasized by the narrator. This character is presented as the stereotypical drunkard, drinking away the money that he manages to extract from Juanito, instead of spending it in a useful way, as Fortunata remarks (I, 486). The 'respectable' working-class character Severiana also reveals a sense of shame at the degradation that drunkenness brings. On one of the occasions when Jacinta comes to visit Severiana's niece Adoración, she asks Severiana about Mauricia, the child's mother. Severiana answers shamefully,

> Señora, no me la nombre [a Mauricia]. A poco de salir de las Micaelas, parecía algo enmendada. Volvió a correr pañuelos de Manila y algunas prendas; estaba en buena conformidad; pero ya la tenemos otra vez en danza con el maldito vicio. Anteanoche la recogieron tiesa en la calle de la Comadre... ¡Qué vergüenza...! (II, 67)

Here, Severiana is equating drinking not only with dissipation and shame but also with work avoidance. Severiana and her family stand for the respectable values of self-improvement, temperance, hard work, thrift and cleanliness. Severiana proudly admits to Jacinta that they can afford to live comfortably because her husband 'no tiene ningún vicio' (I, 366), thereby implying that he is not a drinker. Also, in the scene where she displays to her neighbours the shopping basket she has brought from the market, she is shown to be taking pride in her thriftiness and in her skill in domestic management (I, 365). The description of Severiana as a respectable, orderly and self-sufficient working-class character fits historians' observations that the desire for respectability and self-reliance occurred in the lower classes quite independently of the bourgeoisie's attempt to instil its own ideas and moral values in them.[34] Temperance and sobriety were advocated by sections of the working classes, not just by the upper layers, as forming part of the route to self-improvement and self-respect.[35] This negates the familiar notion of social control, which argues that working-class respectability was imposed from above by a dominant ideology. In Spain, the opinions of many workers' representatives giving evidence to the Comisión de Reformas Sociales reveal an attitude hostile to excessive drinking and the taverns.[36] As in *Fortunata y Jacinta*, the question of temperance was not the preserve of the bourgeoisie but an issue that cut across classes.

It has been noted that a principal target of the anti-alcoholism crusade undertaken by the discourse on public health was the family, as family life was considered to exercise an important influence on the physical and moral health of workers.[37] Within the family unit, women were given an essential role as vehicles for the transmission of the hygienic principles of order, cleanliness and thrift. It was believed that the creation of a homely atmosphere would awaken in the workers a respect for domesticity and family life. This would encourage them to forget the monotony of work and, more importantly, to keep away from taverns, as well as from the destructive influence of radical ideas. The

---

34 See, for instance, F. M. L. Thompson, 'Social Control in Victorian Britain', *Economic History Review*, XXXIV (May 1981), 189–208; and Nicholas Abercrombie, Stephen Hill and Bryan S. Turner, *The Dominant Ideology Thesis* (London, George Allen and Unwin, 1980).

35 Thompson, 'Social Control in Victorian Britain', 204.

36 One observer reporting to the Comisión pointed out that drunkenness was 'el vicio de que más pronto se avergüenza y aparta el obrero culto', *Reformas Sociales* (Información oral y escrita practicada en virtud de la Real orden de 5 de diciembre de 1883. Valencia) (Madrid, Manuel Minuesa de los Ríos, 1891), III, 72. A worker also observed that 'La taberna es un lugar inmundo en que se tejen célebres crespones para toda clase de delitos, y se forjan toda clase de cadenas para los hombres que a ella concurren'; therefore, in order to achieve the workers' 'regeneración', he concluded that it would be necessary to 'cerrar todos esos templos del vicio' (*Reformas Sociales*, I, 235).

37 Campos Marín, 'La instrumentalización de la mujer', 161–73, and 'Casas para obreros', 111–30. The creation of a homely atmosphere was believed to be an essential complement to the building of hygienic housing for workers.

idea that public health experts were trying to propagate was that, if educated into hygienic habits, any woman should be able to create a happy, well-managed, stable home, irrespective of her social station. Any problems arising within the working-class home were therefore attributed not to socio-economic conditions but to women's failure to instil the necessary moral values into it.

In *Fortunata y Jacinta*, Severiana represents the image of the 'ideal woman' that the bourgeoisie, backed by the medical discourse on public health, sought to manufacture, particularly among the working classes. Severiana possesses all the qualities that a housewife needs to create an ideal home. However, although she considers her husband's temperance and hard work as the main factors contributing to their material well-being, she also points out that he has a good enough job to allow them to live a comfortable life (I, 366). Galdós highlights the central role played by financial security when he describes Severiana as being 'la inquilina más ordenada, o si se quiere, más pudiente de aquella colmena' (I, 364–65), implying that she has a clean and tidy house because her husband earns enough money for her to afford it. By emphasizing the importance of material gain, Galdós is implicitly accepting that what were regarded as the weaknesses of the working classes – in this particular case of working-class women – were not necessarily a consequence of their moral failings but, rather, the result of their poverty, thus undermining conservative views that stated that education in matters of hygiene, irrespective of financial circumstances, should suffice to create a stable home.[38]

Despite the space given by commentators to describing the ideal woman, there was also contemporary concern for the issue of the alcoholic woman, considered unable to educate her children and set them a moral example, a problem connected with the burning issue of the degeneration of the race and the damaging role that alcoholic women were believed to play in reproduction.[39] In *Fortunata y Jacinta*, the alcoholic Mauricia is seen by the bourgeois characters, and sometimes by the bourgeois narrator himself, as representing the opposite pole to her

38 The view that domestic order was essential to keep male workers away from drink is endorsed by Galdós in *Misericordia*. Juliana, doña Paca's daughter-in-law, is presented as the image of the ideal woman who morally redeems her husband Antoñito through her hard work (she is a seamstress) and her skills as a housewife. Thanks to his wife's good qualities, Antoñito, who is described as a former drinker and a 'golfo', turns into an 'hombre formal', acquiring 'el hábito y el gusto del trabajo productivo'. The narrator points out, however, that in spite of the fact that they led a 'respectable' life, this was not enough to free them from the poverty in which they lived (117).

39 Campos Marín, 'La instrumentalización de la mujer', 168–70.

sister Severiana. Since, in the bourgeois mentality of the time, alcoholism often appeared linked to 'irregular' or socially unacceptable sexual behaviour (Mauricia had been involved in occasional prostitution), this constituted a dangerous threat in a social climate where women's sexuality had been repressed and where chastity was a sign of moral worth. The sexual threat that Mauricia represents is manifested in her crude utterances against the Las Micaelas' nuns – especially during her first attack – which have clear sexual connotations.[40] Mauricia's wild and uncontrolled fits of derangement in the convent are seen, in the bourgeois mind, as paralleling violent and irrational working-class political uprisings. Women's alcoholism, however, provoked a more negative and moralistic attitude, in view of the dangerous threat it posed to a gendered social system where women's 'proper' role had been clearly defined.[41]

Thus, since Mauricia is unable to submit to the principles of order and morality, let alone to act as a vehicle for the transmission of these principles into the family home, it is not surprising that her daughter Adoración has been left in the care of Severiana. Although Severiana tells Jacinta that Mauricia left Adoración with her ('Aquí me dejó esta criatura' [I, 365]), suggesting that she has been abandoned by her mother, and although Jacinta also assumes that she has been neglected by an unloving mother ('¡Pobre niña!…Su mamá no la quiere' [I, 364]), this account is discredited by Severiana herself when she admits that Mauricia has been interned in Las Micaelas and, after having fled from the reformatory, that they are looking for her in order to lock her up again (I, 365). This suggests that Adoración has been taken away from her mother rather than having been abandoned by her, thereby undermining the negative image that the bourgeoisie, and even her upper-working-class sister, have of Mauricia.[42]

40 As noted by Lucille V. Braun, 'The Novelistic Function of Mauricia la Dura in Galdós' *Fortunata y Jacinta*', *Symposium*, 3 (Winter 1977), 286.
41 In *El pauperismo*, Concepción Arenal, after regretting the pernicious effects of alcoholism on male workers, underlines the much more adverse effects that women's alcoholism has on the home: 'El daño es todavía mayor cuando la mujer da el mal ejemplo […], y hollando deber y honor, acompaña a su marido a las inmundas orgías, y en la borrasca de tantos excesos ni aun deja a los hijos aquella tabla de salvación que se llama *la virtud de mi madre* [author's emphasis]. Mientras ella no cae, es posible que la familia no se hunda, que halle en aquel foco de amor y de abnegación ejemplo y sostén, y que el dolor resignado y la incansable perseverancia en el bien purifiquen el hogar de *los miasmas que exhala el hombre vicioso* [my emphasis]; mas cuando su compañera lo es de desórdenes, difícilmente se ve ni se concibe que los hijos puedan salvarse' (I, 292–93).
42 That Adoración has been taken away from Mauricia is supported by Dulce's reference in *Angel Guerra* to 'esas hijas que tienen separadas de sus madres porque éstas han sido malas' (I, 160).

Moreover, the fact that Mauricia's daughter is presented by Galdós as a model child, clean and well-mannered – to the extent of being loathsome to the modern reader – serves to disprove the contemporary argument of hereditary alcoholism. Similarly, Mauricia's alcoholism is not shown to be inherited in the novel. As Guillermina notes, Mauricia's coarse masculine voice is the product of her drinking, and it used not to be like that (II, 235). Also, we learn through one of the inhabitants of the tenement building, and through Severiana herself, that Mauricia's mother was a respectable working-class woman who used to work as a 'planchadora' in Guillermina Pacheco's house (I, 364, 365).

It is ironic that alcohol was regarded as a poison (indeed, drinking per se was seen as a danger in the sense that it was believed to inevitably lead to drunkenness), yet at the same time being used as a medicine. This again reflects the contradictions and dual values propounded by the ruling classes. Nineteenth-century doctors resorted to alcohol for many of their cures, and it was common to prescribe 'a glass of brandy' for certain complaints.[43] Doctors were often accused of prescribing alcohol, particularly to women, for any real or imaginary complaint, thus encouraging them to drink.[44] In *Fortunata y Jacinta*, doña Lupe shows her disbelief when she finds out that the dying Mauricia has been prescribed alcohol as part of the treatment: '¿Pero de veras le dais... esa perdición?', she asks Severiana in alarm. Severiana's answer is indicative of her awareness of this ambivalent attitude towards drinking: 'Lo ha mandado el médico. Dice que es medicina. Parece aquello de *al revés te lo digo*' (II, 176). Barbarita is also shown giving Juanito tea with brandy when he is recovering from a bad cold at the beginning of the novel (I, 384). Another character in the novel, Sor Marcela, is seen taking doses of brandy that the doctor has prescribed for a stomach complaint. Through this tolerant and sympathetic character the author is not only reflecting the prevalence of this old remedy among doctors but he is also drawing a line between the moderate use of alcohol and excessive drinking, thus implicitly undermining the link between drinking and drunkenness. In the novel, Sor Marcela allows Mauricia to have some of her brandy when she is locked up in the convent's 'dungeon' after her first attack, since, as

43 Shiman, *Crusade against Drink in Victorian England*, 35.

44 Ibid., 249, note 16. Even after 1860, when research proved that alcohol was neither nourishing nor heat-producing, some doctors were still recommending its use as a medicine. Progress on this issue was very gradual, since it was difficult to change the habits of generations; see Shiman, *Crusade against Drink in Victorian England*, 36; and Harrison, *Drink and the Victorians*, 307–08. Campos Marín (*Socialismo marxista*, 98–99) notes the lack of agreement in scientific circles on this issue even at the turn of the century.

she assures Mauricia, 'lo que algunos podrían tener por malo es bueno en medida razonable' (I, 617). Further, according to the narrator, she firmly believed

> que la privación absoluta de los apetitos alimentados por la costumbre más o menos viciosa, es el peor de los remedios, por engendrar la desesperación, y que para curar añejos defectos es conveniente permitirlos de cuando en cuando con mucha medida. (I, 621)

The author's favourable attitude towards moderate drinking manifests itself once more later in the novel, when Guillermina allows Mauricia to have a glass of sherry just before her death in order to calm her down (II, 224).[45] It can be argued that the attitude that allows for moderate drinking may be prompted by the desire to regulate drunkenness; that is, by tolerating drinking in moderation, it is easier to keep it under control. As such, this position is not dissimilar to that adopted towards the regulation of prostitution.

The supposed inevitable connection between drinking and drunkenness helps explain the total abstention of the 'reforming' philanthropist Guillermina, who is twice seen refusing a drink. When Izquierdo, towards the end of the novel, offers her a beer, she replies, '¡Quite usted allá![...] Yo no bebo esas porquerías' (II, 493). The other occasion when she is reluctant to drink is in a bourgeois environment. (The fact that she is offered a drink also shows that it would not have been unusual for middle-class women to drink on special occasions.) The Santa Cruz family, after having learnt that they have won the lottery, decide to celebrate with some friends by opening some bottles of champagne. When Samaniego insists that Guillermina should have a glass of champagne she replies, '¿Pero tú qué has creído de mí, viciosote? ¡Yo beber esas porquerías!...' (I, 383). Her reply is little different from the one she gave Izquierdo, though the use of the suffix '-ote' here, with its affectionate overtones, undercuts her criticism of Samaniego. Drinking clearly loses its negative connotations of 'dissolution' and 'vice' when done by

---

45 Similarly, Nazarín is willing to give the sick Andara some wine when she is hiding in his house after her fight with another prostitute, 'Hubiérale dado él de buena gana un poco de vino, que era lo que ella principalmente apetecía', the narrator comments (41). Finally, Nazarín buys Andara some wine, which she regards as the best medicine (45–46). Nazarín declares vigorously on different occasions in the novel that he does not drink. The author's favourable attitude towards moderate drinking is shown, in the scene discussed above, when he makes Andara say to him, 'Vamos, que el no tener ningún vicio, ninguno, lo que se dice ninguno, vicio también es' (43). Another priest who emphatically refuses to drink is don Tomé in *Angel Guerra*, who is significantly portrayed as childlike and very shy.

the middle classes.[46] Since these classes were considered to be innately 'moral', they would, by definition, be able to cope better with drinking than the innately 'immoral' and 'dissolute' working classes.[47]

The drinking scene at the Santa Cruz household, apart from reflecting relatively liberal attitudes towards middle-class drinking, also illustrates the fact that, although all classes drank, it was usually the working classes who did it in public.[48] This no doubt partly accounts for the association that the middle classes made between drinking and drunkenness: it was the public spectacle of drinking that was not tolerated; as with attitudes to prostitution during this period, it was the 'visibility of

46 Despite Guillermina's reluctance to drink, there are numerous examples in the novels under consideration in this book in which the middle classes are shown drinking, albeit in moderation. One main difference between middle-class and working-class drinking was that the middle classes usually drank good-quality wine, or champagne on special occasions, rather than spirits or adulterated wine, like the working classes. (Drinking beer and wine in moderation was socially more acceptable than drinking spirits, due partly to the fact that it was a popular tradition, and also that they were regarded as healthy drinks – even as a physiological necessity – by many hygienists. On the other hand, distilled drinks were seen as highly toxic and unhealthy, except when their use was specifically therapeutic.) Moreover, middle-class drinking tended to be undertaken during meals. One example of middle-class drinking in Galdós's novels is Isidro Palomeque, the canon in Toledo's cathedral in *Angel Guerra*, who had 'un soberbio Jerez [...] en su armario [...] que reservaba para las grandes solemnidades' (I, 297). The narrator notes that Palomeque only drank his sherry with discretion (I, 299), very much like Sor Marcela in *Fortunata y Jacinta*. The priest Juan Casado is also shown eating and drinking a bottle of wine with Angel in an inn (II, 503 ff.). The fact that Casado would only drink in moderation is reflected by his teasing of the priest Virones when he says to him, 'Haga el favor, amigo Virones, de no acercarse tanto a mí cuando habla, que trae aliento de vinazo' (II, 508). It is also significant that in both Angel Guerra's and Halma's institutions wine is served 'en abundancia' with the meals, as the narrator observes, see *Angel Guerra*, II, 624; and *Halma*, 1844.

47 A contributor to *La Voz de la Caridad* wrote, 'aunque [la embriaguez] sea vicio y abuso que se ve en ricos y en pobres, considerémoslo tan sólo con relación a las clases trabajadoras y pobres, porque en ellas son mayores sus estragos' (15 July 1883), 135. Similarly, Joaquim Salarich commented in respect of drinking and other 'vices', 'Más funestas, delirantes y terribles se ostentan todavía las pasiones, si las consideramos en las clases populares. Entonces se hacen altamente contagiosas, ganan con rapidez individuos y más individuos [...] y los arrastran a veces a actos cuyas consecuencias deploran, cuando han vuelto de su funesta ceguedad' (*Higiene del tejedor*, 192).

48 Alain Corbin, 'Backstage', in Michelle Perrot (ed.), *From the Fires of Revolution to the Great War* (Cambridge, MA, Belknap Press, 1990) (vol. IV of *A History of Private Life*, ed. Philippe Ariès and Georges Duby), 635; and F. M. L. Thompson, *The Rise of Respectable Society: A Social History of Victorian Britain (1830–1900)* (London, Fontana Press, 1988), 308.

the vice' that caused offence. Moroever, like prostitution, drunkenness was established in the bourgeois consciousness as 'filth': a source of disease and contamination. The visibility of drunkenness, like that of rubbish[49] – believed to be an obvious and visible cause of miasma – was perceived in the bourgeois mind as a social danger. The perception was that drink could easily become contagious among the working classes and spread like an epidemic.[50] Immoral and infectious contagion were equated as two parallel pathological phenomena. Whether seen as a source of epidemics or of moral 'plagues',[51] the working classes were conceptualized in bourgeois discourses as a source of infection, and therefore as a threat to the physical and moral health of the nation.

As seen in the previous chapter, in *Fortunata y Jacinta*, the image of the drunken Mauricia sitting on a pile of rubbish in the convent's vegetable garden is symbolic of these associations. This image connects organic decay with prostitution but also with drunkenness – prostitution and drunkenness often being linked by contemporary social observers. Acton had commented, in this respect, that 'as a heap of rubbish will ferment, so surely will a number of unvirtuous women deteriorate'.[52] Mauricia is 'fermenting' inside, just as the compost she is sitting on is fermenting, for she has become internally 'infected' and 'contaminated' by drink. But Mauricia is not just 'infected' or 'contaminated' inside; she is also seen as representing a source of infection or contagion. To borrow an association created by Mayhew, she is portrayed as 'manure' to the country's 'crime-crop'.[53] Drunkenness, like prostitution, is perceived in terms of contagion, filth and disease, as the use of the term 'intoxicación'

---

49 Alain Corbin ('Commercial Sexuality in Nineteenth Century France: A System of Images and Regulations', in Catherine Gallagher and Thomas Laqueur [eds], *The Making of the Modern Body: Sexuality and Society in the Nineteenth Century* [Berkeley and Los Angeles, University of California Press, 1987], 214) discusses the obsession with hiding rubbish away and containing it in refuse dumps in order to prevent infection.

50 In *Angel Guerra* Arístides draws a link between drink and infectious diseases when he tells Angel that Dulce has recovered from the '*enfermedad* diabólica que le *pegó* el tío Pito' (II, 388; my emphasis).

51 Alcoholism was regarded by Restoration commentators as one of the three plagues – alongside tuberculosis and syphilis – that scourged humankind. See Campos Marín and Huertas, 'El alcoholismo como enfermedad social', 263–64.

52 William Acton, *Prostitution Considered in Its Moral, Social and Sanitary Aspects in London and Other Large Cities; with Proposals for the Mitigation of Its Attendant Evils* (London, 1857), 97, quoted by Nead, *Myths of Sexuality*, 121.

53 Henry Mayhew, *London Labour and the London Poor* (1851–62), quoted by Gertrude Himmelfarb in *The Idea of Poverty: England in the Early Industrial Age* (London, Faber & Faber, 1984), 340.

demonstrates.[54] The image of Mauricia sitting on the manure heap represents her deviation from the role of mother and homemaker that society has assigned her, her association with dirt being symbolic of her failure to internalize the hygienic principles – in both their physical and moral senses – advocated by the nuns.

The main device used by Galdós to undermine bourgeois perceptions of the drunken Mauricia is the episode where, after claiming to have seen the Virgin, she tries to steal the monstrance – and does finally steal it in a dream – in order to take the Christ child back to his mother. In this episode Galdós shows that Mauricia's alcoholism is something other than a 'moral disease'. She is presented by the author as a psychologically complex and ambiguous character. Mauricia's vision in Las Micaelas, and her subsequent urge to steal the monstrance, have been interpreted as a reflection of her own anguish regarding her daughter Adoración, who has been taken away from her and put in Severiana's care.[55] Mauricia seems to have been deeply affected by the fact that the Virgin in her vision was crying over the loss of her son. Thus, she says to one of the inmates, '[La Virgen] lloraba mirándome... ¡Se le caían unos lagrimones...! No traía nene Dios; *paicía* que se lo habían quitado' (I, 642). From that moment onwards, Mauricia becomes obsessed with the fact that the child Christ has been taken away from his mother. '¡Oh mi Señora!... Te lo traeré, te lo traeré...' (I, 644), she exclaims when still sitting on the pile of compost in the garden. This serves to place the image of a drunken Mauricia sitting on the rubbish in a different light in the reader's eyes. Her subsequent dream, in which she steals the monstrance, contributes to the author's linkage of her alcoholism with inner psychological motives and emotional longing. In Mauricia's mind it is as if the nuns had taken the Virgin's child away and locked him up in the tabernacle, just as they have separated her from her daughter by keeping her locked up in the convent (the images representing enclosure and deprivation of freedom are commonplace in this episode). Thus, Mauricia takes upon herself the duty of freeing the host at all costs: 'aunque muriera, era preciso cumplir' (I, 647), she thinks to herself. By freeing the

54 Philippe Hauser ('El siglo XIX considerado bajo el punto de vista médico-social', 221), for example, described cholera and other contagious diseases as resulting from an 'intoxicación pútrida'. Similarly, in contemporary Spanish texts, the term 'intoxicación' was used to refer to alcoholic intoxication. Nowadays this word is qualified by the adjective 'etílica' to differentiate it from 'intoxicación alimenticia' (food poisoning).

55 James Whiston, 'The Materialism of Life: Religion in *Fortunata y Jacinta*', *Anales Galdosianos*, XIV (1979), 73; and Braun, 'The Novelistic Function of Mauricia la Dura', 285.

host from the 'power' of the nuns and taking it back to its mother, she can achieve a degree of emotional fulfilment.[56]

Galdós's suggestion that Mauricia has a particular case history that explains her condition may indicate his disagreement with contemporary scientific discourse (based almost exclusively upon organic or physiological explanations) and, in particular, psychiatric degeneration theory. This theory considered alcoholism to be an inherited condition and thus somatic in origin – and reinforced belief in the inherent defects of the working classes. By presenting Mauricia as a differentiated character with individual qualities and specific needs, he is also dismissing the bourgeois image of the working classes as 'the masses'. Moreover, with regard to family values, the author makes clear in this episode that Mauricia has maternal instincts and feelings and that it is only the bourgeois characters in the novel who think, given her addiction to drink and her work as an occasional prostitute, that she would be unable to fulfil the role of mother.

Through her dream, Mauricia can defeat the control of the bourgeoisie in her own way and carry out her plan of freeing the host. Her mind, however, is never completely free from the sense of guilt that the bourgeoisie has instilled in her, which acts as a subtle instrument of control. Thus, there are bourgeois voices in her dream which, speaking through the host, keep reminding her that things should be left as they are; the monstrance should stay in its tabernacle just as she should stay in the convent and away from her daughter:

> "Chica – le decía la voz –, no me saques, vuelve a ponerme donde estaba. No hagas locuras... Si me sueltas te perdonaré tus pecados, que son tantos que no se pueden contar; pero si te obstinas en llevarme, te condenarás." (I, 647)

The bourgeoisie can make her admit that she is a 'bad woman' but, even when she is close to death and the bourgeoisie makes a last effort to restore her to the Catholic religion, her repentance – and therefore her submission to the social norm – is riddled with contradictions. The author persists with these ambiguities to the very moment of her death, when there is a humorous passage in which those who are present at her

---

56 It is significant that Mauricia steals the monstrance in a dream. According to Joseph Schraibman ('Los sueños en *Fortunata y Jacinta*', in Douglass M. Rogers [ed.], *Benito Pérez Galdós* [Madrid, Taurus, 1973]), 'la función más importante del sueño galdosiano es la de profundizar en la presentación de los personajes' (163). As he has further observed, 'Galdós ha podido, mediante su hábil manejo del elemento onírico, trazar a sus personajes no forma unilateral, sino redondeada, desarrollada plenamente, presentándoles como seres de carne y hueso y adentrando en sus secretos nocturnos, verídicos reflejos de sus preocupaciones y deseos diurnos' (168).

death bed doubt whether Mauricia died asking for more sherry or saying that she could already see the other world. As doña Lupe relates to Fortunata,

> Luego la vimos mover los labios y sacar la punta de la lengua como si quisiera relamerse... Dejo oír una voz que parecía venir, por un tubo, del sótano de la casa. A mí me pareció que dijo: *más, más...* Otras personas que allí había aseguran que dijo: *ya.* Como quien dice: 'Ya veo la gloria y los ángeles'. Bobería; no dijo sino *más....* a saber, *más Jerez.* (II, 224–25)

Mauricia is presented as a rebel who resists discipline to the very end. As she proves to be beyond bourgeois control, the threat she poses has to be extinguished through her death. In this sense she is presented in a different light from the drinker Izquierdo, who is shown to be a 'false' revolutionary and not a threat. The fact that Mauricia's character has been developed to a much greater extent than that of her male counterpart Izquierdo – particularly in connection with her reform – may be a reflection of contemporary fears, if not the author's own anxieties, about women's alcoholism, fears that were derived from the different kinds of dangers that male and female alcoholism posed to bourgeois society. Additionally, the fact that the author's undermining of Mauricia's association with vice tends to be presented in an ambiguous way – contrasting with the straightforward dismissal of the association of alcoholism with political revolution through Izquierdo – indicates the anxiety generated by the issue of women's alcoholism. The alcoholic woman, unable to fulfil her educational and moralizing role, constituted a threat aggravated by the spectre of degeneration which, in the case of the drinking female, had particularly pejorative connotations. In *Fortunata y Jacinta*, Galdós dissociates himself from the class bias involved in prevailing contemporary discourses on drink, expressed through his bourgeois characters; but he is unable to free himself completely from the gender bias that regarded drunkenness as more threatening in a woman than in a man.

Drink and Degeneration in *Angel Guerra*

Angel Guerra (1890–91) has generally been analysed from the point of view of Angel's *individual*, spiritual mission to confront poverty, rather than from the wider *social* perspective of changing attitudes to poverty and to the dispensation of charity – attitudes dominated by the growing desire to differentiate between those poor who were deserving of charity and those who were not. The novel's criticism of Angel's utopian Christian ideals has often been seen as a reply to Tolstoy's *What I Believe* (*My*

Religion).[57] It can be argued, however, that beyond this, the novel is firmly rooted in the social debates on the poor that were current in Spain at the time. The distinction established by contemporary social commentators between the deserving and the undeserving poor is highlighted in the novel by the issue of drink.[58] In the wake of social Darwinist thought, theories on racial degeneration, which established a link between degeneration and hereditary alcoholism, began to gain currency, reaching a high point at the time of the publication of *Angel Guerra*. This emphasis on degeneration through hereditary transmission added to the negative perception of alcoholism, fuelling the contemporary debate as to whether alcoholism was a vice or a disease. This section explores how these ideas are echoed and/or subverted in Galdós's *Angel Guerra*.

As explained earlier, excessive drinkers were increasingly seen as responsible for the miserable state in which they lived, and therefore classed as 'undeserving'. As such, they should not benefit from charitable aid, according to the mentality of the period. In *Angel Guerra*, fears concerning indiscriminate charity are expressed by the priest Mancebo, Leré's uncle. When he hears that Angel is going to give his fortune to the poor he exclaims anxiously,

> hay que mirar [...] cómo reparte esos ríos de dinero, porque de repartirlos bien a repartirlos mal, va mucha diferencia para su alma y para el objeto que se propone. Figúrate tú que empieza a soltar, a soltar a chorro libre y sin ningún criterio. Pues no hará más que fomentar la vagancia y los vicios. (II, 375)

In total discord with the views voiced by contemporary commentators, and echoed in the novel by Mancebo, Leré expresses the idea of dispensing charity to whoever needs it, no matter who they are (I, 172).

57 Vera Colin ('Tolstoy and *Angel Guerra*', in J. E. Varey, *Galdós Studies* [London, Tamesis, 1970], 114–35) has noted that many of the ideas of Guerra's doctrine, which he calls 'dominismo', were inspired by Tolstoy's *What I Believe*, in which the Russian author advocated a return to primitive Christianity. This approach has been followed by various critics; see, for instance, Harold L. Dowdle, 'Galdós' Use of Quijote Motifs in *Angel Guerra*', *Anales Galdosianos*, XX (1985), 113–22; Ignacio Elizalde, 'Angel Guerra, su vocación y su religión nacional', *Actas del Cuarto Congreso Internacional de Estudios Galdosianos* (Las Palmas de Gran Canaria, Cabildo Insular de Gran Canaria, 1990), II, 383–92; Monroe Z. Hafter, '"Bálsamo contra bálsamo" in *Angel Guerra*', *Anales Galdosianos*, IV (1969), 39–48; Jennifer Lowe, 'Structural and Linguistic Presentation in Galdós' *Angel Guerra*', *Anales Galdosianos*, X (1975), 45–53; Kathleen M. Sayers, 'El sentido de la tragedia en *Angel Guerra*', *Anales Galdosianos*, V (1970), 81–85; and John H. Sinnigen, 'The Problem of Individual and Social Redemption in *Angel Guerra*', *Anales Galdosianos*, XII (1977), 129–40.

58 The need to differentiate between the deserving and the undeserving poor was an issue constantly highlighted in the pages of the journal *La Voz de la Caridad*.

Although at the beginning of the novel Guerra considers her ideas absurd (I, 172), he eventually accepts her views on the need to support financially all categories of the poor. But his change of attitude, towards the undeserving poor in particular, is shown in the novel not as being based on solid ground or on his own firm convictions, but rather as the result of Leré's captivating influence (I, 174; II, 331).

In the novel, the Babel sons are an obvious example of undeserving poor who become recipients of Angel's charity. The Babel family is depicted from the beginning in a negative light, particularly the three sons involved in Angel's death. The narrator describes the Babeles as 'chusma' (I, 38), and associates them with 'inmundicia' and 'las basuras del muladar', that is, with filth (I, 117). The Babel sons are similarly described as parasitic and incapable of work, living a criminal and dissolute life involving forgery, theft, gambling, smoking and drinking.[59] They constitute what in the jargon of late nineteenth-century social commentary would have been called the products of urban degeneration.

Towards the end of the century, the notion that people *chose* to be poor, or inflicted poverty upon themselves, was challenged – though by no means eradicated – by a new theory of poverty which looked more to the influence of a flawed and unstable socio-economic system and the deleterious conditions of urban life as major factors contributing to the condition of the poor. Drink, idleness, improvidence and irreligiousness began to be seen as symptoms rather than as straightforward causes of a process of physical and moral degeneration spawned by the pressures of city life. It was believed that insanitary living conditions in the cities could produce little else but brutalized and immoral individuals, who would continue degenerating physically and morally through generations of urban existence.[60] The French psychiatrist Bénédict Morel, who first formulated degeneration theory in *Traité des dégénérescences physiques, intellectuelles et morales de l'espèce humaine et causes qui produisent ces variétés maladives* (1857), had established the influence of the social environment as one of the drivers of degeneration. Poor housing, inadequate working conditions and lack of sanitary education were seen as the causes of destitution, alcoholism, prostitution and other social

---

59 Catherine Jagoe, 'Monstrous Inversions: Decadence and Degeneration in Galdós's *Angel Guerra'*, in Lou Charnon-Deutsch and Jo Labanyi (eds), *Culture and Gender in Nineteenth-Century Spain* (Oxford, Oxford University Press, 1995), 164. According to Bénédict Morel, not only alcohol but also other toxins such as tobacco were partly responsible for the degeneration of the race, as noted by Daniel Pick, *Faces of Degeneration* (Cambridge, Cambridge University Press, 1993), 50.

60 Gareth Stedman Jones, *Outcast London* (Harmondsworth, Penguin, 1984), 285–86.

evils.[61] Later in the century, the Austrian Max Nordau, in his book *Degeneration* (1892), argued that the pace of life had increased markedly under capitalism and that the price of progress was inevitable wear and tear on the brain and nervous system, which, in turn, caused the human organism to degenerate.[62] In *Angel Guerra*, the Babel sons are shown to be living in the kind of insalubrious environment that was believed to breed degeneration:[63]

> El aposento era pequeño, con ventanas a un fétido patio, y de la pared pendían formas extrañas, figuras de guiñol, de estúpida cara, una cabeza de toro disecada, un estantillo con varios frascos de reactivos y barnices; libros viejos y sucios; en el suelo, piedras litográficas, montones de periódicos, herramientas diversas, todo en el mayor desorden, maloliente, pringoso, polvoriento. (I, 58)

Although the influence of an adverse social environment was taken into consideration by writers on degenerationism, such studies, it has been observed, tended to be characterized by an excessive biological determinism.[64] Darwinist evolutionary theory inevitably underscored the idea that moral, mental or physical deficiency was hereditary. As Pick notes, 'While seen to stem from acquired diseases (drawn from poverty, immoral habits, unhealthy work and so on), *dégénérescence* tended to imply an inherent physical process, an immanent narrative within the body and across bodies, beyond social determination'.[65] Both in medical

---

61 In spite of admitting the important role of external, environmental influences, Morel still contended that these only affected, in an adverse way, the innate character of the working classes, as discussed by Rafael Huertas, *Locura y degeneración* (Madrid, Consejo Superior de Investigaciones Científicas, 1987), 34.

62 Jagoe, 'Monstrous Inversions', 163.

63 The degenerative effects that the urban environment had on the city poor were often contraposed to the healthy lives led by the rural poor. A contributor to *La Voz de la Caridad* wrote as early as 1875: 'La mayor parte de las guardillas de Madrid constituyen un verdadero foco de infección y [...] a consecuencia de la atmósfera mefítica que en ellas se respira, es frecuente el ver esas caras macilentas y pálidas de los pobres que en ellas se albergan, esos niños raquíticos, entecos y escrofulosos, *verdadera degeneración de la especie humana*, plantel de enfermedades crónicas y de vicios diatésicos. ¡Ah! En Madrid no podemos admirar la robustez y salud que parece conceder la Providencia a los hijos de los pobres que habitan en los pueblos y aldeas...' (my emphasis) (1 December 1875), 282. In *Angel Guerra* Virones associates the country with poverty and filth, subverting the idyllic vision of some contemporaries. As he comments, 'No me gustan a mí las aldeas, donde todo es miseria y basura' (II, 508). Also, in *Nazarín*, the rural poor are shown to be destitute, plague-ridden and, often, brutish.

64 See Pick, *Faces of Degeneration*, 51; and Huertas, *Locura y degeneración*, 75, footnote 29.

65 Pick, *Faces of Degeneration*, 51. It has to be noted that some degenerationists (among them Morel, the Italian criminal anthropologist Cesare Lombroso and the English

discourse and in social thought there arose a conflict between those who viewed poverty as a result of insanitary environment, malnutrition and trade fluctuation, and those who advocated the notion of 'hereditary predisposition', according to which physical, mental and moral failings were transmitted from generation to generation. The poor came to be regarded either as victims of the 'system' or of the social 'deviancy' – itself an effect of industrial capitalism and urban life – that they had inherited from previous generations and would themselves perpetuate and reproduce. Degeneration was thus seen as a product *and* a cause of social evils, constantly and inevitably reproducing itself. It has been argued that the Darwinian overtones of the theory of degeneration, if anything, strengthened what was a moral distinction between the deserving and the undeserving poor.[66]

In his *Traité*, Morel established *hereditary* alcoholism as one of the main factors in the degeneration of the race, a view which had important repercussions in European and especially French psychiatry, and led to a long-lasting link being established between alcoholism and degeneration. Alcoholism was thus believed to act on the individual either directly or

---

psychiatrist Henry Maudsley), following Lamarck's evolutionary theories – according to which acquired traits could be inherited – contended that the effects of industrial urban life were transmitted and intensified from generation to generation, as noted by Jagoe, 'Monstrous Inversions', 163. This is an indication of the strong links established during the period between degeneration and biological determinism. The notion of heredity thus often overshadowed environmental explanations of degeneration.

66 See Stedman Jones, *Outcast London*, 281–314. These matters are also discussed by José Harris, 'Between Civic Virtue and Social Darwinism: the Concept of the Residuum', in David Englander and Rosemary O'Day (eds), *Retrieved Riches: Social Investigation in Britain 1840–1914* (Aldershot, Scolar Press, 1995), 67–87. In Britain the jargon of the 1890s added to the old categories of 'deserving' and 'undeserving' the subdivision of 'unemployable' or 'unfit', a category the Babel sons would seem to occupy. According to the late nineteenth-century commentators Sidney and Beatrice Webb (*Industrial Democracy* [London, Longmans, Green and Co., 1897], 784–89), this new category comprised – apart from the aged and the physically and mentally sick – 'men and women who, without suffering from apparent disease of body or mind, are incapable of steady or continuous application, or who are so deficient in strength, speed or skill that they are incapable, in the industrial order in which they find themselves, of producing their maintenance at any occupation whatsoever'. For a discussion of this categorization, see José Harris, *Unemployment and Politics: A Study in English Social Policy 1886–1914* (Oxford, Clarendon Press, 1972), 45–46. In line with these ideas it was believed that charity should be aimed at those who were in genuine distress and that the degenerate, residual class of the population should be given no encouragement; see Stedman Jones, *Outcast London*, 289.

indirectly through a morbid hereditary transmission, causing serious psycho-physical deterioration. After Morel's identification of 'degeneration through intoxication', alcoholism came to be seen by contemporary writers as the major factor in the degeneration not only of individuals but of the whole human species. Study and treatment of the disease were largely undertaken by degenerationist psychiatrists, such as Magnan and Legrain, who continued Morel's work and who had a definitive influence on Spanish medical discourse during the Restoration.[67] This influence was, however, unsystematic, manifesting itself in a tendency to turn hereditary alcoholism into an easy explanation which could account for all social problems or 'social pathologies'. This association, even confusion, between alcoholism and degeneration of the race reinforced the perception of alcoholism as a working-class vice, rather than as a disease in its own right, with identifiable morbid or pathological symptoms, which logic dictated should be capable of affecting all classes.[68]

The study of alcoholic disease and its links with degeneration reached a high point with Legrain's book *Dégénérescence social et alcoolisme*, published in 1891, the year of publication of *Angel Guerra*. One of the main objectives of scientists during the second half of the century was to investigate the different ways in which inherited characteristics could be transmitted and could manifest themselves, in order to establish a series of laws of heredity. Morel observed that the children of alcoholic parents could inherit their alcoholism. Further, he introduced the concept of 'polymorphous heredity', according to which the alcoholism of a predecessor could become transformed and intensified with each succeeding generation of offspring, giving rise to various degrees of mental alienation and to criminal[69] and other vicious tendencies through successive generations of degenerates, culminating in the exhaustion of

---

67 For a discussion of the association established between alcoholism and degeneration, see Huertas, *Locura y degeneración*, 61–69; Ricardo Campos Marín and Rafael Huertas, 'Alcoholismo y degeneración en la medicina positivista española', *Revista de la Asociación Española de Neuropsiquiatría*, 12, No. 41 (1992), 125–27; and Campos Marín, *Alcoholismo, medicina y sociedad*, 55–81.

68 As observed by Campos Marín and Huertas, 'El alcoholismo como enfermedad social', 271–73 in particular.

69 Lombroso's scientific theories on criminality, which emphasized the notion that hereditary alcoholism was a major cause, had become influential in Spain from the late 1880s, reaching a high point in the mid-1890s. See Luis Maristany, 'Lombroso y España: Nuevas consideraciones', *Anales de Literatura Española*, 2 (1983), Universidad de Alicante; and José Luis Peset and Mariano Peset, *Lombroso y la escuela positivista italiana* (Madrid, Consejo Superior de Investigaciones Científicas, 1975).

the race.[70] The idea that the ravages of alcoholism were transmitted from generation to generation until the final exhaustion of the species was emphasized by Rafael Cervera Barat who, in his work *Alcoholismo y civilización* (1898), asserted that

> 'El bebedor no sólo se hace víctima a sí mismo, sino que hace víctimas a sus hijos y a los hijos de sus hijos. Con rigor inexorable transmite el alcoholismo sus estragos de generación en generación hasta extinguir por completo las familias.'[71]

Cervera described and classified a series of physical and mental pathologies inherited through three different generations, emphasizing how the effects of alcoholism become intensified with each succeeding generation.[72] Among others, he refers to cases of rickets,[73] tuberculosis, meningitis, epilepsy, mental weakness, imbecility, idiocy, hysteria, madness, violence, criminality, prostitution, vagrancy and alcoholism – alcoholism being regarded as both a cause and an effect in the chain of degeneration. One may note that practically all these pathological conditions are found in Galdós's novels. Cervera shows his concern about the 'verdadera resta que el alcoholismo hace al *capital social de inteligencia*' (my emphasis), thereby equating mental and productive capacity.[74] The ideas expressed on this issue by most Spanish texts – which were greatly influenced by French treatises – differed little from this line of thought. The aim of this medical discourse was to alert the medical profession and public opinion to the serious dangers that the abuse of alcoholic drinks posed to the survival of the human species.[75]

70 Huertas, *Locura y degeneración*, 69–79; and Campos Marín and Huertas, 'Alcoholismo y degeneración', 125–27. The forensic experts A. Piga and A. Marioni observed that inherited alcoholism could lead to the transmission of 'toda clase de alteraciones del sistema nervioso […], los torpes, haraganes, viciosos, egoístas, coreicos, epilépticos, locos morales, dipsómanos, erotómanos, lipemaniacos, imbéciles, idiotas y criminales, son los tipos frecuentemente observados' (*Las bebidas alcohólicas. El alcoholismo* [1904], quoted in Campos Marín and Huertas, 'Alcoholismo y degeneración', 126).

71 Rafael Cervera Barat, *Alcoholismo y civilización* (1898), in Antonio M. Rey González (ed.), *Estudios médico-sociales sobre marginados en la España del siglo XIX* (Madrid, Ministerio de Sanidad y Consumo, 1990), 108.

72 Ibid., 109–15.

73 It is worth noting, in connection with this, that in *La desheredada* Isidora's son is born with rickets. In *Angel Guerra* Galdós raises the issue of rickets when, talking about the nephew of the priest Virones, the narrator comments, 'Tenía todo el desarrollo propio de sus seis años, cosa rara en estos tiempos de raquitismo' (II, 536).

74 Cervera Barat, *Alcoholismo y civilización*, in Rey González (ed.), *Estudios médico-sociales sobre marginados*, 114.

75 As argued by Campos Marín and Huertas, 'Alcoholismo y degeneración', 126. Not all contemporary observers subscribed to the view that alcoholism could be inherited.

Although *Angel Guerra* reflects some of the stock assumptions of the
time about the issue of urban degeneration through the description of
the Babel sons as an example of the degenerate residuum, the notion of
hereditary alcoholism as the major cause of degeneration is not presented
in a consistent way. The two women with whom Guerra is involved in
the novel, Dulce and Leré, come from degenerate families. Leré's father
was an alcoholic who produced several 'monsters' (as Leré describes them),
of which only one survived.[76] The Babel family are morally degraded, in
particular Arístides, Fausto and their cousin Policarpo (don Pito's son),
the three responsible for Angel's death. Dulce is rachitic and has a
chlorotic complexion, and her mother, doña Catalina, is described as
mad. Both Dulce and her uncle don Pito suffer from alcoholism. Don Pito
is a semi-invalid and Fausto walks with a limp.[77]

However, in spite of what at first sight might seem like a straightforward endorsement of the degeneration doctrine, the novel challenges
some of its basic assumptions. Don Pito, for instance, the most obvious
example of alcoholic intoxication, is not associated with degeneration;
rather, his alcoholism is presented as resulting from his personal circumstances. The drinking of the Babel sons – particularly Fausto and Policarpo – is the case most clearly linked to moral degeneration. They are
shown to be given to alcohol from the beginning of the novel, in a scene
in which don Pito calls everybody into his room to have a few drinks and
Policarpo and Fausto have to be thrown into the street by doña Catalina
so that they do not over-indulge (I, 60). Fausto appears in connection
with drink and filth – in this case verbal filth – when he is hiding in
Zacarías's house. As Leré comments, 'se ha puesto entre el pecho y la
espalda una chuleta como la rueda de un carro, y todo el vino que había
[…] No hace más que dar patadas y echar mil herejías indecentes por
aquella boca…' (II, 541). Policarpo, don Pito's son, is similarly portrayed
in negative terms. The narrator describes him as idle, dissolute and rowdy,
and given to drinking and gambling, referring to his 'vida callejera,
tabernaria y disoluta' (I, 49). However, Galdós is not here necessarily
legitimizing degenerationist theories of hereditary alcoholism. Although,
at the beginning of the novel, the narrator mentions the rumours that
circulate about Policarpo and *Naturaleza* (don Pito's sons) having been

---

Concepción Arenal, for example, expresses her scepticism when she writes, 'No
creemos, como algunos, que haya una organización propia para la embriaguez y que
se trasmita por herencia' (*El pauperismo*, I, 293).

76 Also, one of Leré's brothers is described as a genius, which was regarded by
Lombroso as another sign of abnormality linked to degeneration.

77 Jagoe ('Monstrous Inversions', 164) makes this observation.

born of the same parents, and although he tells the reader that 'no son del caso estas averiguaciones' (I, 48), the subject is brought up again towards the end of the novel when the alcoholic don Pito admits that the drunk-ard Policarpo is not his real son. Thus, when don Pito finds out that Policarpo, together with his nephews Fausto and Arístides, have come to Guadalupe looking for Angel's protection, he discloses that his only son is *Naturaleza*:

> Poli no es mi hijo, me lo pasó de contrabando la bribona aquella, y yo hice lo que los de la Aduana cuando les untan [...] Mi hijo es *Naturaleza*, y nadie más que *Naturaleza*, aquel cacho de ángel, bueno y leal... (II, 621)

The author's implicit dismissal of the notion that alcoholism is heredi-tary is not, however, entirely clear cut. Although don Pito's son *Natural-eza* appears completely inoffensive, he is also presented as idle (he does not do much apart from eat and sleep and is completely useless for work) and slow-minded (the narrator observes his 'falta de agudeza y pron-titud', and describes him as 'tardo de lengua y más de pensamiento'[I, 47]). Both idleness and mental weakness were regarded as signs of degeneration. To add to the ambiguity, the scene in which don Pito reveals that *Naturaleza* is his son is presented in a humorous way and he is of course drunk when he makes his claim. When Angel comes back from Toledo, one of the 'asilados' tells him that don Pito

> vagaba por las espesuras hecho una lástima, a ratos como lelo, a ratos dando brincos, y sin acertar a decir más que una sola frase, esto es, que él era el *padre de la Naturaleza.* (II, 622)

However, *Naturaleza*, like the other Babel sons, is not shown to be degenerating physically. As his nickname indicates, he is depicted as very healthy and robust. The nickname *Naturaleza* is also an ironic reference to the fact that he is illegitimate, an 'hijo natural'. Similarly, Jagoe has pointed out that the other Babel sons, in contrast to their moral degradation, are all described as good-looking and of noble appearance, thereby contradicting Lombroso's scientific theories on criminality, according to which the criminal nature of an individual manifests itself in external signs of primitive physiognomy.[78]

In *Angel Guerra*, the protagonist's charitable attitude towards the Babel sons conflicts with late nineteenth-century ideology, which stated that the undeserving poor – the residual class of the population – should not be entitled to charitable aid. Towards the end of the novel Angel offers them financial protection when, in hiding from the law, they are

---

78 Jagoe, 'Monstrous Inversions', 164.

shown to be living in the most degrading conditions. The state of moral degeneration into which the Babel sons have sunk is paralleled by the state of physical filth they live in. This association of the degenerate poor with filth links the social 'residuum' to the physical residuum. It should be remembered here that the term 'residuum' was used by contemporaries to refer to both organic and human waste.[79] As the narrator notes,

> Guerra observó el local [...] [,] que más parecía depósito de inmundicias que habitación de seres humanos [...] Mirando bien se podían distinguir pilas de distintas formas, pellejos inflados, sacos de greda, y broza de tenerías, más perceptible al olfato que a la vista. (II, 586)

Here, the Babel sons are further associated with foul odours, which, like filth, were connected during this period to the residual groups of the population. Moreover, the description of Fausto's appearance as animal-like links him with savagery and the 'pre-civilized', reinforcing his state of degeneration.[80] Here we see the contradictory nature of degeneration theory, which posited degeneracy as resulting from progress and, at the same time, from 'under-civilization'. In this episode, Guerra's indiscriminate charity is called into question when Arístides reveals that the money that Angel was supposed to be delivering to them via their friend, the drinker Zacarías, has been gambled away. Arístides makes an acerbic comment, mocking Guerra's Christian mission, his sarcastic tone accentuated by his use of Christ's words on the cross:

> El pobrecillo tuvo una mala tentación, se fue maquinalmente al garito, y cátate que una mal intencionada sota le escamoteó lo que el filántropo de Guadalupe destinaba al socorro de nuestras miserias. Perdónale, que no sabe lo que se hace. (II, 591)

Critics have noted that the failure of Angel's 'dominista' project suggests the author's suspicion of the practicability of some of his ideas.[81]

---

79 A contemporary observer commented about the social residuum, 'Everywhere no doubt there is a certain percentage who are almost beyond hope of being reached at all. Crushed down into the gutter, physically and mentally by their social surroundings, they can but die out, leaving, it is hoped, no progeny as a burden on a better state of things' (quoted by Stedman Jones, *Outcast London*, 289). This part of the population was described by another contemporary commentator as 'the waste products of our nineteenth century civilisation' (quoted by Harris, *Unemployment and Politics*, 46).

80 José Harris ('Between Civic Virtue and Social Darwinism', 67–68) has observed that, in the wake of Darwinist evolutionary theory, the poor in great cities were increasingly identified as 'primitive tribes' and 'savages', separated from the 'civilized' by an ineradicable 'hereditary gap'.

81 See, for instance, Colin, 'A Note on Tolstoy and Galdós', and Dowdle, 'Galdós' Use of Quijote Motifs in *Angel Guerra*'.

Angel dies towards the end of the novel at the hands of the undeserving Babel sons who, after being put up by him, rob him in order to escape to Portugal. This suggests that the author disagrees with Angel's insistence on giving protection and financial support to those poor regarded as undeserving by contemporary observers. Angel's death could thus be read as a kind of punishment imposed by Galdós on his character. The point here is that Galdós's implied criticism of Angel's utopian ideals is not just a reply to Tolstoy's *What I Believe* but part of a contemporary debate, in Spain as elsewhere, on attitudes to poverty and the poor.

Paradoxically, it is the alcoholic ex-sailor don Pito — an undeserving character according to the criteria of contemporary moral commentators — who, more in line with contemporary ideas, thinks that society should not give charity to such loafers and rascals as the Babel sons, but should contain them and punish them by subjecting them to a form of 'state slavery' system. As he tells Guerra,

> La sociedad debía tomar una determinación con tantísimo tunante y tantísimo holgazán. Debiera hacerse una leva de ellos cada poco tiempo, y colocarlos a trabajar, mediante un tanto por cabeza. Llámelo usted esclavitud... ¿Y qué? Yo no me asusto de ninguna palabra, aunque suene a demonios. Pues sea esclavitud, ¡Carando!, o llámelo usted el trabajo obligado de los que no quieren trabajar. Crea usted que con este ten con ten habría más dinero, y nadie dejaría de tener su tanto más cuanto. (II, 356–57)

Don Pito's statement reflects the ideas of the time, which stated that the undeserving poor were not only unproductive but also a drain on the national economy, their proper place being outside society.[82]

The issue of drunkenness appears in the novel on several other occasions in connection with vice and degeneracy. As mentioned above, the description of Leré's father seems to associate alcoholism with hereditary degeneration since he is said to have produced several 'monsters', among them the one depicted in the novel. Leré's father is described as the stereotypical drunken worker — a figure that gained currency in the

82 The 'state slavery' system referred to by don Pito — who traded slaves during his years as a sailor — is not too dissimilar to the one proposed by the late nineteenth-century British social investigator Charles Booth. His plan was to shift the casual poor, that part of the population that he saw as costly to society and of little use from a productive point of view, into labour colonies where their 'idle' and 'unregulated' ways of life could be subject to surveillance and control. As any form of state slavery would have been politically unacceptable, he proposed that life should be made otherwise impossible for this group of the population; in this way they would have no other alternative but to accept a state of semi-slavery. See Charles Booth, *Life and Labour of the People of London* (London, Macmillan and Co., 1902), I, 165–68. For a fuller discussion of Booth's plan, see Stedman Jones, *Outcast London*, 307.

late nineteenth century[83] – whose addiction causes him to lose his job, to waste away his money in taverns and to resort to domestic violence. As Leré tells Guerra,

> aquella desgracia de la bebida le perdió [...] [C]rea usted que sin el maldito vicio hubiera salido adelante; pero el pobre, en cuanto cogía dinero, a la taberna derechito; volvía furioso a casa y pegaba a mi madre. (I, 120)

The description of Leré's father's alcoholism, however, is not totally devoid of humour. Thus, Leré explains to Guerra that her father was dismissed from Toledo Cathedral choir because on one occasion, under the effects of alcohol, he began to sing 'coplas de zarzuela' in the middle of the mass. The introduction of this humorous incident weakens to some extent the negative overtones attached to his drunkenness.[84]

Drinking is again connected with dissolution and vice via the character Zacarías, the husband of the woman recovering from an operation to remove her breasts, whom Leré is looking after, with the help of Guerra, in her own house.[85] Zacarías appears as the archetype of the drunken worker expelled from the sword factory 'por faltón y pendenciero' (II, 582), leaving his family destitute. He is described as surly, bad-tempered and inhuman, showing lack of consideration for his sick wife and

83 See Campos Marín, *Alcoholismo, medicina y sociedad*, 109–19, and 'La instrumentalización de la mujer', 164.

84 Galdós's description of Leré's father's symptoms during his last days (I, 122) seems to correspond to one of the stages of the disease known as 'locura ebriosa', a sign of which was, according to Santero (*Elementos de higiene privada y pública*, I, 372), the 'manía a poto', characterized by a proclivity to break and destroy things. Interestingly, despite his apparent description of alcoholism as a disease, Santero uses the term 'borrachera' rather than 'alcoholismo', which reflects the difficulty in overcoming the moral overtones attached to alcoholism during this period.

85 Like the episode of Mauricia's death, this one provides another example of 'hospitalidad domiciliaria', regarded by contemporaries as the most useful and rational way of assisting the sick poor. The good results obtained from home assistance to the sick poor are reflected in *Angel Guerra* by the swift recovery of Zacarías's wife. As the narrator comments, '[el médico] aseguró que en los hospitales rara vez se obtienen tan excelentes y prontos resultados, y que en toda su carrera clínica no había visto un caso semejante' (II, 579). As we saw, this was also the most interventionist form of charity. It is significant that in *Angel Guerra* Mancebo regards Angel's 'beneficencia domiciliaria' as intrusive, although here his reluctance and suspicion are shown to be linked to his fear of being arrested. Thus, he says to Angel in a humorous sequence, 'Ese Zacarías será todo lo bruto que se quiera, pero es dueño de su casa y jefe de su familia, y nosotros, con fines muy santos y muy buenos, eso sí, nos hemos colado en su domicilio, *somos unos intrusos*, y nada tendría de particular que el hombre se amoscara y nos pusiera en la calle. De modo que, a mi juicio, lo primero es traernos un permiso de la autoridad para *allanar moradas caritativamente*' (II, 565; my emphasis).

children. He is also violent and quarrelsome, and is shown to be involved with delinquents such as Fausto and Arístides. When Mancebo finds out that, knife in hand, he threatened to cut his niece Leré's throat (believing she had told the police about his hiding Fausto Babel in his house), the former associates drunkenness with violent behaviour when he comments, 'La causa no la sé; pero no hay que discurrir causas, sabiendo que ese Zacarías empina el codo un día sí y otro también' (II, 548). Similarly, in keeping with contemporary thought, Mancebo associates temperance with respectability. His brother-in-law Roque, disabled by an accident at work,[86] represents for him the image of the deserving poor, among other things because he does not drink. As he says to Guerra, 'Roque es un pedazo de pan. El ni taberna; él ni juego; él ni comilonas con los amigos, ni trasnochadas' (I, 248).[87] Roque and his wife, Justina, represent the respectable working classes, very much like Severiana and her family in *Fortunata y Jacinta*. Mancebo's association of temperance with respectability is stressed by the narrator when he describes Roque as 'un hombre como pocos, muy sentado y sin vicio ninguno' (I, 238). Mancebo makes this association once more when he comments to Angel about Leré's suitor: 'es de lo más excelente que usted puede figurarse, bien plantado, sin ningún vicio' (I, 251). Here, 'vicio' has become virtually synonymous with drunkenness.

However, Zacarías is not presented as a stereotypical drunkard, for the narrator notes that after a while he becomes more human and also begins to show more gratitude to his wife's benefactors (II, 567, 581). On one occasion he is referred to as 'el desdichado armero' (II, 581). The stereotypical image of the dangerous and violent drunkard is also partly undermined in the humorous episode when Zacarías asks Angel to come with him to see somebody (meaning Fausto and Arístides) in hiding and needing his help. On their way through the dark and solitary streets of Toledo, Zacarías asks Angel if he does not fear being attacked by him, and he is surprised and annoyed when Guerra retorts that he does not fear anything from him. When they are nearing the end of their walk Zacarías insists that Angel should confess that he has been afraid of him.

---

86 In connection with the issue of invalidity as resulting from unsafe scaffolding, see Chapter 1, note 29.

87 Mancebo sees himself and Roque's family, which he has to support financially, as highly deserving of Angel's charity – hence his concern about which 'casta de pobres' is going to benefit from it and his suspicions about Angel's projected institution (II, 374). As he exclaims, '¡Buena estará la Orden, sí, buena, buena! Apuesto que será para proteger a toda esa pillería, so pretexto de enmendarla y corregirla, o para poner a mesa y mantel a tantísimo holgazán. En cambio, los verdaderos necesitados [...] no tocamos pito en esas magnas funciones de la caridad de teatro' (II, 389).

To Angel's negative reply, he exclaims, in anger, '¡Ajo!¡Dios!, que sí, que
me temió [...] Pues qué, ¿soy yo algún mariquita? Yo quiero que, después
de tenerme miedo, me agradezcan el no haberle hecho nada' (II, 585).
Similarly, when Angel asks Leré about the episode in which Zacarías
threatened to kill her, she replies, 'Fue más el ruido que las nueces' (II,
594). Zacarías is portrayed more as a braggart than as a really dangerous
man. As such, he is much like the drinker José Izquierdo in the novel
Fortunata y Jacinta.

The character through whom the novel most clearly dismisses contemporary associations between drink, on the one hand, and vice and
degeneration, on the other, is don Pito. Don Pito stands out as a deserving
character, particularly by comparison with the rest of the Babeles.
Through this character, the author establishes a sub-category of 'deserving' within the social group classified as 'undeserving' by contemporary
commentators. In the case of don Pito, the issue of alcoholism – along
with the related theme of racial degeneration – is used by the author to
highlight what, as we shall see in the next chapter, is a major problem in
Angel Guerra as well as in other novels studied in that chapter: that of
distinguishing between the deserving and the undeserving poor. Don
Pito is not presented as the stereotype of the undeserving, disreputable
drunkard often depicted by social and moral observers. Guerra's personal relationship with don Pito and his tolerance towards the old sailor's
drinking illustrate this. Whereas the genuineness of Angel's Christian
attitude and feelings towards the Babel sons (particularly towards the
cynical Arístides) are called into question, since they appear to have been
prompted by Angel's desire to follow to the letter Leré's doctrine,[88] there
are never any doubts about his charitable feelings towards don Pito.

Don Pito's alcoholism is not associated with degeneration. Like
Mauricia la Dura in *Fortunata y Jacinta*, don Pito can be said to have his
own case history: this runs counter to psychiatric degeneration doctrine,
which stressed the somatic origin of the disease by claiming that alcoholism was inherited. Also, the fact that don Pito is a sailor – sailors being
traditionally associated with drink – may similarly indicate the author's
disagreement with contemporary medical thought. Don Pito finds life in
Madrid, away from his beloved sea, unbearable, and drinking becomes
his only consolation. As the narrator comments, 'No era feliz don Pito en
aquella vida de inválido, amenizada con turcas, vida holgazana, humillante
y aburrida lejos de su elemento propio, el mar' (I, 204). Later in the novel,
don Pito himself tells Guerra that alcohol is the only thing that keeps him

---

88 Lowe ('Structural and Linguistic Presentation in Galdós' *Angel Guerra*', 51–53)
    comments on this.

alive, puts him out of his misery and allows him to escape boredom (I, 294–95). As the narrator observes, don Pito would not get used to life in Madrid even if he were living in luxury. The narrator comments that, being used to deprivation, don Pito did not mind the discomforts of living in poverty as long as he had tobacco and drink (I, 204–05). This undermines contemporary thinking, which regarded the building of good housing and the stability of family life as key elements in the diversion of workers from drink and the taverns.[89]

Don Pito appears in the novel as a totally non-threatening, inoffensive character. From the outset he is described in a very different light from the rest of the Babel family. When Guerra, after the frustrated revolutionary uprising, is hiding from the law, he expresses his fears of being betrayed by the Babeles but has no doubts about don Pito. The narrator's use of humour when describing don Pito's fondness for drinking, as well as his drunken rantings and hallucinations when walking about the streets in Madrid imagining he is at sea (the narrator establishes a parallel between the 'mareo' caused by alcohol and that produced by the sea), diverge considerably from perceptions of alcoholism as a vice and social threat. One such scene takes place when don Pito first arrives in Toledo and meets Guerra in the street by chance. After exchanging a few words, don Pito enquires about the closing times of taverns in Toledo: 'Y dígame, ¿en este pueblo cierran muy tarde las…, los… establecimientos?', he asks Guerra (I, 290). The use by don Pito of the term 'establecimientos', in an attempt to make his drinking sound more respectable, introduces a humorous note, which is amplified when he mistakes the cathedral for a tavern. The use of maritime jargon by both don Pito and the narrator underlines the humour surrounding don Pito's drunkenness: what we have here is the traditional comic figure of the drunken sailor, not the late nineteenth-century stereotype of the undeserving working-class drunkard.

Guerra's benevolent attitude towards don Pito, and in particular his tolerance of don Pito's drinking, clinches the novel's dissociation of this character from degeneration and vice. Don Pito is shown to enjoy Guerra's company, because Guerra always invited him to have as many drinks as he wanted (I, 313). Angel's feelings towards don Pito are summarized by the narrator when, on one occasion when the sailor's tongue is loosened by a few drinks, he observes, 'Guerra le miraba con lástima benévola, viendo en él, más que perversidad, abandono y miseria' (I, 293). A clear sign of Guerra's tolerance towards the old sailor is his decision to offer him protection in his asylum while allowing him to

---

89 In this regard, see Campos Marín, 'Casas para obreros'.

carry on drinking. Don Pito's fears about being turned away because of his drinking are presented in a comic light in a scene in which he discloses his thoughts to Guerra. Here, don Pito's reference to Angel's institution as an 'establecimiento' (he had previously described taverns as 'establecimientos') adds to the humour:

> en ese establecimiento de religión, llámese como se llame, Carando, ha de haber mucho catolicismo, ¡me caso con Judas!, y mucho melindre de confesionario; y le sacarán a uno el mandamiento, y la tabla de Moisés, haciéndonos creer que en el infierno se trinca y en la gloria no. Pues yo digo, con perdón, que si me quitan el consuelo no hay quien me embarque, porque el beber, más que vicio, es en mí naturaleza, y dejarme en agua pura es lo mismo que condenarme a muerte. Y si no, dígame, ¿qué va ganando mi alma con que yo beba agua, convirtiendo mi estómago en una casa de baños? No, señor, en mí no quita lo bebedor a lo cristiano'. (II, 441)

To this, Guerra retorts,

> Descuide usted [...] que todo se arreglará. ¡Lucida estaría una religión en que se permitiera la embriaguez! Pero para todo hay bula, compañero, y no estoy porque se condenen en absoluto los hábitos arraigados en una larga vida, y que al fin de ella vienen a ser la única alegría del anciano [...] Cada edad, cada estado, cada naturaleza tiene su sed. Unos la aplacan en este vaso, otros en aquel. El tuyo no es bueno, pero no seré yo quien te lo quite. (II, 442)

In a later humorous scene, on returning from Toledo, Angel is surprised not to see don Pito in his 'asilo', and the narrator comments,

> extrañó Guerra no ver a don Pito por ninguna parte. Dijéronle que había dormido en Turleque, y recelando que engolfado en su feo vicio se hallaba [...] fue allá con ánimo de exhortarle, no a la templanza, cosa imposible, sino a emborracharse decorosamente, pues eran ejemplo muy feo en Turleque aquellas turcas hondas, monumentales, empalmando el día con la noche. (II, 622)

Here, the mixture of colloquialisms on the one hand and quasi-biblical language on the other seems to play down not only the importance of don Pito's drunkenness, but also the significance of Angel's Christian mission. The idea that it is possible to 'emborracharse decorosamente' seems to poke fun at the contemporary equation of temperance with respectability.

Guerra's tolerance towards don Pito continues to the end of the novel. When, mortally injured, Guerra draws up his will, he stipulates that

> A don Pito se le daría cada dos días una botella del licor que él mismo designara, y todos los sábados cinco duros en metálico para que se los gastara libre y alegremente como mejor le conviniese, sin que nadie pudiera coartarle en la caprichosa satisfacción de sus deseos. Esto sin perjuicio de

atender a su subsistencia en el caso (muy probable, ciertamente) de que las hermanitas no quisieran tenerle consigo. (II, 648)

Guerra's liberal and sympathetic attitude towards don Pito's alcoholism contrasts with contemporary views on it, as reflected in the quotation above, in which Guerra is almost certain that the 'hermanitas del socorro' will refuse to give shelter to an alcoholic. Whereas most contemporary commentators did not deny the fact that workers needed to consume fermented drinks such as wine and beer in order to recover their strength, they did warn against the dangers of distilled drinks; and they also disapproved of drinking as a means of achieving temporary relief from the pressures of life.[90] Furthermore, Guerra's way of dealing with don Pito's drinking does not have much in common with the measures proposed by degenerationist psychiatrists to combat alcoholism. These believed that most alcoholics could be cured through the appropriate therapy, and integrated into social and productive life. Pick has pointed out the contradictions involved in the language of degeneration. As he observes, theories about degeneration and heredity were articulated in the context of a social medicine that was committed, in other respects, to the amelioration and cure of disease, that is, to the mastery of disease. The alcoholic, at least in the first stages, was not perceived as an 'incurable degenerate'.[91] Although don Pito is presented as 'unrecyclable' since, as Angel notes realistically, his alcoholism is too deeply rooted in him to be reformed, it is not suggested that this makes him naturally undeserving. Thus, the author does not write off all alcoholics as dissolute and degenerate.

A further contradiction, noted above, inherent in the issue of degeneration is the notion that it is a result both of progress and of lack of civilization. In the novel, the issue of drink and degeneration appears in connection with savagery and 'under-civilization' mainly through the character of Tirso, the Guadalupe shepherd. The narrator, after stating

90 Campos Marín (*Alcoholismo, medicina y sociedad*, 127–35) discusses this issue; see also *La Voz de la Caridad* (15 July 1883), 135–36.

91 Pick, *Faces of Degeneration*, 49. The rehabilitation of alcoholics was mainly based on control through moralization – in keeping with the perception of alcoholism as a vice or a 'social pathology' – and the imposition of total abstinence as a therapy. These therapeutic aims were closely related to those of control: even when alcoholics were defined as sick, they were still regarded as a social danger. The projected 'asilos para bebedores' therefore had to fulfil the double task of protecting and rehabilitating the sick person *and*, at the same time, acting as an instrument of social order. The psychiatrists Magnan and Legrain pioneered this initiative in France, and it was taken up in Spain by, among others, Pedro Dorado, a specialist in criminal law and a translator of Lombroso. See Campos Marín and Huertas, 'Alcoholismo y degeneración', 127; and Huertas, *Locura y degeneración*, 97–103.

that Tirso's moral sense 'parecía muy embrionario en él', goes on to say,

> el bruto aquel se relamía de gusto cada vez que empinaba el codo. Esto y
> salir a tirar algunos tiros era su mayor delicia, en lo cual se confirmaba la
> observación de que lo primero que el salvaje acepta de las razas civilizadas
> es la pólvora y el aguardiente. (II, 334)

Ironically, what makes Tirso a 'savage' is the alcohol he obtains from
the civilized world. The association of Tirso with savagery is made not
only by the narrator but also by don Pito, who calls him 'Tatabuquen-
que' because he reminds him of a 'cacique de negros' he met in Africa. He
goes so far as to say that 'savages' like Tirso should be declared racially
inferior and sold as slaves: 'el mundo está perdido con esta libertad que
hay ahora y esta igualdad de pateta. ¿Por qué hemos de ser todos iguales,
todos amos, todos señores?' (II, 356). Don Pito's words are a reflection of
the anthropological racism of the period, a key element in degeneration
theory: he also often refers to blacks as barbaric and instinctively
violent. It is ironic that the alcoholic don Pito regards Tirso as a savage
and as a member of an inferior race when he himself would also have
been classed by contemporary bourgeois discourse as a member of the
'savage', 'uncivilized' and morally and intellectually 'inferior' working
classes. Pick has argued that degeneration must be primarily understood
in the context of nineteenth-century racist imperialism, which projected
'savagery' and 'moral pathology' on to the non-European world in an
attempt to shore up European cultural hegemony and to create a sense of
social coherence at home. In spite of the attempt to divert attention from
internal divisions, however, the spectre of degeneration at home constantly
haunted imperial discourse on internal unity. The word *dégénérescence*
would eventually come to characterize both 'primitive' peoples and 'alien'
groups at home, making it increasingly unclear whether degeneration
was caused by civilization or by its absence.[92]

92 Pick, *Faces of Degeneration*, 21, 37–44. The perceived 'social pathologies', such as
    alcoholism, crime and prostitution, were regarded as a danger to European races in
    the sense that they constituted a degenerative process within them. In fact Morel
    argued that the intellectual inferiority of an individual from another race was not as
    serious as that of the 'degenerate' in the civilized world, because, as he stated, 'The
    first, in fact, is susceptible of a radical modification, and his descendants can revert
    to a more perfect type. The second is susceptible only of a reslative amelioration,
    and hereditary influences will fatally weigh upon his posterity' ('An analysis of a
    treatise on the degenerations, physical, intellectual and moral of the human race,
    and the causes which produce their unhealthy varieties...', *Medical Circular*, 10–12
    [1857–58], quoted by Pick, *Faces of Degeneration*, 41). It needs to be taken into
    account that Morel was writing before Darwin's *The Origin of Species* (1859), which
    led to the classification of non-European races as biologically inferior.

In *Angel Guerra*, the issue of alcoholism and degeneration is presented not only in relation to class but also to gender. Female alcoholism is portrayed via the character of Dulce, don Pito's niece and Angel's mistress. Dulce takes to drink under don Pito's influence after being callously abandoned by Angel. There is an important difference between the description of don Pito's alcoholism and that of Dulce, reflecting the different attitudes adopted at the time towards male and female alcoholism. This was partly related to the damage to racial strength that female alcoholics were thought to be inflicting through reproduction. In this sense, although don Pito's drunkenness is very often seen in a humorous light, Dulce's alcoholism takes on particularly negative overtones, even when don Pito is shown to be responsible for it. If don Pito's drunkenness and its connections with vice are often underplayed, the picture that the narrator portrays of Dulce when she is under the effects of alcohol has altogether different connotations. When Angel comes to the Babeles' house wishing to break definitively with Dulce, she becomes associated with degradation and filth. The narrator describes Angel's shock, repulsion and disbelief when he first sees her:

> le salió al encuentro la persona que buscando iba, la propia Dulce; pero¡en qué facha, Dios poderoso, en qué actitudes! El tristísimo espectáculo que a sus ojos se ofrecía dejó a Guerra suspenso y sin habla. Desmelenada, arrastrando una falda hecha jirones, los pies en chancletas, hecha un asqueroso pingo, descompuesto y arrebatado el rostro, la mirada echando lumbre, Dulce salió por una puerta que parecía de cuadra o cocina, y corrió hacia él echando por aquella boca los denuestos más atroces y las expresiones más groseras. Angel dudó un momento si era ella la figura lastimosa que ante sí tenía, y algún esfuerzo hubo de hacer su mente para dar crédito a los sentidos. La que fue siempre la misma delicadeza en el hablar, la que nunca profirió vocablo indecente, habíase trocado en soez arpía o en furia insolente de las calles. La risilla de imbecilidad desvergonzada que soltó al ver a su amante, puso a éste los pelos de punta. (II, 348)

As with Mauricia la Dura in *Fortunata y Jacinta*, Dulce's drunkenness is associated not only with moral filth but also with physical and verbal filth. In the scene above, Dulce is also linked with lunacy. The description of her physical appearance ('desmelenada, [...] los pies en chancletas, [...] descompuesto y arrebatado el rostro, la mirada echando lumbre') remind the reader of the drunken Mauricia during her second fit in Las Micaelas, when she is similarly depicted as a lunatic. As the narrator comments, '[las madres] vieron aparecer a Mauricia, descalza, las melenas sueltas, la mirada ardiente y extraviada, y todas las apariencias, en fin, de una loca'

(I, 652).[93] In both cases, drunkenness is also equated with animality. Just as Mauricia was compared to a bull being released into the ring (I, 483), so Dulce is described as a 'res brava' (II, 349).[94]

Dulce is again linked to lunacy when don Pito tells Angel that Casado and the Babel family are trying to cure her from 'esa locurilla que tiene' (II, 358). It is ironic that the alcoholic don Pito himself refers to his niece's alcoholism as a 'locurilla'. It is worth noting that, in both *Angel Guerra* and *Fortunata y Jacinta*, drunkenness is linked with lunacy particularly in connection with women, reflecting the contemporary gender bias that regarded alcoholism as more threatening in a woman than in a man. Although don Pito's alcoholism is associated with lunacy towards the end of the novel, this is done in a specific legal context. When he is taken to make a statement to the judge, the narrator points out that the latter did not believe him, 'creyéndole borracho y demente' (II, 644). Here, the link is made by the judge, rather than by the narrator; this illustrates the psychiatric profession's increasing influence in the law courts, in late nineteenth-century Spain as elsewhere in Europe.[95] It is interesting that

93 Like drunkenness, lunacy was at the time perceived in terms of insubordination and lack of discipline, being, therefore, mostly associated with the working classes. Alvarez-Uría (*Miserables y locos*) has written, in this respect: 'Tras los desórdenes de la locura se leen los gritos y las agitaciones de un pueblo salvaje' (158). 'Alborotador, perturbador, irracional', this critic continues, '[el loco] es un peligro para sí y para los que le rodean. Foco de inestabilidad, rompe el equilibrio familiar y social convirtiéndose en una *peste pública*' (116) (my emphasis). Lunacy was thus also associated with contagion: as with drunkenness and other working-class 'vices', it was feared that it would spread like an infectious disease. As Alvarez-Uría observes (*Miserables y locos*, 116), 'la locura es una especie de *cólera cerebral contagiosa*' (my emphasis). Historically, the Spanish term 'cólera' could refer to both the disease and the unexpected 'fits' and 'criminal fury' of the working classes, who were visualized at times as united by the infectious ties of a plague (whether physical or moral) in the same way that they could become united in insurrection. Alvarez-Uría (*Miserables y locos*, 96) notes that during this period the lunatic became the archetype of the ungovernable, threatening and 'diseased' working class.

94 Fernando Alvarez-Uría ('La cárcel o el manicomio', in Julia Varela and Fernando Alvarez-Uría [eds], *El cura Galeote asesino del obispo de Madrid-Alcalá* [Madrid, La Piqueta, 1979], 150, footnote 1) has pointed out in this regard the relationship established, from the end of the eighteenth century, between socially alienated groups and animals. He notes that in the 1870 Spanish Penal Code lunatics were equated with 'animales feroces y dañinos'.

95 For a discussion of these matters, see Alvarez-Uría, 'La cárcel', 149–730, and *Miserables y locos*, 181–243. Luis Maristany ('Lombroso y España', 369) has noted, in connection with this, that the Madrid Ateneo was in the early 1880s the focus of heated debates between doctors and magistrates as to whether criminals should be regarded as insane and, therefore, not responsible for their acts, this reflecting the growing power that psychiatrists were gaining in the law courts. It was the forensic

don Pito is arrested after Angel has been injured by the Babel sons, reflecting the association during this period of alcoholism with criminality. At the same time, by showing that don Pito had nothing to do with Angel's tragedy Galdós implicitly undermines a view that dismissed all alcoholics as inevitably criminal.

When Dulce, under the effects of alcohol, uses the same swear words as don Pito, they lose their humorous effect, as, for instance, when she exclaims, on seeing Angel,

¡Hola, canallita...! ¿qué..., crees que te quiero? [...] Ya no, ya no... Me caso con tu madre, y maldita sea su alma...¡yema! ¡Qué feo eres, qué horroroso te has puesto, ¡je, je! con la beati..., con la beatitud...!¡Carando!, lárgate de aquí. No sé a quién buscas..., no sé. Yo también me he santifiqui..., fiquido, ficado, ¡je, je!, y me caso con... (II, 348)

Dulce's image is particularly shocking to Angel – and to the narrator – because of the stark contrast with the image of the ideal woman that she used to represent, that is to say, sweet-natured (as her name indicates), domestic and totally devoted to him. In this sense, Dulce is not dissimilar from the character of Fortunata.

But although Dulce's alcoholism is described in much more pejorative terms than don Pito's, it is not presented in the novel as a case of hereditary alcoholism, despite the fact that Dulce is a member of the Babel family. Dulce, like don Pito, drinks to forget the cause of her unhappiness. The fact that she has been callously abandoned by Guerra, after devoting herself to him and accepting a life lived according to his revolutionary ideals (it must be remembered that they did not get married because it went against Angel's ideas), makes her appear in a more positive light in the eyes of the reader.[96] When, at the beginning of the novel, don Pito asks the members of the Babel family to come into his

---

doctor Pedro Mata (*Tratado de la razón humana con aplicación a la práctica del foro* [1858]) who laid the foundations for the medicalization of crime, advocating the extension of medical power to the field of penal law. As he wrote, 'Es mi propósito irrevocable arrancar de las garras del verdugo, de los presidios y de las cárceles a ciertas víctimas de su infeliz organización o de sus dolencias, y trasladarlas a los manicomios, o establecimientos de orates, que es donde les está llamando la humanidad a voz en cuello' (quoted by Alvarez-Uría, *Miserables y locos*, 186–87). It is noteworthy that Mata is mentioned by Galdós in *Fortunata y Jacinta* (I, 144).

96 Geoffrey Ribbans ('Woman as Scapegoat: The Case of Dulcenombre Babel in Galdós' *Angel Guerra*', *Bulletin of Hispanic Studies* [Glasgow], LXXVI [1999], 487–97) examines Dulce's victimization and degradation by both Angel and the Babel family within a rigid society which 'make[s] a scapegoat of the female victim instead of the male perpetrator' (496).

room for a few drinks, Dulce replies, '¿Yo?¡Qué asco!' (I, 59), whereas
Policarpo and Fausto are willing to indulge in drinking. In spite of the
narrator's more negative picture, Dulce's alcoholism cannot therefore be
wholly associated with vice and immorality. The fact that religion is
shown to be useless as a remedy for her problem may suggest Galdós's
dismissal of the notion that alcoholism is a moral issue. Although both
the Babeles and the priest Casado, who is put in charge of her moral
guidance, seem to think that religion has cured her, the narrator's reference to her passivity and lack of will during her disease suggests, rather,
that she was merely unable to offer any resistance to the priest's attempts
to indoctrinate her:

> desde aquella noche empezó don Juan a catequizarla, conociendo que su
> alma necesitaba de enérgica medicina. Y la verdad, no encontró grandes resis-
> tencias, porque la infeliz joven padecía entonces principalmente de un desmayo
> de la voluntad, como quien habiendo agotado su fuerza en descomunal
> lucha, cae postrado y sin aliento; todas las iniciativas y erguimientos de su
> carácter habían cedido, y se entregaba, exánime y desgranada, para que
> hicieran de ella lo que quisiesen. (II, 397)

Dulce's lack of will is reinforced when, a few pages later, the narrator
observes,

> Su característica en aquella temporada era el decaimiento de la voluntad, y
> si conforme la condujeron a la iglesia, la hubieran metido en un sitio de
> escándalo y corrupción, su pasividad habría sido quizá la misma. (II, 401)

Ironically, the result of her religious indoctrination is that Dulce eventually comes to like religion too much, revealing, to the shock of her mother,
her wish to become a nun rather than marry the man her mother had
chosen for her.

Galdós at times echoes contemporary beliefs on degeneration, but he
is not consistent. The Babel sons, for example, are depicted in a rather
stereotyped fashion as the products of modern urban degeneration.
Similarly, the shepherd Tirso appears as the prototype of the uncivilized
'degenerate'. However, the issue of degeneration in respect of hereditary
alcoholism is presented more ambiguously. Unlike Zola, Galdós does not
systematically describe the history of a family suffering the effects of
hereditary alcoholism through several generations. Moroever, alcoholism
does not always appear in connection with degeneration and vice. The
author is not writing off all alcoholics as dissolute and degenerate. By
introducing characters such as don Pito, who do not fit neatly into any of
the standard classifications established by social and moral commentators, Galdós suggests that, although there are people, such as the Babel

sons, who are morally undeserving or 'degenerate', the system of categorization and labelling implemented by the late nineteenth-century bourgeoisie does not always work. If the author, through the character of don Pito, refuses to comply with contemporary views on alcoholism in connection with class, it has to be admitted that when confronted with female drinking he presents a much more conservative picture.

Chapter 4

The New Poor:
Changing Attitudes to
Poverty, Mendicity and Vagrancy

There has been a tendency to regard the novels discussed in this chapter as the product of Galdós's search for the spiritual. As seen in the previous chapter, Angel Guerra's charitable mission has been analysed from the perspective of Angel's Tolstoyan religiosity. Similarly, the other three novels under consideration – *Nazarín*, *Halma* and *Misericordia* – have traditionally been seen as a reflection of Galdós's spiritual dimension, and often as forming part of a trilogy.[1] (Although in this chapter each section discusses a particular novel, where relevant, reference is at times also made to other novels.) On the other hand, little attention has been devoted to these novels as a product of the material, in particular the social and class transformations that characterized late nineteenth-century Spain. I would like to argue that these novels are not simply concerned with spiritual issues, but are deeply reflective of contemporary social problems and controversies, especially the vibrant debates that occurred at the time on poverty and the dispensation of charity. I hope not only to show how these contemporary discourses throw new light on the novels under consideration here, but also to elucidate Galdós's position with regard to these debates.

The Deserving and Undeserving Poor in *Angel Guerra*

Angel Guerra, disillusioned with politics, and after a series of upheavals in his life such as the death of his daughter and mother, decides to spend the inheritance left to him by his bourgeois mother on setting up a charitable

---

1   See, for instance, Joaquín Casalduero, *Vida y obra de Galdós* (Madrid, Gredos, 1961); Vera Colin, 'A Note on Tolstoy and Galdós', *Anales Galdosianos*, II (1967), 155–68; Gustavo Correa, *El simbolismo religioso en las novelas de Pérez Galdós* (Madrid, Gredos, 1962); G. G. Minter, '*Halma* and the Writings of St Augustine', *Anales Galdosianos*, XIII (1978), 73–97; Ciriaco Morón Arroyo, '*Nazarín y Halma*: Sentido y unidad', *Anales Galdosianos*, II (1967), 67–81; Alexander Parker, '*Nazarín*, or the Passion of Our Lord Jesus Christ according to Galdós', *Anales Galdosianos*, II (1967), 83–101; and John H. Sinnigen, 'The Search for a New Totality in *Nazarín*, *Halma*, *Misericordia*', *Modern Language Notes*, 93, No. 2 (1978), 233–51.

institution in the countryside. Guerra's philanthropic impulses are, to a great extent, influenced by the mystic Leré, his dead daughter's governess. After the death of Guerra's mother, Leré has a conversation with him, which is central to a major theme in the novel: that of the deserving and undeserving poor and the indiscriminate giving of charity. In this conversation Leré tells Guerra that it would be sinful if, being in possession of a large fortune, he kept it to himself instead of giving it away to those who are in real need. Guerra, surprised by what he first regards as an eccentric idea, replies, 'De modo que yo peco por no dedicarme a sostener vagos' (I, 171). To Leré's insistence that he must try to decrease, with his charity, the number of needy people, he retorts, '¿Y qué necesitados son ésos? ¿Con qué *criterio* debo buscarlos y elegirlos? (I, 172; my emphasis). Through Angel's words, Galdós is echoing one of the fundamental social problems in Spain in the last half of the nineteenth century: that of the perceived need to differentiate between those poor who were regarded as deserving charitable assistance and those who were not. As argued in Chapter 1, this need for discrimination has to be understood in a historical context of changing attitudes towards poverty, which led to the older classification between the deserving and the undeserving poor being accentuated. In Spain, where poverty and mendicity often became associated during this time, the distinction between the deserving and the undeserving was frequently made in terms of 'true' beggars, also called 'pobres vergonzantes', and 'false' or professional beggars. The importance of investigating real needs was stressed: charity needed to be scientifically organized and administered, in keeping with the rational ethos that was beginning to characterize modern production. The ordaining of charitable aid could, it was said, save society a great deal of unnecessary expenditure.[2]

---

2 See, for instance, Concepción Arenal's *El pauperismo* (Madrid, Librería de Victoriano Suárez, 1897), I, 403. The most efficient and practical way of dispensing charity, as Arenal and other writers for *La Voz de la Caridad* observed, was the system of 'beneficencia domiciliaria', or home assistance to the poor. This form of charity enabled the philanthropist to be in direct contact with the poor and therefore to be able to investigate their real needs, away from the street, where needs might be fabricated. It was believed that the existing forms of public and private charity could neither give efficient 'socorros a domicilio' nor thoroughly investigate real needs: see, for instance, the issues of 1 June 1883, 102–03; 15 August 1876, 163; and 15 February 1883, 354. It is noteworthy that in a letter of 1865 to the Buenos Aires newspaper *La Nación*, Galdós praised this system of 'beneficencia domiciliaria', emphasizing that, unlike official charity, it was motivated by a genuine charitable feeling and was not hampered by bureaucratic red tape; see W. H. Shoemaker (ed.), *Los artículos de Galdós en 'La Nación'* (Madrid, Insula, 1972), 170. An important manifestation of this kind of charity was the so-called 'hospitalidad domiciliaria', of which Galdós's novels, as we saw, provide some examples.

Writers on social and moral issues, including public health experts, philanthropists and criminologists, propounded the ethic of work and warned against unthinking charity. According to Concepción Arenal, an indiscriminate distribution of charitable funds could only encourage vagrancy and immorality. In her writings she described mendicity, even in those cases when the needs were considered real, as leading to idleness and loss of dignity,[3] and proposed a series of measures to classify beggars into different categories. According to Arenal, this would assist in the distribution of charity according to real needs, thereby eradicating mendicity. A main theme, both in Arenal's book *El pauperismo* (1897) and through the pages of her journal *La Voz de la Caridad* (1870–1883), is the distinction drawn between those who cannot work (because of old age, illness or temporary unemployment) and those who do not want to work; or, in other words, between 'el que pide por necesidad y el que pide por vicio'.[4] In Arenal's view, those who cannot work should not really be classified as 'mendigos'. Santero, writing in 1885, established the same distinction, and warned that

> Deben [...] evitarse esas caridades mal entendidas por medio de las que se socorre y da de comer a todo el que lo solicita, sin averiguar si es o no un verdadero necesitado. La antigua sopa boba de los conventos servía, más bien que a satisfacer necesidades, a crear holgazanes y vagos.[5]

In accordance with this pragmatic utilitarian spirit, Bernaldo de Quirós and Llanas Aguilaneido similarly insisted on the requirement to investigate real needs:

---

3 As Concepción Arenal wrote in *La Voz de la Caridad*, 'la mendicidad rebaja, envilece, desmoraliza'. Arenal considers that even when mendicity is caused by genuine necessity it eventually leads to moral degradation; thus, she continues, 'El mendigo está ocioso y sufre la influencia moral de la ociosidad; enérvanse las facultades que no ejercita, viene el tedio de la inacción indefectible en un ser como el hombre, esencialmente activo, y para combatirlo, los acres estimulantes del vicio o la atonía de un embrutecimiento pasivo' (15 May 1880), 63. Arenal emphasized these ideas nearly twenty years later in *El pauperismo*, I, 381ff.

4 Arenal, *La Voz de la Caridad* (1 June 1880), 79. In *El pauperismo* she wrote, along the same lines, 'Hasta que no se lleve a cabo la distinción o clasificación fundamental entre los que piden por necesidad y los que piden por oficio, no podrá haber ni justicia ni orden' (I, 401). The preoccupation with this theme was also pursued in the conservative journal *La Epoca*: see the various issues from the 1880s and 1890s collected by Angel Bahamonde Magro and Julián Toro Mérida in 'Mendicidad y paro en el Madrid de la Restauración', *Estudios de Historia Social*, 7 (1978), 353–84.

5 Francisco Javier Santero, *Elementos de higiene privada y pública* (Madrid, El Cosmos, 1985), II, 491.

Un espíritu práctico y previsor, estudiaría las condiciones en que había de dar la limosna, de manera que satisficiera una necesidad real, sin que el organismo social se perjudicara con ello en breve ni en corto plazo.[6]

A few pages later they repeat this idea when they comment, 'En otro tiempo se decía "haz bien sin mirar a quién". Hoy no puede prevalecer este aforismo. Hay que dar a cada uno el bien que necesite, *mirándolo mucho*' (my emphasis).[7] Quoting Arenal, Bernaldo de Quirós and Llanas Aguilaneido stated that, if in the old days charity was essentially 'pathological', nowadays it should be 'hygienic', meaning that '[la limosna] no debe darse al pobre sino en condiciones tales, que le sea provechosa, sin correr el riesgo de enemistarle con el trabajo honrado, convirtiéndole en un holgazán sucio e incurable, que sólo perjuicios puede traer a la sociedad'.[8] According to them, unthinking alms-giving constituted a major contributor to pauperism, which was the scourge of nations, 'propagándose como una lepra' – as a commentator writing in 1890 put it – 'secuestrando por millares obreros válidos y sacándoles de una sociedad honrada, laboriosa y acomodada para echarlos a la de los holgazanes y vagos que viven de la crápula, que tienen sus costumbres especiales, que viven en inmundos lupanares y que piden su alimento a la conmiseración pública'.[9] Mendicity is associated here with filth, disease, parasitism and dissolution, and described as a social threat. Like other kinds of deviant behaviour, mendicity is conceptualized in terms of a plague, as a source of contamination and infection. Significantly, beggars were often described in the contemporary press as a 'plaga' infesting the streets.[10]

6 Constancio Bernaldo de Quirós and José M. Llanas Aguilaneido, *La mala vida en Madrid* (Madrid, B. Rodríguez Serra, 1901), 345.

7 Ibid., 348. In order to achieve this aim, the authors stated that one should follow the advice of the 'Charity Organisation Society'– the organisation that coordinated charitable relief in Britain – which included, among other rules and guidance, 'No dar jamás a quien mendiga en la vía pública sino recomendaciones para una sociedad benéfica', and '[n]o otorgar nunca socorros sin previa información' (348–49). Similarly, Francisco Giner de los Ríos ('La prohibición de la mendicidad y las Hermanitas de los Pobres', *Boletín de la Institución Libre de Enseñanza*, 5 [1881], 49) wrote that in order to eradicate mendicity people should not 'dar limosna sin conocimiento de causa'. Like other commentators of the period, he regarded the 'limosna indiscreta' as the 'hija y heredera directa de la sopa de los conventos'.

8 Bernaldo de Quirós and Llanas Aguilaneido, *La mala vida en Madrid*, 348.

9 Quoted by Bernaldo de Quirós and Llanas Aguilaneido in *La mala vida en Madrid*, 348.

10 See, for example, *La Época* (3 October 1889) in Bahamonde Magro and Toro Mérida 'Mendicidad y paro', 372. Already in the eighteenth century, Padre Feijoo had described beggars – in the same way as other Enlightenment writers – as 'basura' and 'inmundicia' polluting the streets, as noted by Pedro Trinidad Fernández in

Being non-productive, the beggar was perceived as an economic liability in a society increasingly seeking economic advance. Giner de los Ríos defined the 'mendigo' as the man 'que no tiene otra profesión que la de pedir limosna sin devolver nada a la sociedad a cambio de ella' and proposed 'la transformación del mendigo en miembro útil de la sociedad'.[11] The image of the undeserving poor was mainly constructed in economic terms. In *La Voz de la Caridad*, for example, undeserving beggars were described as 'esa mendicidad funesta y vergonzosa que [...] defrauda al Estado de multitud de brazos que, pudiendo serles útiles para la agricultura u otros trabajos, le son del todo inútiles y funestos, llegando en ocasiones a turbar la paz de los pueblos'.[12] A contributor to the conservative newspaper *La Epoca* drew attention to the waste that indiscriminate alms-giving represented for the nation. Writing about the swarms of beggars that invaded the streets of Madrid, he pointed out that

> Su aglomeración es una carga para el vecindario, que invierte en limosnas una suma con la cual podría sostenerse un asilo que diese albergue a los verdaderos necesitados que carecen de todo recurso, evitándose al mismo tiempo las falsificaciones.[13]

In *Angel Guerra*, the priest Mancebo, as we saw in the previous chapter, is the character through whom Galdós echoes the anxiety felt during this period about the indiscriminate dispensation of charity. When Justina, Mancebo's sister, tells him that she has heard that Angel is going to give all his fortune to the poor, he asks 'con vivísima inquietud',

---

'Penalidad y gobierno de la pobreza en el Antiguo Régimen', *Estudios de Historia Social*, 48–49 (1989), 50.

11 Giner de los Ríos, 'La prohibición de la mendicidad', 49–50. Nearly half a century earlier, Ramón de Mesonero Romanos (*Escenas matritenses*, ed. María Pilar Palomo [Barcelona, Planeta, 1987], 278 [originally published in 1836–42]) expressed very similar views when, writing about the creation of the San Bernardino asylum, he observed, 'El antiguo sistema de "hacer bien sin mirar a quién" es más generoso que político; las sociedades modernas han considerado justamente que los dones indiscretos hacen florecer la mendicidad, que la holganza ningún derecho tiene a ser mantenida por el trabajo ajeno, y que todo el que reclame el auxilio de sus semejantes, es preciso que sea a cambio proporcional del que les preste con el suyo'. Interestingly, *Escenas matritenses* is among the books in Galdós's private library. Later in the century, Juan Giné y Partagás (*Curso elemental de higiene privada y pública* [Imprenta de Narciso Ramírez y Cñía, Barcelona, 1872], II, 435) wrote, in a similar fashion, '*Trabajo y pan*: tal debe ser el lema de [...] [los] establecimientos benéficos'.

12 *La Voz de la Caridad* (15 August 1874), 164.

13 *La Epoca* (25 March 1881), quoted by Bahamonde Magro and Toro Mérida, 'Mendicidad y paro', 367.

¡A los pobres! ¿Pero qué pobres son ésos?¡zapa! No serán los que pordiosean por la calle…, no serán los que ejercen la mendicidad como un oficio, ¡zapa, contra zapa! (*Furioso*), y entre ellos conozco algunos que son unos solemnísimos bribones. (II, 374)

To which Justina replies, 'No dijeron qué *casta de pobres* serían los que van a heredarle' (II, 374; my emphasis). In Mancebo's view, indiscriminate charity would only foster idleness and vice (II, 375). In another scene, later in the novel, when Mancebo is reluctantly helping Guerra take care of the wife of the drinker Zacarías in the latter's house, he discovers some suspect material in the house that leads him to believe that Zacarías is forging money. His warning to Angel is a reflection of the new discriminatory conception of charity:

Don Angel de mis entretelas, gran cosa es la caridad, pero hay que ver dónde y cómo se ejerce. Claro que no debe haber distinciones, y así lo mandó nuestro Señor Jesucristo […] Pero una cosa es la conciencia y otra la sociedad. Porque figúrese, don Angel, que estamos aquí tan descuidaditos, hechos unos santos, y viene la Policía y muy santamente nos coge a todos y ¡zapa!, nos lleva a la cárcel…, con muchísima santidad. ¡Qué susto, qué vergüenza! (II, 568)

In this instance, the humorous tone of Mancebo's words serves to expose his self-interest, rather than being a criticism of Angel's way of practising charity.

Contrary to Mancebo's belief, Leré is of the opinion that charity should benefit all categories of poor and that no distinctions should be made, thereby challenging dominant views. Thus, when a sceptical Guerra asks her, 'De modo que, según tú, a todos los perdis que me pidan dinero o que intenten estafarme les debo abrir cuenta corriente', she replies,

Yo no me fijo en este ni en aquel caso. (*Con resolución y convencimiento.*) Digo y repito que hay que socorrer a los menesterosos […] Disminuya usted la necesidad y disminuirá los delitos […] Lo que he dicho se llama caridad. (I, 172)

Not only were the undeserving poor seen as non-productive, but also as a social burden since they were draining society's resources. This economic perception is echoed by Guerra when he talks, sarcastically, about opening a current account for those (undeserving) poor who ask him for money. To Guerra, Leré's ideas are foolish, in the same way as contemporary writers on this issue regarded indiscriminate alms-giving as absurd. Thus, he says to Leré, 'Perdona, hija, pero tu socialismo evangélico es un disparate' (I, 172). Angel's words may reflect fears of a government system that would distribute money indiscriminately among the poor. In *La Voz de la Caridad* Arenal expresses fear of state intervention when she insists that the state, its laws and its agents are incapable of dealing with the categorization of the 'mendigos' and, therefore, of administering charity in an efficient way.[14]

Leré regards poverty as a sign of belonging to Christ, a conception which is in agreement with the beliefs of early Christians and with the doctrine of divine providence (Guerra makes this point when he talks about her 'socialismo evangélico'). When she rejects the practical Mancebo's plan to marry her to a rich suitor – a marriage which would put an end to the family's economic plight – she underlines the idea that poverty is a sign of Christianity. Thus, she doesn't mind that Justina and her children have to live in poverty:

> ¡La pobreza es el signo visible de pertenecer a Cristo!¡El *eres mío* con que nos marca en la frente! [...] El mal, el verdadero mal es el pecado [...]¡Pero la pobreza!,¡mirar como mal la carencia de medios de fortuna! [...] [E]l accidente del tener o el no tener, colocado entre el nacer y el morir, significa bien poco. ¡Si no muriera el rico, si su riqueza le asegurara un puesto preferente en la otra vida!... Pero¡si muere como el mendigo, y tan polvo es el uno como el otro! (II, 330)

Here Leré voices the traditional belief that earthly distinctions of class or rank make no difference in the sight of God. As commentators noted in the second half of the century, attempting to dismiss ancient ideas and beliefs about poverty, Christianity treated the poor as the object of a special predilection of divine providence. Primitive Christians believed that giving alms to the poor was equivalent to giving them to God himself, from which it follows that beggars were respected and called 'miembros de Jesucristo'.

This image of the poor belonging to Christ was highlighted by the Catholic theological tradition.[15] Leré's view on charity is, in fact, that of the traditional Catholic Church prior to the mid-nineteenth century.[16]

---

14 As Concepción Arenal wrote, 'No es un agente de policía ni una autoridad más elevada el que ha de clasificar a los mendigos, sino personas con aptitud moral, intelectual y material' (*La Voz de la Caridad* [1 June 1880], 80). In *El pauperismo*, Arenal stresses this idea when she states, 'El gobierno jamás llegará por sí solo a clasificar a los mendigos en desgraciados y pícaros' (I, 392). A few pages later she once more emphasizes that 'El Estado, por medio de agentes pagados, no llegará jamás a clasificar bien a los desvalidos, ni a distribuir bien los socorros' (I, 403).

15 See Jacques Soubeyroux, 'Pauperismo y relaciones sociales en el Madrid del siglo XVIII', *Estudios de Historia Social*, 12–13 (1980), 143.

16 The traditional Catholic Church, however, did not require the faithful also to be poor, except for some religious orders, whose members took vows of poverty. Laxity towards vows of poverty had frequently provoked criticism of the Church and campaigns for reform, as, for example, in the case of the Franciscans.

According to the hygienist Pedro Felipe Monlau, the evangelical doctrine, erroneously interpreted and often exaggerated, had been the main cause of the growth of pauperism since the Middle Ages, when the number of beggars, renowned for their audacity and completely idle ways, considerably increased.[17] Bernaldo de Quirós and Llanas Aguilaneido similarly contrasted the new attitudes towards poverty and mendicity with old conceptions based on primitive Christianity:

> De muy distinta manera se consideró en otro tiempo la mendicidad, cuando haciéndose del socorro a los pobres la virtud cristiana por excelencia, se practicaba la doctrina de "la limosna por la limosna" [...] Tan a la letra se tomaba que debemos mirar en el pobre a la propia persona de Jesucristo y tan en la memoria se tenía que la primitiva Iglesia predicaba que el mendigo es hermano del emperador, que *la mendicidad estaba casi santificada*.[18]

Ideas on the providential origin of poverty and the notion that both poor and rich would find themselves on equal terms after death – although by the nineteenth century they had begun to be replaced by more rational and pragmatic attitudes towards the poor – were never completely displaced. The Church continued to recommend resignation to the poor and teach that material goods could never lead to happiness.[19] In an article published in *La Voz de la Caridad* and entitled 'Deberes de los ricos y de los pobres', its author talks about a pamphlet written by the archbishop of Paris and translated into Spanish, in which he presents as an incontrovertible truth that 'el dinero por sí solo no es ni puede ser fundamento sólido para las felicidades de esta vida'.[20] These ideas, which regarded poverty as the lot assigned by God to the poor in this world and a means of gaining access to the riches of the after-life, were a powerful instrument of social stability at a time when social tensions had begun to increase. The continual preaching of resignation to the poor was a means of slowing working-class social mobility, while encouraging it in the middle classes. The development of capitalism, particularly after its full onset, had begun to displace old views on poverty, the possibility of social mobility undermining old beliefs that attributed one's position in this life to providence. Nonetheless, in rural areas traditional beliefs stubbornly survived.

---

17 Pedro Felipe Monlau, *Remedios del pauperismo* (Valencia, Imprenta de Mariano Cabrerizo, 1846), 10.

18 Bernaldo de Quirós and Llanas Aguilaneido, *La mala vida en Madrid*, 321 (my emphasis).

19 See Jenifer Hart, 'Religion and Social Control in the Mid-Nineteenth Century', in A. P. Donajgrodzki (ed.), *Social Control in Nineteenth-Century Britain* (London, Croom Helm, 1977), 108–33.

20 *La Voz de la Caridad* (1 May 1883), 55.

The idea that begging is a sign of sanctity is voiced by Leré when she declares to Angel,

> ¿Qué diferencia esencial hay entre recibir de un administrador o del habilitado el pedazo de pan y tener que pedírselo al primero que pasa? Cuestión de formalidades, que en el fondo no son más que soberbia...¡Que Justina tenga que mendigar! ¿Y qué? Es lo único que le falta para ser santa. De limosna vivimos nosotras. (II, 330)

In spite of Leré's statement that the 'hermanitas del socorro' live on charity, the 'órdenes mendicantes' were not seen at the time in the same pejorative terms as beggars. Giner de los Ríos, for example, observed that the 'órdenes mendicantes' could not be considered within the same category as the 'mendigos', as their members begged in order to satisfy a social interest; or, in other words, they were delivering a service to society in exchange for the money that they received.[21] *La Voz de la Caridad* also includes an article which in effect praises 'las Hermanitas de los Pobres' and the nuns who comprise the mendicant order.[22] Also writing for this journal, Arenal, although she did not attack mendicant orders (their members, she observes, worked and inspired respect), admitted the influence that the history of mendicity in Spain had on developing social attitudes towards it. Arenal regards the growth of mendicant orders in the past and the habit of all religious orders of giving alms at the entrance to monasteries and convents as 'un antecedente histórico que predispone la opinión pública a ser tolerante con la mendicidad y un obstáculo más para enfrenarla'. Thus, she concludes that

> en un país donde se ha mendigado en tan grande escala, por tanto tiempo y con tanta honra y provecho, la mendicidad tiene que haber echado profundas raíces, y la opinión pública no puede serle tan hostil como sería necesario para reprimirla.[23]

Two decades later Bernaldo de Quirós and Llanas Aguilaneido emphasized this same idea when they wrote, 'En Madrid, por costumbre tradicional, o por no haber pensado la mayoría de las gentes en las gravísimas consecuencias sociales que un socorro imprudente tiene, la limosna inconsiderada y en la vía pública, sigue siendo una institución más difícil de desarraigar de lo que pudiera creerse'.[24]

In an article of 14 April 1887 published in *Política española*, Galdós expressed his disagreement with the idea that self-enforced poverty and

---

21   Giner de los Ríos, 'La prohibición de la mendicidad', 49.
22   *La Voz de la Caridad* (15 September 1879), 198.
23   Arenal, *La Voz de la Caridad* (1 June 1880), 73–75.
24   Bernaldo de Quirós and Llanas Aguilaneido, *La mala vida en Madrid*, 344.

resignation to one's impoverished lot in life should be regarded as a virtue. He regarded as a serious problem the fact that, in Spain, this view was deeply rooted in many people's minds. As he wrote, 'la idea de que pobreza y honradez son sinónimos, no se desarraigará fácilmente de muchos entendimientos'.[25] Galdós argues that this 'culto a la pobreza', which in Spain still prevailed in the mainly agricultural areas of the central part of the country, was responsible for the reluctance shown by some entrepreneurs and politicians to engage in large-scale business enterprise 'por respeto a aquella opinión de la pobreza erigida en santidad sólo por ser tal pobreza',[26] a view that had led to the association, in the popular mind, of big business and material progress with immorality. This unquestioning 'espiritualismo malsano', as Galdós calls it, which had prevailed in Spain for centuries, is considered by Galdós as the main cause of Spain's economic backwardness in comparison with other European countries. Against this traditional and widespread perception of poverty as a virtue he argues that 'si no es cosa probada que el hombre para ser bueno y merecer la gloria eterna deba ser por necesidad pobre, menos lo es que las naciones para ser grandes y figurar dignamente en la historia, deban ser miserables y no tener sobre qué caerse muertas'.[27] In contrast to primitive Christian ideas that viewed the ability to work and make money as sinful and immoral, Galdós endorses in this article the Protestant work ethic – which, as seen in Chapter 3, had an important influence on Catholicism as a result of capitalist development – criticizing

25 Alberto Ghiraldo (ed.), *Política española*, I, vol. III of his *Obras inéditas de Benito Pérez Galdós* (Madrid, Renacimiento, 1923), 299–310. Galdós finishes his essay with an ironic remark, observing that if big business continues to be associated with immorality, the day will come when governments will be discouraged from such enterprises, which would mean that 'Tendríamos un poder legislativo resueltamente espiritual, y esto podrá ser muy bonito y muy cristiano, pero nos convertiría pronto en pobres de solemnidad' (303).

26 Ibid., 301.

27 Ibid., 301. Continuing in this line, in an article of 1885 for the Buenos Aires newspaper *La Prensa*, Galdós asks if the exaltation of religious feeling in Spain could have hampered the nation's scientific progress. He comes to the conclusion, contrary to the opinion of some of his contemporaries, that mysticism may have had a negative impact on the development of science. As he wrote, '¿Dónde está nuestro Galileo, nuestro Leibnitz, nuestro Keplero, nuestro Copérnico, nuestro Newton? He aquí una serie de santos que faltan,¡ay!, en nuestro cielo tan bien poblado de ilustres figuras en el orden de la poesía y del arte. Porque las eminencias científicas de por acá no son astros de primera magnitud como los Calderones, Cervantes y Teresas en el cielo del arte: son personalidades subalternas y un tanto oscuras, que no van delante del progreso científico, sino detrás, que no guian, sino que son guiados'; see W. H. Shoemaker (ed.), *Las cartas desconocidas de Galdós en "La Prensa" de Buenos Aires* (Madrid, Cultura Hispánica, 1973), 148–49.

Spain's traditional hostility to work. In several articles written for the Buenos Aires newspaper *La Prensa* in the 1890s, Galdós continues to show a strong interest in industrial and scientific progress, praising people's capacity for work and attacking idleness.[28] The views expressed here by Galdós are significant, given that it has been generally assumed that he rejected the material for the spiritual in his work of the 1890s. I would like to argue that Galdós conceived the spiritual as an ethical use of the material, rather than as the opposite to the material. What he condemned was hedonistic materialism and excessive rationalism rather than material, civilizing progress.

Although in the course of the novel Guerra's ideas on charity begin to change under Leré's influence, and he finally comes to accept her view that he should help the needy without making distinctions, the narrator explicitly states that Angel is acting under the fascination exercised on him by Leré, moved by a desire to imitate her in every possible way. Angel's actions are described as mechanical and instinctive, rather than rational:

> fascinado por Leré, y sometido a una especie de obediencia sugestiva, ponía en práctica casi maquinalmente alguna de las máximas contenidas en los estrafalarios sermones de la iluminada. Esta le había dicho: 'Socorre a los necesitados, sean los que fueren', y él sentía inclinación instintiva hacia ellos. (I, 174)[29]

---

28 See, for example, *La Prensa* (18 October 1890) in Shoemaker (ed.), *Las cartas desconocidas de Galdós*, 408–15 and *La Prensa* (11 January 1891) in *Las cartas desconocidas*, 435–37, in which Galdós applauds the advances in hygiene and medicine; and *La Prensa* (15 June 1890), in *Las cartas desconocidas*, 395–401. This last article, written to mark the occasion of the 1 May workers' demonstrations, salutes Barcelona and the considerable development of its industry, which had made the city into a 'emporio de riqueza y actividad'. As the author comments, 'Tejidos y maquinaria, industrias suntuarias, librería y cerámica, porque todo cabe y todo prospera en la esfera grandiosa del trabajo catalán' (398). After commending the capacity for work of the Catalan people, Galdós launches a harsh attack against the anarchist minority, which was coercing workers into stopping work, describing them as 'individuos sin hábitos de trabajo [...] que patrocinan el escándalo y la holgazanería' (400–01).

29 This point is reinforced later in the novel, when the narrator observes, 'las ideas expuestas con tanto donaire y sencillez por su amiga le seducían y cautivaban sin meterse a examinarlas con auxilio de la razón. Había llegado Leré a ejercer sobre él un dominio tan avasallador, se revestía de tal prestigio y autoridad, que llegó a representársele como la primera persona de la Humanidad, como un ser superior, excepcional, investido de cualidades y atributos negados al común de los mortales; y cediendo a una ley de gravitación moral, sentíase atraído a la órbita de ella, llamado a seguirla y a imitarla' (II, 331).

Thus, the genuineness of Guerra's newly inspired charitable feelings and the validity of his change of attitude towards the poor are called into question. Guided by Leré, and following to the letter Christ's doctrine, Guerra declares that his idea of founding an institution for the poor is based on the desire to 'amparar al desvalido, sea quien fuere' (II, 527). As he explains to the sceptical priest Casado,

> Toda persona que necesite nuestros auxilios, ya por enfermedad, ya por miseria, ya por otra causa, llamará en esa puerta, y se le abrirá. Nadie será rechazado, a nadie se le preguntará quién es, ni de dónde viene. El anciano inválido, el enfermo, el hambriento, el desnudo, el criminal mismo, serán acogidos con amor. (II, 524)

Guerra's projected utopian religious order bears no resemblance to other nineteenth-century 'casas de beneficencia', which were mainly designed for the 'containment', control and recycling of the poor. Although his 'fundación' can be considered a 'controlling' institution to an extent, in the sense that Angel tries to exercise control through the teaching of pure Christian values, his approach is not characterized by the aggressiveness of contemporary philanthropic institutions, aimed at the imposition of bourgeois moral values on those perceived as deviant groups. When Casado enquires, 'Y las dolencias morales, veo que también tendrán aquí su medicina, o por lo menos su higiene' (II, 526), Guerra explains his programme of moral rehabilitation in the following terms:

> El tratamiento del cariño, de la confraternidad, de la exhortación cristiana, sin hierros, sin violencia de ninguna clase. El pecador que aquí venga no podrá menos de sentirse afectado por el ambiente de paz que ha de respirar. Si los medios que se empleen para corregirle no hacen eco en su corazón; si se rebela y quiere marcharse, no le faltará puerta por donde salir, con la ventaja de que pudo entrar desnudo y sale vestido, pudo entrar hambriento y sale harto. Descuide usted, que ya volverá. (II, 526)

Moreover, as this quote reveals, Guerra's ideas about giving the 'asilados' complete freedom as to when to enter and leave the institution do not arise from the need, particularly felt in the second half of the century, to 'fix' a nomadic population that did not work and had become a social problem. This freedom of movement contrasts with the 'encierros' of beggars picked up in the streets in contemporary Madrid, a novelistic reflection of which is found, for example, in the cases of Benina and Almudena in *Misericordia*. Similarly, in *Fortunata y Jacinta*, Mauricia la Dura, who is locked up in Las Micaelas twice (the second time after managing to escape), provides another fictional example of the desire to 'fix' the population. As will be discussed later in this chapter, beggars were picked up by the police and taken by force to 'casas de beneficiencia', such as San Bernardino or El Pardo, which were, in reality, prison-like institutions used as mere detention centres. In order to enter most private 'asilos' they needed a 'recomendación', which entailed that they would have needed to have been categorized as deserving.[30]

The major moral – and controlling – objective that contemporary asylums were expected to fulfil was to make their inmates useful to society through the imposition of habits of work, something with which Guerra's project does not comply. A commentator writing for *La Voz de la Caridad*, in an article entitled 'Hospicios y Casas de Beneficencia', observed in this regard,

> Desde tiempo muy antiguo comprendieron las naciones la necesidad de crear casas de refugio y misericordia, para evitar los males que siempre ha causado la ociosidad [...] La ociosidad en que viven [los mendigos] ¿no puede conducirlos, y con frecuencia los conduce a todos los excesos del vicio? Recogidos en los hospicios y cuidados con esmero, *serían elementos de la prosperidad del país los que antes eran gravosos*, trabajando a medida de sus fuerzas [...] La embriaguez, la blasfemia, el hurto, el olvido de Dios, el odio de su prójimo y demás vicios, que lleva tras sí la ociosidad y vida vaga-bunda, se extinguen radicalmente en estos establecimientos con un método de vida laborioso y cristiano; la instrucción religiosa que en ellos se da [...] les inspira indudablemente el amor a la virtud y al trabajo; el horror a la ociosidad y al vicio. (my emphasis)[31]

This author, like others during this period, believed that the creation of workshops in these institutions would foster 'la afición al trabajo productivo, afición que es siempre una ventaja grande para todos'. He finishes his article urging the government to increase the number of such 'útiles y piadosos establecimientos'. Also following this line of thought, Santero wrote,

> Los asilos no deben ser centros en que, a la sombra de las necesidades satisfechas, se cree un plantel de miembros inútiles o perjudiciales para la sociedad; sino, por el contrario, un verdadero arsenal de buenos ciudadanos que devuelvan a la sociedad el bien que de ella han recibido [...] El trabajo es la ley impuesta a la humanidad, y desde luego debe inculcarse en los asilados la idea de que sólo por el trabajo pueden reconquistar en la sociedad el puesto que les pertenece.[32]

---

30 See, for example, *La Época* (22 December 1896), in Bahamonde Magro and Toro Mérida, 'Mendicidad y paro', 375; and Carlos Plá, Pilar Benito, Mercedes Casado and Juan Carlos Poyán, *El Madrid de Galdós* (Madrid, Lavapiés, 1987), 94–101 in particular.

31 *La Voz de la Caridad*, 15 August 1874, 164–67.

32 Santero, *Elementos de higiene privada y pública*, II, 216.

The new conception of poverty implied that charity had to serve a utilitarian end. As the above quotation shows, Santero also emphasizes the view that the 'asilados' had to give something in return for the benefits received from society through their work. In the novel, when the deserving priest Virones, after having been refused the 'curato' that would have brought him out of his poverty, accepts Angel's protection, he immediately asks him, 'Dígame, señor y dueño mío, qué tengo que hacer aquí, pues en algo he de ocuparme, y los beneficios que recibo, en alguna forma he de pagarlos' (II, 532). Guerra, however, does not institute work as a compulsory part of his 'moralizing' programme, which is based on the *spiritual* conversion or reform of the 'asilados', as opposed to the inculcation of good habits through mechanical and imposed tasks. According to his plan, if the 'asilados' choose to do any physical work they may do so; however, if they prefer to devote themselves to a contemplative life or to enjoy the countryside, they may also choose to do that (II, 532–33), in keeping with his belief that freedom of choice is the key to their achievement of spiritual reform.

Although Virones offers his work in return for Angel's protection, some of the 'asilados' are portrayed as idle and often taking advantage of Angel, which implies the author's suspicions of the protagonist's indiscriminate charity. Among them is the undeserving *Maldiciones*, a grudging and insolent beggar. When, after having been admonished by Guerra on account of his bad behaviour, he decides to leave, the narrator notes,

> Recogió sus alforjas vacías y se fue. No podía vivir sino en la mendicidad vagabunda, y sentía la nostalgia de las puertas de las iglesias, en las cuales llevaba veinte años de honrada profesión de cojo. (II, 535)

This quotation confirms the contemporary view that mendicity bred inactivity and idleness and that it was difficult to make beggars abandon these deeply rooted habits. In this context, the reference by the narrator to *Maldiciones*' years of mendicity in the 'honrada profesión de cojo' is highly ironic.[33]

When the starving *Maldiciones* decides to return to Guerra's 'finca', the latter, loyal to his Christian ideals, welcomes him and another beggar he brings with him. At this moment in the story, work had already started on levelling the ground where the order's buildings were to be erected, with some of Guerra's 'protegés' (Virones among them) lending a

---

33 It must be noted that it was generally agreed that, as an antidote to idleness, even semi-invalids and the aged should be employed in doing some work in accordance with their physical abilities. This view was expressed, for instance, by Arenal, *La Voz de la Caridad* (1 June 1880), 76, and *El pauperismo*, I, 397; and Giner de los Ríos, 'La prohibición de la mendicidad', 49.

helping hand. Here, the narrator makes the point that the two beggars did not join in the work, painting a picture in which mendicity, idleness and immorality are once more associated:

> Uno y otro fueron bien recibidos, y por cubrir el expediente hicieron como que trabajaban; pero no hacían más que charlar y fumar cigarrillos, esperando las horas de comida y cena. (II, 562)

The narrator also comments that don Pito was not keen on physical work. Don Pito's 'idle' stay in Angel's 'asilo', however, is not described in negative terms. He is usually presented by the narrator in a humorous context, either trying to win the rough Jusepa's heart, or teasing the ignorant shepherd Tirso. This tolerance towards the old alcoholic sailor fits with the liberal attitude adopted by both the narrator and Angel Guerra towards his drunkenness, as seen in the previous chapter. Although Guerra's attitude towards such undeserving poor as the beggar *Maldiciones* is implicitly criticized by Galdós – in the same way as he implicitly criticizes Guerra's protection of the degenerate Babel sons – the author does not always endorse contemporary discourses on the deserving and the undeserving poor. Indeed, as we saw when discussing the issue of drink, the introduction of characters such as don Pito, who do not fit neatly into any of these categories, undermines attempts to classify and label the lower layers of the population.

Another recipient of Angel's charity who would no doubt have been classed as undeserving of charity by contemporary commentators, but who is not depicted as such in the novel, is Gurmesinda, a neighbour of the sick woman that Guerra is protecting, and one of her carers. Gurmesinda is presented as an honest and completely unselfish working-class woman. Galdós describes her as 'una mujer dispuesta y agradable como pocas, alma expansiva, corazón puro, joya oscurecida y olvidada, como otras mil, en medio de la tosquedad de las muchedumbres populares'. The narrator continues, 'Sentíase Guerra humillado por aquella mujer que practicaba la caridad sin ninguna petulancia, que se sacrificaba por sus semejantes sin dar importancia al sacrificio, que era buena sin decirlo y hasta sin saberlo' (II, 580). Gurmesinda's husband, a building worker temporarily unemployed due to '*parálisis* de obras', as Gurmesinda puts it, is an example of the instability of the building industry during the period and the forced unemployment that many workers suffered.[34]

---

34 Angel Bahamonde Magro ('Cultura de la pobreza y mendicidad involuntaria en el Madrid del siglo XIX', in *Madrid en Galdós, Galdós en Madrid* [Madrid, Comunidad de Madrid, Consejería de Cultura, May 1988], 172) observes that the building sector generated the highest rates of unemployment and casual employment.

When Guerra decides to protect them, offering the husband a job as a labourer on his estate, Gurmesinda admits to him with obvious embarrassment that they are not married. Interestingly, she also comments that some ladies – presumably philanthropists in charge of 'beneficencia domiciliaria' or 'visitadoras de pobres'– had been to see her about getting the papers in order so that they can be married:

> *Monifacio* y yo no somos *mismamente* casados. Vivimos así..., pues [...] Queremos casarnos por la Iglesia; pero el sacar los papeles y el tanto más cuanto de la vicaría nos imposibilita, porque viceversa no tenemos dinero. Unas señoras que hablan para casar a los que viven en familia, le dijeron a una servidora que nos traerían los papeles y toda la incumbencia para las bendiciones; pero no han vuelto a parecer. (II, 580)

Angel offers to help Gurmesinda to obtain the official papers they need to get married. However, he makes the important point that he will still protect them even if they are not married: 'Claro está que lo mismo les protejo casados que solteros' (II, 580), he tells Gurmesinda. Galdós is using Gurmesinda's case to criticize the religious establishment, as well as contemporary beliefs that associated the great number of illegal unions among the working classes with the dissolution, immorality and lack of religious feelings they perceived as inherent in this social group. A similar attitude was adopted by an observer reporting to the Comisión de Reformas Sociales, who criticized the Church for voicing this opinion when, in fact, the Church itself, because of the bureaucratic and financial obstacles it put in the working classes' way, was responsible for the frequency of such illegal unions.[35] Through the positive portrayal of Gurmesinda and through Guerra's tolerant attitude towards her and her family, the author dismisses the standard classification of the poor into deserving and undeserving as understood and defined in the late nineteenth century.

This reinforces the conclusion drawn in the previous chapter: the fact that Angel dies at the hands of the Babel sons suggests that Galdós disagrees with the protagonist's financial support of the category of poor that they represent. However, the author does not disapprove of Angel's protection of other characters who, although regarded as immoral and undeserving according to the criteria of many of his contemporaries, are not described in the novel as such. Galdós suggests that, although there are people who are morally undeserving, such as the degenerate Babel sons or the beggar *Maldiciones*, it is sometimes difficult to draw a line between the various categories applied to the poor by the society of the time.

---

35 See *Reformas Sociales* (Información escrita practicada en virtud de la Real orden de 5 diciembre de 1883. Madrid) (Madrid, Manuel Minuesa de los Ríos, 1890), II, 433.

Nazarín's Challenge: Begging and Indiscriminate Charity

Like *Angel Guerra, Nazarín* (1895) has tended to be seen as concentrating on its protagonist's *individual*, spiritual mission.[36] In this context, critical studies of the novel have often focused attention on the ambiguities and contradictions of his character, his selfishness and self-interested motives and the final failure of his utopian project.[37] Departing from this critical tradition I shall here analyse the novel in terms of its *social* context, highlighting the new, more rational and pragmatic approach to poverty and mendicity that had begun to emerge in the nineteenth century – particularly in the last third – and its coexistence, to an extent, with prevailing older, more tolerant conceptions of the problem. Through the ambiguities and inconsistencies that surround the character Nazarín, I would argue, Galdós is calling into question the wider social implications of Nazarín's actions rather than simply his individual spiritual mission. As in *Angel Guerra*, Galdós's questioning of Nazarín's views, rather than being solely a reply to Tolstoy's *What I Believe*, is part of the contemporary debate on poverty, mendicity and the dispensation of charity.

Despite the emergence of new perceptions of charity and new attitudes towards the poor, Nazarín's endorsement of poverty, like Leré's,[38] illustrates the persistence in the late nineteenth century of old beliefs

---

36 A shorter version of this section was presented as an unpublished paper, entitled 'A Diseased Morality: Begging and "Rebellious" Charity in *Nazarín*', to the Modern Languages Association Convention (Panel on 'Deviancy and Control in Galdós'), Chicago, 29 December 1999.

37 Critics have clearly demonstrated how the author, through the use of ambiguity and irony, makes the reader wary of the ideas expressed by Nazarín. See, in particular, Peter A. Bly, '"Nazarín": ¿Enigma eterno o triunfo del arte galdosiano?', *Cuadernos Hispanoamericanos*, 124 (1981), 286–300, and *Pérez Galdós: Nazarín* (London, Grant & Cutler, 1991); Brian J. Dendle, 'Point of View in *Nazarín*: An Appendix to Goldman', *Anales Galdosianos*, IX (1974), 113–21; and Peter B. Goldman, 'Galdós and the Aesthetic of Ambiguity: Notes on the Thematic Structure of *Nazarín*', *Anales Galdosianos*, IX (1974), 99–112. A clear example of this, Bly notes ('"Nazarín": ¿Enigma eterno?', 291–92), is the scene where Nazarín first appears in the novel, in which he is shown to be complaining about the fact that he has been robbed. As Bly has observed, it is ironic that someone like Nazarín, who aspires to total poverty and argues against private property, should complain so vehemently about having been robbed. Also, Nazarín's plaintive tone in this scene contrasts with his later lack of concern about the theft itself and his statement that private property does not mean anything to him.

38 Nazarín's self-imposed poverty and resigned attitude to life is not dissimilar to Leré's in *Angel Guerra*. Nazarín's description, however, is more negative, as he often appears to be moved by a pursuit of self-satisfaction. In this respect, it has to be remembered that Angel Guerra's motives were also shown to be self-interested, in the sense that his actions were often motivated by a desire to get closer to Leré.

that sanctified the state of poverty on the grounds that Christ himself was poor. The view that the poor, who had to endure their sufferings and afflictions with resignation, had been placed by God in a favourable position to earn a place in heaven (and from this perspective possessed immense riches) is echoed by Nazarín when he tells his 'disciples', Andara and Beatriz, 'Nosotros no somos pobres, somos ricos porque tenemos el caudal inmenso y las inagotables provisiones de la conformidad cristiana' (120). Later in the novel he repeats this idea when he says to the two women that 'los pobres de solemnidad son los verdaderos ricos' (143).[39] The tolerance towards alms-giving, which persisted in public opinion in spite of the attempts to make the distribution of charity more rational,

39 It is significant that Nazarín is supporting a view that was often used by contemporary moral commentators and clergymen as an instrument of social stability. It has been observed, in this regard, that Nazarín's message in the novel – his endorsement of poverty as a solution to social unrest and injustice, his resignation and disregard for material progress – may have been used by Galdós to deflect the threat of political revolution; see Jo Labanyi's introduction to her translation of *Nazarín* (Oxford, Oxford University Press, 1993), xii–xiii. Similarly, Goldman has noted that in 1885 Galdós regarded with pessimism the possibility of socialism as a solution to the problems and conflicts created by industrialization and urban growth. As Galdós wrote, 'Spiritualism perhaps comes closest to a solution, since it proclaims contempt for wealth and Christian resignation, and counteracts an inequality based on externals with the consolation of an eternal equality, that is, the noble levelling of human destinies in the sanctuary of our inner conscience' (*Política española*, II [vol. IV of Ghiraldo (ed.), *Obras inéditas de Benito Pérez Galdós*], 273–74, quoted by Peter B. Goldman, 'Galdós and the Nineteenth-Century Novel: The Need for an Interdisciplinary Approach', in Jo Labanyi [ed.], *Galdós* [London, Longman, 1993], 146). In an article in *La Prensa* of 26 October 1893, Galdós stated, along similar lines, 'El mal humor y la displicencia de las clases humildes es cada día mayor. Falta el contrapeso de la idea religiosa, de las compensaciones anunciadas para la otra vida, en la cual han empezado a perder la fe algunos desheredados de la fortuna'; see Shoemaker (ed.), *Las cartas desconocidas de Galdós*, 487. Labanyi (*Nazarín*, xii–xiii) has argued that the author's message in the novel is contradictory and ambiguous, as he voices, through the character of Andara, the opposite view to Nazarín: that is, that material goods can help in life and that the victims of injustice should fight to defend their rights. Also, Nazarín's penultimate dream in the novel, in which Andara is portrayed as a triumphant warrior fighting injustice and the forces of oppression, would seem to support Andara's more rebellious posture. But this episode only adds to the ambiguity, as Labanyi has shown, since it is presented by the narrator as a product of a diseased mind, Nazarín being delirious with typhus. As mentioned earlier, Galdós was not opposed to material progress and often propounded industrial and scientific development in his journalistic writings of the 1880s and early 1890s. In light of these, it is difficult not to agree with Labanyi's argument that Galdós may be using Nazarín's message as a weapon against the threat of social violence. This threat may also justify the disregard for wealth and economic progress that Galdós voiced in his articles noted here.

was particularly strong in rural areas. Bernaldo de Quirós and Llanas Aguilaneido observed,

> La vida mendicativa a través de los caminos y alrededor de pueblos y aldeas, es aún feliz en la ventura y próspera en los rendimientos. Almas sencillas, llenas de una piedad supersticiosa, aún quieren ver en los mendigos elegidos del Señor. La cara venerable de algunos, semejantes a apóstoles de retablo [...] impresionan aún a los creyentes, que viéndoles marchar socorridos de sus manos temen o confían si serán enviados del Señor [...] o acaso el Señor mismo, descendido a la tierra para probar a sus fieles.
>
> Existen todavía ermitaños, solitarios y aun penitentes que en despoblado reciben y socorren a los pobres. *Hospitalillos, pajares para pobres* y otras instituciones de rústica beneficencia, existen en muchos pueblos, y no falta en ninguno algún vecino piadoso que preste asistencia a los vagabundos pordioseros.[40]

However, attitudes towards mendicity were far less tolerant in the city, due to a more rational conception of charity, which explains why Nazarín leaves the city for the country. As Bernaldo de Quirós and Llanas Aguilaneido pointed out, 'En la ciudad, efecto de las nuevas ideas y prácticas en materia de asistencia, es harto más difícil la existencia del mendigo'.[41] This also accounts for the fact that some of the country people whom Nazarín and the two women meet during their 'peregrinación' display a lenient attitude towards them when they are begging for alms. However, in the novel, Nazarín, Andara and Beatriz are more often regarded with suspicion and mistrust by the characters they encounter, demonstrating that older perceptions of poverty were being increasingly discarded. *Nazarín* shows how its protagonist's beliefs regarding poverty and begging were becoming obsolete.

In the interview that takes place at the beginning of the novel between Nazarín, the narrator and his journalist companion, Nazarín's views on begging are shown to be the same as those expressed by Leré in *Angel Guerra*. When the narrator-interviewer asks him, '¿Y no cree usted que la dignidad de un sacerdote es incompatible con la humillación de recibir limosna?', Nazarín replies, 'No, señor; la limosna no envilece a quien la recibe ni en nada vulnera su dignidad' (27). These words contradict starkly Arenal's statement in *La Voz de la Caridad* that 'la mendicidad rebaja, envilece, desmoraliza'.[42] Nazarín's 'credo', like Leré's, conflicts strongly with contemporary views, which regarded begging as degrading and undignified. This interview is also used by the author to raise an issue

40 Bernaldo de Quirós and Llanas Aguilaneido, *La mala vida en Madrid*, 337.
41 Ibid., 337.
42 *La Voz de la Caridad* (15 May 1880), 63.

previously treated in *Angel Guerra*: that of the deserving and undeserving poor. Nazarín's statement that private property has only been created by human selfishness, and particularly his declaration that all things should belong to those who need them ('[n]ada es de nadie. Todo es del primero que lo necesita' [19]), necessarily poses the question of who exactly the really needy are. As the narrator-interviewer retorts,

> ¡Bonita sociedad tendríamos si esas ideas prevalecieran! ¿Y cómo sabríamos quién era el primer necesitado? Habríamos de disputarnos, cuchillo en mano, ese derecho de primacía en la necesidad. (19)

It is significant that Nazarín is not only presented in the novel as a beggar, but also as a dispenser of charity. It is even more significant that, like Leré and Angel Guerra, he is portrayed as practising charity in an indiscriminate way, rebelling therefore against newer views. When the narrator-interviewer says to him, 'Y es de presumir que algo de lo que usted reciba pasará a manos de otros más necesitados *o que lo parezcan*' (27; my emphasis), he is implying that he might be helping the undeserving poor. Nazarín thus is seen to be fostering poverty and idleness, as he gives alms to the needy without distinction. The old gypsy makes this point when he tells the narrator and his reporter friend,

> Señores […] ¿se *pue sabé* si le dieron *guita* a ese *venturao* de don Najarillo? Porque más valiera que lo diesen a *mujotros*, que así nos ahorrábamos el trabajo de subir a pedírselo, o se quitaban de que lo diera a malas manos… Que muchos hay […] que le sonsacan la caridad, y le quitan hasta el aire santísimo, antes de que lo dé *a quien se lo merece*… (32; my emphasis)

This issue is brought up again later by *Chanfaina*. When she notices the smell of Andara's perfume wafting from Nazarín's window, she points out to him,

> me parece que sale por esa ventana un olor… así como de esa perfumería condenada que usan las mujeronas… […] Claro, no es novedad. Como entran a verlo a usted personas de todas castas, y usted no distingue, ni sabe a quién socorre… (48)

Here, the use of the term 'casta' is reminiscent of the use that Galdós makes of it in *Angel Guerra*, in the sequence in which the priest Mancebo is concerned about the 'casta de pobres' who are going to inherit Angel's money. Also, in the same way as Angel Guerra declares to the priest Casado that nobody will be rejected in his projected institution and that whoever knocks on the door will be admitted, so Nazarín shelters all sorts of people under his roof. Nazarín's attitude towards the poor would have been considered reprehensible by proponents of the emergent liberal-economic discourse. Arenal wrote in this respect,

> La mendicidad [...] es culpa o delito que el mendigo no puede cometer solo,
> porque, si no hubiera quien diese *sin discernimiento*, no habría quien pidiera
> *sin necesidad*. El público puede considerarse como cómplice, y aun como
> coautor del delito, puesto que sin él no podría cometerse, y aunque esté de
> buena fe, y aunque ceda a un sentimiento humano y noble, siempre habrá
> imprudencia temeraria en dar sin saber a quién y sabiendo que hay tantos
> que abusan de su ignorancia. [43]

In the novel the reporter regards individual, disorganized alms-givers
like Nazarín as 'immoral' because he believes that they act against the
interests of the state, hence his harsh attack on Nazarín:

> Y yo pregunto: ¿ese hombre, con su *altruismo* desenfrenado [author's
> emphasis], hace algún bien a sus semejantes? Respondo: no. Comprendo las
> instituciones religiosas que ayudan a la Beneficencia en su obra grandiosa.
> La misericordia, virtud privada, es el mejor auxiliar de la Beneficencia,
> virtud pública. ¿Por ventura, estos misericordiosos sueltos, individuales,
> medievales, acaso contribuyen a *labrar la vida del Estado*? [my emphasis]
> No. Lo que ellos cultivan es su propia viña, y de la limosna, cosa tan santa,
> dada con método y repartida con criterio, hacen una granjería indecente.
> (29–30)[44]

Here, once more, the rational and methodical distribution of charity is
contrasted with the emotional and unthinking giving of alms. Nazarín's
acts are not only seen by the reporter as morally reprehensible from the
point of view of his attitude towards the undeserving poor; his self-
enforced poverty also makes him a parasite, or an idler, in society's eyes,
that is, he is perceived as undeserving himself. The reporter's view of
Nazarín as an idler and a scrounger is echoed by Andara and three other
prostitutes. It is ironic that they accuse Nazarín of being unwilling to
work and of living off other people, when prostitutes themselves were
often associated with idleness:

> ¿Quién es él, ni que significan sus hábitos negros de ala de mosca, si no hace
> más que vivir de gorra y no sabe ganarlo? ¿Por qué el muy simple no se
> agencia bautizos y funerales, como otros clerigones que andan por Madrid

---

43 Arenal, *El pauperismo*, I, 391.

44 The reporter's words here, 'Comprendo las instituciones religiosas que ayudan a la
    Beneficencia en su obra grandiosa,' are at odds with Galdós's pessimistic attitude
    towards institutionalized charity, both public and private; see, in this respect, Plá et
    al., *El Madrid de Galdós*, 89–113; and Arnold Penuel, *Charity in Galdós* (Athens, GA,
    University of Georgia Press, 1972), especially chapter II. Public institutions (including
    hospitals) always appear in Galdós's novels as the last resort. Private institutions,
    such as Las Micaelas or La Misericordia, are not offered as a solution either. The
    utopian institutions depicted in *Angel Guerra* and *Halma* are also shown to fail.

con muy buen pelo?... Misas a granel salen para todos, y para él nada:
miseria, y chocolate de a tres reales, hígado y un poco de acelga, de lo que
no quieren las cabras...¡Y luego decir que le roban!... (17–18)

It should be noted that the narrator is not shown to share the reporter's
very negative view of Nazarín. Although this is not made explicit (Galdós's
dislike of the mayor at the end of the novel is made more obvious),
Galdós's choice of two different characters in the scene of the interview
with Nazarín alerts the reader to the fact that there might not be a complete agreement between them with regard to their judgement of Nazarín.
The reporter's views on Nazarín are likely to be those of Galdós's middle-
class readers (as a journalist he would take care to reflect public opinion).
Open criticism of the reporter would possibly have alienated the author
from his readers at this very early stage in the novel. The creation of a
character-narrator allows the author to distance himself from the ideas
expressed by the press, that is, from commonly held beliefs on poverty
and mendicity (a major topic in the press at the time), without provoking
the reader's hostility. Towards the end of the novel, however, Galdós is
in a safer position to make his views more explicit. Therefore, he does not
hide his dislike for the mayor of the village where Nazarín is arrested,
whose ideas are not dissimilar to the reporter's. This does not necessarily
imply, however, that Galdós supports Nazarín's doctrine. Rather, he
presents this character as an enigma: Nazarín represents a challenge to all
the accepted views on poverty and charity during this period. The
difficulty of determining where Galdós stands in the first part of the
novel is compounded in the rest of the novel by the fact that there is
confusion as to who is the real narrator of the 'crónica'.

The suspicion and distrust shown by most characters towards
Nazarín, Andara and Beatriz reflects the pejorative connotations of
begging and vagrancy in the late nineteenth century. These are voiced
by *Pinto*, Beatriz's ex-boyfriend, when he says to her, in the episode
where they meet as she goes to get water from the fountain, 'Bien te dije
que te habías de ver perdida, pidiendo limosna, como una callejera
vergonzante o sin vergüenza' (136).[45] The fierce don Pedro de Belmonte
offers another example of the hostile attitude adopted towards beggars
and vagrants. As he says to Nazarín, 'No acostumbro dar a los holgazanes
y vagabundos más que una buena mano de palos cuando se acercan a mi
casa' (101), thus associating mendicity with idleness. As this quotation

45 It should be noted here that the expression 'pobres vergonzantes' was used to refer
    to the deserving poor (and not the undeserving, as Pinto's words suggest). The
    author may have used this pun to poke fun at Pinto, criticizing his total lack of
    consideration for Beatriz and his association of her with the undeserving poor.

shows, Nazarín and the two women are not only seen as beggars but also as vagrants: these social categories were seen as synonymous in the period, since their mobility resisted attempts to 'fix' or settle them.[46] When later in the novel Nazarín and the two women arrive in Villamantilla to help the victims of the epidemic, the narrator similarly notes the suspicion shown by the people who they meet on their way to the village square. The mayor of the village also greets them with a hostile remark when he says, 'aquí no hay lugar para la vagancia' (128).

Both begging and vagrancy become linked with dissolution because they are seen to be transgressing, in a threatening way, the political and economic interests of the nation. Nazarín, as a beggar, is perceived as non-productive and, therefore, of little use to society. It is significant that Galdós has chosen a prostitute and a fallen woman as Nazarín's disciples: like beggars, prostitutes were commonly regarded as unproductive. This explains the mistrust shown by some people in the novel towards Nazarín, Andara and Beatriz. The image of the beggar is once more constructed in economic terms in a passage in which the reporter comments about Nazarín,

> Este hombre es un fanático, un vicioso del parasitismo, y bien puede afirmarse que no tiene ningún otro vicio, porque todas sus facultades se concentran en la cría y desarrollo de aquella aptitud [...] La sociedad, a fuer de tutora y enfermera, debe considerar estos tipos como corruptores de la Humanidad, *en buena ley económico-política*, y encerrarlos en un asilo benéfico. (29; my emphasis)

To the reporter, Nazarín is a scoundrel who is making a living out of begging. The only other explanation of his behaviour is that he is insane:

> Este hombre es un sinvergüenza [...], un cínico de mucho talento, que ha encontrado la piedra filosofal de la gandulería; un pillo de grande imaginación que cultiva el parasitismo con arte [...] [S]i no es un cínico, sostengo que no tiene la cabeza buena. (28–29)

It is significant that the reporter associates insanity with non-compliance with the social norm. If Nazarín is not a 'cínico', a parasite or a scoundrel who does not work and who lives on begging, he necessarily has to be mad. His 'credo'– that of self-imposed poverty and total passivity allied to his lack of interest in improving his position within the religious establishment – is not understood because it constitutes a complete reversal of nineteenth-century ideas on work and progress emanating from the development of industrial capitalism. The third alternative is

---

46 In this regard, the stress on constructing housing for workers in the last third of the century also complements the need to 'fix' the 'dangerous' groups of the population.

that he is a 'santo', because of his strict practice of the Christian doctrine and his concern for the poor. But, as one of the guards tells Nazarín on their way to Madrid,

> No tenga cuidado, padre, que allá le absolverán por loco. Los dos tercios de los procesados que pasan por nuestras manos, por locos escapan del castigo, si es que castigo merecen. Y presuponiendo que sea usted un santo, no por santo le han de soltar, sino por loco; que ahora priva mucho la razón de la sinrazón, o sea que la locura es quien hace a los muy sabios y a los muy ignorantes, a los que sobresalen por arriba y por abajo. (201)

As this quotation shows, the emphasis is laid, once more, on what is useful or productive. *Chanfaina* comments, in this respect, 'en estos tiempos de tanta sabiduría [...], ¿para qué sirve un santo más que para divertir a los chiquillos de las calles?' (31). If Nazarín is to be acquitted, as the mayor declares later in the novel, his lawyer will have to plead insanity (160), for in the context of late nineteenth-century Spain, Nazarín's ideas can only be understood as being the product of an insane mind. In *Halma* (1895), which constitutes a sequel to *Nazarín*, the priest Manuel Flórez admires Nazarín's spiritual perfection, but at the same time regards him as 'un ser dislocado, completamente fuera del ambiente social en que vivía' (1815). Nazarín poses a threat because he acts independently, on the fringes of society, and he rejects progress. He does not conform to the social norm as he acts beyond the accepted boundaries established by the Church: at this point, sanctity becomes insanity. As Flórez observes,

> Yo no sé si es santo; pero lo que es a pureza de conciencia no le gana nadie. Desde luego le declararía yo digno de canonización, si su conducta al lanzarse a correr aventuras por los caminos no me ofreciera un punto negro, la rebeldía al superior... (1809)

Flórez is unable to draw the line between the 'santo' and the 'loco'. If madness is equated with non-compliance, submission to society's rules is regarded as a symptom of the recovery of reason. When Halma takes upon herself the task of Nazarín's restoration to society, she asserts, 'No [...] será difícil restablecer en él el hombre de conducta ejemplar, el sacerdote sumiso y obediente' (1818). Don Remigio, the priest of San Agustín – a village close to Pedralba – believes that Nazarín is completely recovered because he is obedient and willing to defer to authority: 'Es tan humilde [...], y su comportamiento tan ejemplar, su obediencia tan absoluta, que si de mí dependiera, no tendría inconveniente en darle de alta' (1865). Similarly, in *Fortunata y Jacinta*, Fortunata is considered 'fit' to leave the convent because she is docile and submissive to discipline (I, 633).

In *Nazarín*, the protagonist's passivity conflicts strongly with the new ethos of work. As the reporter observes, 'Tanta pasividad traspasa los límites del ideal cristiano, sobre todo en estos tiempos en que cada cual es hijo de sus obras' (28), reflecting the influence of the Protestant self-made-man ethos. The reporter is here referring to the fact that people are judged by their aptitude for work. Work, or more precisely the 'work ethic', had become the basis of capitalist society, referred to by the reporter as a 'social law':

> La ley social, y si se quiere, cristiana, es que todo el mundo trabaje, cada cual en su esfera. Trabajan los presidiarios, los niños y ancianos en los asilos. Pues este clérigo muslímico-manchego[47] ha resuelto el problema de vivir sin ninguna especie de trabajo, ni aun el descansado de decir misa [...] Y me temo que saque discípulos, porque su doctrina [...] de fijo tendrá indecible seducción para tanto gandul como hay por esos mundos. (30)

The reporter's opinion of Nazarín is repeated later in the novel by the mayor, when he tells Nazarín, in a similar sarcastic tone,

> no vea en mí más que el amigo [...] a quien le hace mucha gracia usted y su cuadrilla, y la *sombra* con que ha convertido la vagancia en una religión muy cómoda y desahogada... [...] No crea, ya sacará discípulos, sobre todo si el Gobierno sigue recargando las contribuciones... (170–71)

It is significant that both the reporter and the mayor observe that Nazarín's doctrine is likely to attract many followers, echoing contemporary fears that pinpointed mendicity as a source of contagion. It should be noted, however, that the mayor is depicted in a very sarcastic way, and therefore the author can distance himself from the views expressed by this character, in the same way as he detached himself from the reporter at the beginning of the novel. The idea that insanity is contagious is also voiced by Manuel Flórez in *Halma* when, in a state of total confusion after one of his conversations with Nazarín, he comments, 'este hombre me ha trastornado, ha llenado mi cabeza de confusión. No, no vuelvo a verle más. La sinrazón es contagiosa... Un loco hace mil. No más, no más' (1815). Both insanity and mendicity are perceived as a plague. It is worth noting, in respect of the seclusion and isolation of those social groups perceived as diseased, Nazarín's insistence on mixing with the victims of the plague-ridden villages, which demonstrates his opposition to fears of 'contagion' and ideas on the containment of disease, both physical and moral. The stress laid by Galdós (in *Nazarín* and, similarly, in *Halma*) on issues such as undeserving poverty, begging and vagrancy,

---

47 The fact that Nazarín is seen to operate outside the rational Western capitalist order may explain why he is perceived in the novel as 'Arab'.

idleness, the work ethic, submission to discipline, insanity and contagion is a reflection of his concern for contemporary attitudes towards the poor, and lessens the emphasis traditionally placed on Galdós's spiritual tendencies during this period.

Although Nazarín does not disapprove of begging, and although he does not intend to improve his position in life, he is not shown in the novel to be unwilling to work. Thus, he will offer his work in exchange for the hospitality given to him by the 'Peludos' couple, after his house burns down. Although the husband does not think that a priest should work ('¡Un señor eclesiástico!¡Dios nos libre!...¡Qué diría la *sociedaz*, qué el santo cleriguicio!...') (67), his wife has different ideas, as the narrator comments humorously:

> La señora *Peluda* no tomó por lo sentimental los planes de su huésped, y como mujer *práctica* [my emphasis], manifestó que el trabajo no deshonra a nadie, pues el mismo Dios *trabajó* para fabricar el mundo [author's emphasis], y que ella sabía que en la estación de las Pulgas daban cinco reales a todo el que fuera al acarreo del carbón. (67)

Nazarín is also seen on other occasions offering his labour, for which he often gets money or food.[48] The most obvious example in the novel is, of course, the protagonist's charitable work helping the diseased people in the plague-ridden villages. Also, as discussed later, Nazarín is seen carrying out hard physical work in Halma's institution, and to be enjoying it (1847). As the narrator explains, Halma decides to take Nazarín to her institution with the intention of 'devolverle *sano y útil* al poder eclesiástico' (1842; my emphasis). Don Remigio is also shown exposing Nazarín to hard intellectual work (1837). Thus, Halma and don Remigio regard work as the ideal cure for Nazarín's insanity, mirroring contemporary ideas. Towards the end of the novel don Remigio considers Nazarín recovered, not only because of his absolute obedience but also because of his unflagging capacity for work (1865). Similarly, in *Fortunata y Jacinta*, the nuns link Mauricia's recovery from her fits to her obedience and her willingness to work, whereas her rebelliousness and reluctance to work – that is, her non-conformity with the rules of behaviour imposed in the convent – are equated with lunacy. As the narrator observes,

---

48 It is significant that on one of these occasions Nazarín and the two women are associated with filth and putrefaction, as they help some men to clean a trough full of mud and 'sustancias en putefacción' (151). This episode, though, is not devoid of humour, as a non-poisonous snake coils round Beatriz's foot, causing hilarious laughter among those present.

Las monjas la consideraban lunática, porque si las más de las veces la
sometían fácilmente a la obediencia, haciéndola trabajar, entrábale de golpe
como una locura y rompía a decir y hacer los mayores desatinos. (I, 611)[49]

In *Nazarín*, the protagonist is not only associated with insanity but
also with criminality. At the end of the nineteenth century insanity was
often linked with criminality in the context of the working classes.[50]
Nazarín, who is by no means a prototype of the undeserving working classes
(he acts as a beggar but also as a philanthropist), displays rebellious, anti-
establishment behaviour. This poses a threat to society, and from this
perspective he is perceived, like the working classes generally, as
dangerous, destructive, irrational and irresponsible, a perception which,
along with the need felt to 'fix' these sectors of the population and to subject them to discipline, led to the equation of lunacy with criminality.[51]
In *Halma*, Consuelo Feramor associates insanity and criminality when,
talking about Nazarín, she asks Flórez, '¿es cierto que traerán a casa a ese

49 Mauricia echoes these bourgeois associations when, after having been locked up in a
    cage-like room following one of her fits, she requests Sor Marcela, 'Sáqueme pronto
    de aquí, y trabajaré como nunca, y si me mandan fregar toda la casa de arriba a
    abajo, la fregaré' (I, 617). For Sor Marcela, Mauricia's subservient attitude is a sign of
    her recovery of reason. Thus, she replies to Mauricia, 'Me gusta verte tan entrada en
    razón' (I, 618). Fernando Alvarez-Uría (*Miserables y locos: Medicina mental y orden
    social en la España del siglo XIX* [Barcelona, Tusquets, 1983], 206–07) has noted, in
    respect of institutions for the reform of 'social deviants' – such as asylums or prisons
    – that 'la conformidad con las normas y preceptos se traduce siempre en signos
    positivos de curación. Y a la inversa, la actitud rebelde, la violencia, la resistencia, la
    suciedad [...] son síntomas inequívocos de los progresos de la enfermedad'.
50 In *Fortunata y Jacinta* Mauricia's alcoholism is linked by middle-class characters,
    and very often by the narrator, not only with lunacy but also with criminality,
    particularly in the chapter 'Las Micaelas por dentro'.
51 The link between criminality and insanity, along with the issue of the responsibility
    of the criminal, had begun to be discussed in the Madrid Ateneo in the early 1880s.
    Towards the end of this decade, when Lombroso's theories on criminality had
    become influential in Spain, the focus of the debates in the Ateneo was no longer
    whether criminals were responsible for their acts, but the impossibility of redeeming
    them, as it was argued that the causes of their 'abnormality' were congenital. Since
    'social deviants' could not be cured or reformed, it was believed that the problem
    could only be eradicated, a view that justified the death penalty. During the 1890s
    the issues of criminality and insanity gave rise to a great number of publications in
    Spain, the influence of Lombroso's doctrine reaching a height in 1895, the year of
    publication of *Nazarín*. See Luis Maristany, 'Lombroso y España: Nuevas considera-
    ciones', *Anales de Literatura Española*, 2 (1983), Universidad de Alicante, 361–81;
    and Jo Labanyi's introduction to her translation of *Nazarín*. As Labanyi has
    observed (xiv), it is significant that in *Halma*, the courts consider Nazarín insane
    and therefore exempt from criminal responsibility, which reveals the influence on
    Galdós of the doctor Tolosa Latour, an advocate of penal reform.

pobre demente..., o criminal..., vaya usted a saber?' (1804). This link is again a reflection of Galdós's desire to echo social issues. Further, Nazarín's association with criminality, particularly in the novel *Nazarín*, arises from the connection made during this period between begging and vagrancy on the one hand, and criminality on the other. Beggars (that is, those of the undeserving kind) were perceived as thieves who deceived the public and exploited people's compassion for the benefit of their own idleness and other personal vices. It was also felt that they were diverting money that could be used to help legitimate beggars. When Nazarín asks for shelter at a house in the outskirts of Madrid on the first day of his 'peregrinación' (he asks if he can sleep in a corner of the yard), he is not well received by the owner of the house, who begins to shout abuse at him, saying that 'ya estaba harto de albergar ladrones en su propiedad' (77). Later, when Nazarín, Andara and Beatriz approach Belmonte's estate, the property's guard, who is alerted by the dogs' barking, exclaims, '¡Váyanse de aquí, granujas, holgazanes, taifa de ladrones!' (98).

Mendicity was often described as a business or full-time occupation, hence the expression 'mendigos profesionales', which was used in opposition to 'pobres vergonzantes' or deserving beggars. In 1889, according to *La Epoca*, eight out of ten beggars were 'mendigos industriales'.[52] In another article published in this newspaper in 1891, it was reported in this respect, 'Como la caridad abunda, es lo cierto que hay mendigo en Madrid que recibe en limosnas lo que no ganan como premio a su trabajo, hombres inteligentes y laboriosos. Como el negocio marcha, la plaga crece.'[53] The perception of mendicity as a business is echoed in the novel when, shortly after Nazarín sets out for the country, away from Madrid, the narrator comments on his encounter with other beggars, who look at him with suspicion and distrust:

> Al pasar el puente, unos mendigos que allí *ejercían su libérrima industria* le miraron sorprendidos y recelosos, como diciendo: '¿Qué pájaro es éste que viene por nuestros dominios *sin que le hayamos dado la patente?*...' (70; my emphasis)

It is significant that here it is not just the narrator but also the beggars themselves who describe mendicity in terms of a business that they have set up in a definite territory, for which they believe they have an exclusive

---

52 *La Epoca* (3 October 1889), in Bahamonde Magro and Toro Mérida, 'Mendicidad y paro', 372.

53 *La Epoca* (5 August 1891), in Bahamonde Magro and Toro Mérida, 'Mendicidad y paro', 374. The abundance of professional beggars is easily explained if one takes into account that they could earn through begging as much as, if not more than, unskilled workers, as noted by Bahamonde Magro, 'Cultura de la pobreza', 168.

'patent'. Similarly, when the narrator refers to Nazarín's first try at begging, he comments humorously, 'Ensayó allí Nazarín su flamante *oficio* de pordiosero' (76; my emphasis). A few pages later Nazarín is described by the narrator as 'el aspirante [a mendigo]' (79). Here, Nazarín's self-imposed poverty and his desire to become a beggar are not taken seriously by the narrator. Also on this first day of his 'peregrinación', Nazarín meets a shepherd who, once more, associates mendicity with a 'profession' when, looking at Nazarín warily, he says,

> *Paíce* que *seis* nuevo en el *oficio* [my emphasis] [...] y que nunca *anduviéis* por acá [...] Pues pongo en su conocimiento que los *ceviles* tienen orden de coger a toda la mendicidad y de llevarla a todos los *recogimientos* que hay en Madrid. Verdad que luego la sueltan otra vez, porque no hay allá *mantención* para tanto vago... (75–76)

Here, the shepherd is also referring to the rounding up of beggars carried out by the authorities during this time. Nazarín, Andara and Beatriz, like beggars and vagrants, were perceived as a 'floating population', which had to be swept up from the streets and secluded or 'fixed' in asylums. The foundation in Madrid of the asylums of San Bernardino in 1834 and El Pardo in 1868 arose out of the need to contain the threat represented by the increasing influx of beggars to the capital.[54] The creation of San Bernardino was complemented by the appearance of 'La Ley de Vagos' in 1845 (which identified the 'vago' with the 'parado')[55] and a 'Real Orden' which specified that people, of any sex or age, found begging for alms *in the streets* were to be rounded up by the authorities. The subsequent 'Ordenanzas Municipales' prohibited begging on the public highway, and ordered municipal agents to bring beggars to the authorities so they could be taken to the appropriate charitable establishments.[56] These measures explain the shepherd's warning to Nazarín in the above quotation, as well as Nazarín's and the women's arrest later in the novel (although Nazarín and Andara are arrested for other reasons also). Far from being a route to salvation, mendicity and vagrancy had

---

54   These establishments were, since their foundation, pauper prisons, rather than the charitable institutions whose aim had initially been, according to a contemporary source, 'dar a todos los asilados instrucción primaria y trabajo en los talleres'; see Plá et al., *El Madrid de Galdós*, 100–01. As the shepherd tells Nazarín in the novel, these asylums were insufficient to contain the number of beggars that invaded the streets of the capital. See also note 123 in this regard.

55   Similarly, article 258 of the Penal Code of 1849 identified, although in a less precise way, 'vago' with 'parado'. The reform of this article in 1868 reinforced the understanding of the two terms as synonymous. See Angel Bahamonde Magro and Jesús A. Martínez, *Historia de España siglo XIX* (Madrid, Cátedra, 1994), 479–80.

56   See Plá et al., *El Madrid de Galdós*, 99.

become legally associated with criminality.[57] As the dwarf Ujo tells Nazarín and the two women in his grotesque language, '*desapartaos* de la Guardia *civila*, pues *diz* que si *vos* coge, *vos* lleva como *relincuentes* públicos y criminales, ¡Caraifa!' (149). The mayor of the village where Nazarín and the two women are taken after being arrested tells Nazarín that by law he is a criminal, and that the only way of being acquitted is to plead insanity:

> supongo que su abogado le defenderá por loco, porque cuerdo no hay cristiano que le defienda, ni ley que no le condene [...]¡Pero, por Dios, padre Zaharín, echarse a una vida de vagabundo, con ese par de pencos!... (160)

The negative connotations of vagrancy in the case of the character Nazarín are aggravated by the fact that he is a priest. (As the mayor tells him in a recriminatory tone, '¿Le parece a usted que está bien que un señor eclesiástico ande en estos trotes...?' [160].)[58] In the mayor's view, anyone who, at the end of the nineteenth century, tries to put Christ's doctrine into practice, thereby disregarding material progress and the work ethic, cannot be sane, as he declares to Nazarín:

> ¿Y cómo he de creer yo que un hombre de sentido, en nuestros tiempos prácticos, esencialmente prácticos, o si se quiere de tanta ilustración, puede tomar en serio eso de enseñar con el ejemplo todo lo que dice la doctrina? [...] Yo no creo que se pueda llevar a la práctica todo lo que dijo y predicó el gran reformador de la sociedad [...] El fin del hombre es vivir. No se vive sin comer. No se come sin trabajar. Y en este siglo ilustrado, ¿a qué tiene que mirar el hombre? A la industria, a la agricultura, a la administración, al comercio [...] [Q]ue haya la mar de fábricas..., vías de comunicación..., casinos para obreros..., barrios obreros..., ilustración, escuelas, beneficencia pública y particular... ¿Y dónde me deja usted la higiene, la urbanización y otras grandes conquistas? Pues nada de eso tendrá usted con el misticismo, que es lo que usted practica; no tendrá más que hambre, miseria pública y particular... (162–63)

While Nazarín's views are not to be trusted, due to the ambiguities that surround this character, the reader is clearly not meant to agree with the

---

57 Arenal (*El pauperismo*, I, 381) expressed her disagreement with this association, stating that although government measures and unjust laws had linked mendicity to crime and vice, mendicity should be considered as 'un capítulo aparte'. The fact that writers like Bernaldo de Quirós and Llanas Aguilaneido, as criminologists, devoted considerable attention to the issues of poverty and vagrancy is an indicator of the criminalization of poverty during this period.

58 In *Halma*, the priest Manuel Flórez also makes this point when he comments, 'la mendicidad, fuera de las órdenes que la practican por su instituto, es contraria al decoro eclesiástico' (1816).

mayor's defence of pragmatism and his rejection of spiritual values, since he is presented by Galdós as rude, cynical and ignorant (Galdós makes him use the incorrect form 'haiga' in order to highlight and mock his false erudition, 163). It is significant that in *Halma*, the administrator of the state of Pedralba, who expresses similar ideas to the mayor, is also portrayed in pejorative terms. His materialistic approach is reflected in his words to don Remigio: 'Si yo no siembro, nada cogeré, por más que me pase el día y la noche engarzando rosarios y potras. [T]odo eso del misticismo eclesiástico y de la santísima fe católica es cosa muy buena, pero hace falta trigo para vivir' (1858). So the advice that he gives Halma is 'pues yo que la señora me dejaría de capillas y panteones y de toda esa monserga de poner aquí al modo de un convento para observantes *circun-spetos* y *mendicativos*' (1844). The administrator's plan is to cultivate the land and to make a profit out of it, because, as he says, '¿De qué sirve lo *espertual* sin lo otro?' (1844).[59] The administrator, like the mayor in *Nazarín*, is depicted as uncouth and ignorant (Galdós also highlights here the administrator's incorrect language).

It is noteworthy that, although at first Halma rejects the idea of making a business out of the land because she considers it to be at odds with the humble life she intends to live (1841), she finally decides to exploit it and make the most of it. Thus she tells Amador, 'me decido, señor don Pascual, me decido. Hay que sacar del suelo de Dios todo lo que se pueda' (1850). As seen earlier, Galdós approved of material progress, but he attacked narrow materialism and excessive rationalism and pragmatism, propounding instead an ethical use of the material. If Nazarín's spirituality makes him disregard material progress, the materialistic attitude of the mayor is completely devoid of ethical principles. Both the mayor in *Nazarín* and the administrator in *Halma* are representatives of the authorities, criticized by Galdós for their 'scientific', rational attempts at categorization and labelling at the expense of more humane attitudes.

In *Nazarín*, Galdós portrays on several occasions this contemporary zeal for separating or isolating the various groups of the population perceived as dangerous or threatening. After Nazarín's interview with the mayor, the narrator comments that the latter and the local magistrate had discussed the prisoners' transfer, which would have to be postponed for a day due to the arrival of other 'vagabundos' and 'criminales'. Among

59 Another character in *Halma* who is typically representative of excessive rationalism and materialism is, of course, Halma's brother Feramor. In total contrast to Feramor, Halma's choice of poverty is, according to the priest don Remigio, 'la más grande maravilla de estos tiempos de positivismo, de estos tiempos de egoísmo, de estos tiempos de materialismo' (1838). As in *Angel Guerra* and *Nazarín*, the issue of poverty in *Halma* has wider social implications.

these there was an old beggar, a person who had committed parricide, and someone arrested for stealing from churches (169). Here, the narrator is drawing attention to the indiscriminate mixing of people with very different kinds of offences. When Nazarín, Andara, and Beatriz set off on the road to Madrid along with other criminals and beggars (once more a sign of the close association drawn between the two at the time) under the surveillance of the civil guards, the narrator once more emphasizes the mixture of different categories under one common label, commenting,

> La triste caravana emprendió su camino por la polvorienta carretera. Iban silenciosos, pensando cada cual en sus cosas, que eran,¡ay!, tan distintas... Cada cual llevaba su mundo entre ceja y ceja, y los caminantes y campesinos que al paso les veían formaban de todas aquellas existencias una sola opinión: 'Vagancia, desvergüenza, pillería.' (171)

Here, people with very different life histories are bracketed together under the label of 'vagrants' and 'delinquents', forming a category that differentiates them clearly from the 'normal' elements of the population. When they arrive in Navalcarnero, Nazarín has to spend one night in its prison in the company of an old beggar and a bunch of hardened criminals (178). In this respect it is noteworthy that in an article of 1884 in *La Prensa*, Galdós criticized the 'mixing together', in the Madrid prison El Saladero, of prisoners with very different kinds of offences.[60]

Similarly, the novel implies a critique of attempts at categorizing filth and disease. Galdós was an active but partially critical contributor to contemporary debates on public hygiene and the control of 'filth'. In several articles that he wrote for *La Prensa* on the cholera epidemic of 1885, he attacked the inefficiency, inflexibility and lack of humanity of the public health measures taken by the authorities, which were mainly aimed at the isolation or cordoning off of the disease, and whose only effect was to create panic among the population.[61] In *Nazarín*, the author

---

60 *La Prensa* (31 January 1884), in Shoemaker (ed.), *Las cartas desconocidas de Galdós*, 46–47.

61 Galdós's letters to *La Prensa* were later collected, edited and published in different volumes by the Argentinian journalist Alberto Ghiraldo. The titles of each volume, and those of the articles included in each volume, were Ghiraldo's. As Shoemaker has observed, Ghiraldo did not always reproduce these articles in their entirety. Also, he did not keep a chronological order, grouping the articles according to their topic and sometimes splitting an article into different sections, each of which appears under different headings or even in different volumes; see Shoemaker, *Las cartas desconocidas de Galdós*, Introduction. Most of Galdós's articles on the 1885 cholera epidemic are included in the first volume of *Cronicón*, 1924, vol. VI of Ghiraldo's *Obras inéditas de Benito Pérez Galdós*. This epidemic affected 2,207 people in Madrid, causing 1,366 deaths, or 61% of total deaths: see Alfredo García Gómez-

implicitly condemns this attitude by making Nazarín go into the plague-
stricken villages to help the isolated victims of a smallpox epidemic who
had been abandoned to die by the 'healthy' members of the population,
as 'la *señá* Polonia', a friend of Beatriz's, informs Nazarín (121). Nazarín,
however, shows his willingness to go to visit the infected villages to help
the diseased. As the narrator notes, 'A Nazarín no se le cocía el pan hasta
no meterse en el foco de la peste' (123). Thus, Nazarín tells Andara and
Beatriz, 'El Señor nos ha deparado una epidemia, en cuyo seno pestífero
hemos de zambullirnos, como nadadores intrépidos que se lanzan a las
olas para salvar a infelices náufragos' (123).

Galdós, by disagreeing with the system of isolation propounded by
the government, was refusing to fall in behind the authorities' discourse
on the control of filth.[62] In an article of 1884 in *La Prensa*, after attacking
the severity with which the government had applied the principle of sanitary cordons and 'lazaretos', Galdós comments, 'Todo esto sería ridículo

---

Alvarez, 'La sobremortalidad de la clase obrera madrileña a finales del siglo XIX
(1880–1900)', in Rafael Huertas and Ricardo Campos (eds), *Medicina social y clase
obrera en España (Siglos XIX y XX)* (Madrid, Fundación de Investigaciones Marxistas,
1992), I, 152.

62 Galdós's criticism of the system of sanitary cordons and 'lazaretos' was partly
related to the fact that, at the end of the century, theories of contagion were still
being debated. In an article of 17 November 1884 Galdós wrote about the 'conta-
gionistas' and the 'anticontagionistas' and the futile battles between them in the
'Consejo de Sanidad', stating that 'siendo aún un misterio las causas de la infección
epidémica, todo lo que allí se dice sirve para aumentar el barullo y empeorar la
situación' (*Cronicón*, I, 74–75, in Ghiraldo's *Obras inéditas de Benito Pérez Galdós*).
(The contagionists believed that diseases could be transmitted through direct
contact [i.e. through touch] whereas the anticontagionists argued that they were
transmitted through the air. According to anticontagionist theories, the system of
sanitary cordons and 'lazaretos' was pointless.) As Galdós stated in another article
on the subject (27 July 1884, *Cronicón*, I, 23–25), there was still a great deal of speculation surrounding the microbe and its biological conditions, an issue which, according to Galdós, was given extensive coverage in the press of the time. As Galdós noted,
during this period there were conflicting positions among scientists regarding the
validity of disinfection theory and the efficacy of disinfection; see *La Prensa* [4
November 1884 and 25 December 1884, in Shoemaker (ed.), *Las cartas desconocidas
de Galdós*, 121; and an article of 8 October 1884, *Cronicón*, I, 35–53. Faced with the
battle over this issue, Galdós asks, '¿Es la desinfección una verdad o un embuste
propalado por el vulgo y consagrado torpemente por la ciencia?' (8 October 1884,
Cronicón, I, 48). In another article, which Ghiraldo significantly entitled 'La especulación del miedo' (19 June 1885, *Cronicón*, I, 200), Galdós sarcasticamente criticized the
inflexibility shown by the government in applying its fumigation and disinfection
policies. Interestingly, in *Nazarín*, among the material aid sent to Villamantilla from
Madrid was '[un] sin fin de drogas para desinfectar personas y cosas' (132).

si no fuera altamente deplorable'.[63] As he argued, 'El sistema gubernamental de cordones y lazaretos ha traído lo que popularmente ya es designado con el nombre de *cantonalismo sanitario*'.[64] Six years later, when writing about the sanitary precautions taken in Portugal in order to prevent the spread of the cholera epidemic which had been declared in some areas of Western Spain, Galdós draws attention once more to the inhumanity and brutality of such measures, which he describes as 'grotescas' and 'contra-producentes', stating that 'No cabe sistema más contrario a la ciencia y a los últimos descubrimientos biológicos'.[65] He continues by pointing out that those who wish to travel to Portugal are isolated and secluded in 'inmundos lazaretos', where they are treated as 'animales dañinos'.[66] Galdós is criticizing here the association of infection, filth and animality. It is significant, in this respect, that in Spain, the Penal Code of 1870 juxtaposed lunatics and 'animales feroces y dañinos', thus reflecting the connection established between animality and savagery on the one hand and, on the other, the 'diseased' groups of the population.[67]

In these articles, Galdós often criticized the government for interfering in public health matters and for using hygiene as a political weapon. The excesses committed by the Spanish government in the name of public hygiene had led to what Galdós calls an 'inquisición sanitaria'.[68] As he wrote: 'El ministro de la Gobernación [...] [a]vezado en las campañas electorales, hizo de la higiene una bandera política, y afiliándose a la escuela contagionista,[69] planteó el sistema preventivo y preservativo con un lujo de detalles que causa maravilla'.[70] Galdós closes his attack on the

63 *La Prensa* (4 November 1884), in Shoemaker (ed.), *Las cartas desconocidas de Galdós*, 119. In connection with this, it is worth noting Angel Guerra's attack on 'esas reglas anticristianas de la higiene moderna que ordenan mil precauciones ridículas contra el contagio' (II, 526), as discussed earlier.

64 Ibid., 119.

65 *La Prensa* (6 September 1890), in Shoemaker (ed.), *Las cartas desconocidas de Galdós*, 417. Galdós is probably referring here to the discovery by Koch in 1883 of the 'vibrio cholerae', the bacteria found to cause cholera. This discovery meant that the system of isolation used to prevent the spread of the epidemic was senseless.

66 Ibid., 417.

67 Fernando Alvarez-Uría, 'La cárcel o el manicomio', in Julia Varela and Fernando Alvarez-Uría (eds), *El cura Galeote asesino del obispo de Madrid-Alcalá* (Proceso médico-legal reconstruido y presentado por Julia Varela y Fernando Alvarez-Uría) (Madrid, La Piqueta, 1979), 150, note 1.

68 *La Prensa* (4 November 1884), in Shoemaker (ed.), *Las cartas desconocidas de Galdós*, 120.

69 With regard to the contagionists see note 61.

70 *La Prensa* (4 November 1884), in Shoemaker (ed.), *Las cartas desconocidas de Galdós*, 120. The following year Galdós wrote, in a similar vein, 'Como el gobierno se ha erigido en guardián de la salud pública, a los ministeriales les sabe muy mal que se

government's interference and its attempts at containing and isolating
the victims of epidemics, asserting,

> Convengamos en que no es de la incumbencia de los gobiernos hacer el
> papel de Providencia más que dentro de ciertos límites muy prudentes
> [...]¡La acción gubernamental alcanzando a detener la marcha de la epidemia
> cuyos caracteres patológicos no son bien conocidos aún por la ciencia! Cosa
> más chusca no se ha visto ni se verá. ¡Un ministro cerrando el paso al
> invisible, indecifrable [*sic*], incomprensible y misteriosísimo microbio del
> cólera! ¿Y por qué medio?...¡Por la Guardia Civil!¡*Como si el cólera fuera una*
> *cuadrilla de ladrones o una partida de revolucionarios*! [my emphasis][71]

In this quotation, Galdós once more criticizes the association of disease
with deviancy, in this case with criminality and revolution.[72] He believed
that the government's attitude towards the epidemic was fostering
confusion and panic among the population.[73] In an article of 1865 in the
Buenos Aires newspaper *La Nación*, when writing about the cholera epidemic that broke out that year, Galdós described panic as a 'segunda
epidemia'.[74] Twenty years later, he repeated the idea that panic aggra-
vates the ravages of epidemics, when he stated,

> Pueblos hay que dejándose vencer del terror, han visto duplicado el número
> de víctimas por causa del abandono y de la precipitación [...] Allí, donde el
> egoísmo ha decretado los aislamientos, se ha dado el caso de permanecer
> insepultos los cadáveres, infestando la atmósfera. Muchos enfermos, a
> quienes una regular asistencia habría salvado, han perecido en espantosa
> soledad... Tardarán mucho los pueblos en comprender que la serenidad es el

---

quite importancia a la epidemia reinante [...] Nunca hemos visto aquí un furor de
limpieza semejante, ni un rigor más inflexible para hacer cumplir ciertas prescrip-
ciones municipales que atañen a la salud pública [...] Toda la gente de oposición no
ve en los casos ocurridos sino enfermedades comunes, y un comodín para poner en
juego mil resortes gubernamentales que ayudan al gabinete para contener la ruina
que lo amenaza [...] El Gobierno se defiende de su propia destrucción con toda esa
marimorena de los lazaretos y de las fumigaciones. La higiene, que Letamendi llama
medicina política, viene a ser uno de tantos recursos para *ir tirando* y entretener a las
fuerzas que lo combaten' (13 June 1885, *Cronicón*, I, 194–95).

71 *La Prensa* (4 November 1884), in Shoemaker (ed.), *Las cartas desconocidas de Galdós*,
    121.

72 It is worth noting in this respect the growing political violence in 1890s Spain, and
    the influence on contemporary debates of Lombroso's theories which equated
    insanity and criminality with political revolution and terrorism. See Maristany,
    'Lombroso y España', 361–81.

73 This view is also emphasized in an article which Ghiraldo entitled 'La especulación
    del miedo', 19 June 1885, *Cronicón*, I, 197–202.

74 *La Nación* (15 October 1865), in Shoemaker (ed.), *Los artículos de Galdós en 'La Nación'*,
    170.

mejor dique que se puede oponer a esa asoladora epidemia, y que el cólera, atacado con prudencia, oportunidad y energía, es una de las enfermedades que menos víctimas causan.[75]

In *Nazarín*, the protagonist seems to take this view when he decides to plunge into the infected village and fight the epidemic – although it is not cholera but smallpox in this case. The consequences of panic in the village population are voiced by 'la *seña* Polonia' when she says, 'no hay quien asista a los enfermos y los sanos salen despavoridos' (121). When Nazarín, Andara and Beatriz spend a night in an inn on their way to Villamantilla, the narrator emphasizes again the isolation of the diseased and the resulting deaths brought about by panic:

> Pidieron hospitalidad en una venta, y cuando allí les oyeron decir que iban a Villamantilla, tuviéronles por locos, pues en el pueblo había muy poca gente a más de los enfermos [...] [T]odo era allí desolación, hambre y muerte (127)

A similar attitude towards isolation and the 'control' of infection was found in *Angel Guerra*, where the protagonist criticized the 'absurd' rules imposed by modern hygiene, describing them as 'anticristianas' and declaring that contagion should not be feared:

> En nuestras casas se proscribe el aislamiento riguroso, y se prescinde de esas reglas anticristianas de la higiene moderna, que ordenan mil precauciones ridículas contra el contagio. Se prohíbe temer la muerte, y huir de las enfermedades pegadizas. El que se contagia, contagiado se queda, y si se muere, se le encomienda a Dios. No habrá más higiene que un aseo exquisito y las precauciones del sentido común. (II, 526)

Guerra's views on contagion may be related to the doubts that still surrounded this issue. Just as Galdós described the system of cordons and 'lazaretos' as 'ridículo' and 'deplorable', Guerra similarly regards the hygienic precautions against contagion as 'ridículas'. In a letter of 1893 to *La Prensa*, Galdós ridicules the exaggerated concern for hygiene when he speaks humorously of 'el aforismo novísimo que simplifica extraordinariamente la ciencia hipocrática: *Todo es mentira. Sólo es verdad la higiene.*'[76] Against these excesses committed in the name of hygiene, both

---

75 4 August 1885, *Cronicón*, I, 255.

76 *La Prensa* (17 July 1893), in Shoemaker (ed.), *Las cartas desconocidas de Galdós*, 480. Nearly thirty years earlier, in an article in *La Nación*, Galdós had attacked, in a highly sarcastic tone, the hygienic measures recommended against the epidemic, such as to avoid 'las impresiones fuertes'; see issue of 15 October 1865, in Shoemaker (ed.), *Los artículos de Galdós en 'La Nación'*, 140–41. The contemporary obsession with hygiene is also mocked by Galdós in his fiction. In *Fortunata y Jacinta*, for instance, the narrator notes that one of the traders in the market advertises his

Galdós and his character Angel Guerra recommend cleanliness as the main basis of hygiene.[77] In the same way as Guerra propounded 'un aseo exquisito' as the main hygienic measure to be used in his institution, Galdós stated in an article of 1892 in *La Prensa* that 'limpieza' and 'aseo' were the best prevention against epidemics.[78] In this article, which deals with the cholera epidemic in Hamburg, it is significant that Galdós not only associates hygiene with cleanliness, but also with 'las costumbres morigeradas' of the city's population, thus echoing contemporary discourses that linked physical and moral hygiene.[79] As he observed, dissolution and vice were cordoned off, restricted to a particular 'arrabal', and therefore constituted a kind of ghetto within the city. Galdós expressed the view that such a separation was a positive one, and regretted the difficulty of applying this system to other European cities. In this instance, Galdós's approval of a *cordon sanitaire* to contain vice and deprivation contrasts with his opposition to placing areas affected

---

'turrones' as 'turrones *higiénicos*' as a way of attracting customers (I, 395; my emphasis). In *Halma*, Laínez, a provisional doctor at Pedralba and a representative of the medical establishment in the novel, aspires to become the director of Halma's institution because, according to him, 'la señora condesa ha querido fundar un *instituto higiénico* hablando más propiamente, un sanatorio médico-quirúrgico con vistas a la religión' (1857; my emphasis). Laínez's words also reflect how the medical profession was gaining increasing power during this period, at the expense of the religious establishment.

77   Guerra's fostering of cleanliness in his institution contrasts with the deplorable hygienic conditions of most charitable institutions and hospitals in Madrid, which were the object of harsh criticism on the part of commentators of the period. At the end of the nineteenth century Spain still lived in a state of extreme sanitary backwardness. Most people were unaware of the need for hygiene in order to avoid infection or contagion. The growth of the city and the new scientific discoveries were in stark contrast to the lack of hygiene and the old-fashioned methods used in the treatment of diseases. See Plá et al., *El Madrid de Galdós*, 101–07; and María Mercedes Gutiérrez Sánchez, 'La Beneficencia Pública en Madrid durante el último tercio del siglo XIX', in Angel Bahamonde Magro and Luis E. Otero Carvajal (eds), *La sociedad madrileña durante la Restauración (1876–1931)* (Madrid, Comunidad de Madrid, Consejería de Cultura, 1989), 427–28 in particular.

78   *La Prensa* (2 October 1892), in Shoemaker (ed.), *Las cartas desconocidas de Galdós*, 464.

79   In *Halma*, Galdós also makes this association between physical and moral cleanliness through the novel's protagonist. As the narrator comments, 'Al adoptar la vida pobre, la señora condesa no estimó que debía renunciar a sus hábitos de pulcritud; decía que el aseo exterior, por causa de la educación y la costumbre, afectaba al alma, y que la suciedad del cuerpo era pecado tan feo como la de la conciencia. No vacilaba, pues, en aplicar estas ideas a la realidad, manteniendo en su cuarto y persona la misma esmerada limpieza de sus mejores tiempos de vida cortesana. "El aseo – decía – es a la pureza del alma lo que el rubor a la vergüenza." No comprendía el ascetismo de otro modo' (1842).

by the disease under quarantine. In another article in *La Prensa*, Galdós similarly seems to comply with contemporary views that associated disease with dissolution. Thus, writing about several cases of cholera that had arisen in Toledo, he comments,

> Hay motivos para sospechar que la alarma producida por los misteriosos casos de la Ciudad Imperial es infundada. En París la epidemia es benigna; dicen que sólo ataca a los alcohólicos, a los disolutos, a los que hacen vida relajada y a los que viven en moradas estrechas y en barrios insalubres. Es un consuelo relativo, pero consuelo al fin.[80]

By stating in the majority of his articles on the cholera epidemic that cholera victims should not be cordoned off and contained, Galdós dissociates physical and moral infection from those social groups perceived as dissolute. In the articles mentioned above, he would seem, however, to follow the contemporary tendency to categorize and marginalize immorality and vice. Of course, there is the problem here that what moral commentators of the period categorized as 'dissolute' or 'deviant' behaviour was not always regarded by Galdós as such. When discussing *Angel Guerra* we saw how, although Galdós at times invests in contemporary discourses, he also established a subdivision within the group classed as 'undeserving'. The message that the author would appear to want to put across is the difficulty of defining and drawing a demarcation line between the various categories of the poor.

Nazarín's ideas could not be implemented in a society that regarded mendicity and vagrancy not only as vices but also as crimes, a society in which the distribution of charity was becoming increasingly pragmatic and rational. Galdós's position with regard to these new attitudes towards mendicity is not always clearly defined in the novel. If, on the one hand, the ambiguous presentation of Nazarín leads the reader to question his views on self-imposed poverty, indiscriminate distribution of charity and disregard for material progress, on the other Galdós implicitly criticizes the desire to label and control certain groups of the population associated with immorality and filth: a categorization process that is shown to be arbitrary.

Halma: The Undeserving Poor Reconsidered

Halma (1895), another novel which has tended to be examined from the perspective of Galdós's rejection of materialism in favour of spirituality,

---

80 *La Prensa* (19 December 1884), reproduced in Shoemaker (ed.), *Las cartas desconocidas de Galdós*, 129–30.

echoes some of the ideas previously expounded by Galdós in *Angel Guerra* and *Nazarín*. Like Guerra, Halma proposes to use her inheritance to found an institution for the poor in the countryside. She discloses her plans for the charitable institution to Manuel Flórez, the family's priest and friend, also informing him of her decision to reserve a certain amount of the inheritance money for distribution among the needy. Manuel Flórez, who plays a similar role to the priest Mancebo in *Angel Guerra*, voices contemporary concerns and anxieties about the indiscriminate giving of charity when, to Halma's decision to distribute a certain sum of money among the needy, he replies,

> Sí; pero eso es difícil, porque no tendríamos ni para empezar. La caridad debe hacerse con método, apoyándose en el criterio de la Iglesia, y favoreciendo los planes de la misma. No vale dar limosna sin ton ni son. Falta saber a quién se da y cómo se da. (1797)

Halma, however, does not understand the priest's more rational criteria. As she admits, '¿Sabe usted, mi buen don Manuel, que no entiendo bien eso?' (1797). She expresses the view that money is only a 'material vil y despreciable', and its distribution should not be submitted to any rational set of rules: '[su] reparto no debe someterse a ninguna regla de orden y gobierno. Las leyes económicas de mi hermano me parecen una de las más infames invenciones del género humano' (1798). Flórez's reply to Halma is not dissimilar to Angel Guerra's when, near the beginning of the novel, he dismisses Leré's ideas on indiscriminate charity. As he says: 'De modo que usted, señora mía, ¿cree que para despreciar al dinero y castigarlo por su vileza debe dársele al primer loquinario que lo pide, sin que sepamos en qué lo ha de emplear?' (1798). Halma's belief is that money, in the end, will always satisfy a need, no matter who it is given to, as she explains to Flórez:

> Creo que el empleo final de la moneda es siempre el mismo, dése a quien se diere. Caiga donde caiga, va a satisfacer necesidades. El manirroto, el disipado, el vicioso mismo, lo hacen pasar a otras manos, que lo aprovechan en lo que debe aprovecharse. Lance usted un puñado de billetes a la calle, o entrégueselo al primer perdido que pase, al primer ladrón que lo solicite, y ese dinero, como van todas las aguas a los ríos, y los ríos al mar, irá a cumplir su objeto en el mar inmenso de la miseria humana. Cerca o lejos, aquí o allá, con ese dinero arrojado por usted a la calle se vestirá alguien, alguien matará su hambre y su sed. El resultado final de toda donación [...] es siempre el mismo. (1798)

Here Halma seems to endorse a free market economy in the service of philanthropy rather than profit. The effect that Halma's words have on Flórez, as the narrator notes, is one of bewilderment: 'Señora mía – dijo don Manuel un poco aturdido –, no seamos paradójicos..., no seamos

sofísticos. Si usted me permite que la contradiga, que le haga una demos-
tración clara de su error en esa materia…'(1798). The narrator stresses the
priest's anxiety and uneasiness about Halma's beliefs when he comments, 'El hombre no podía expresarse bien. Estaba sofocadísimo, sentía
calor y se abanicaba con su teja' (1798). Halma insists on her idea that
there must be no distinctions established between the poor, because
money will eventually come to satisfy 'legitimate' needs. Through her
words the narrator highlights the difficulty of deciding who are the
really needy, an issue that occupied many commentators of the period:

> Por más que usted diga […] yo creo que la limosna consiste esencialmente en
> dar lo que se tiene al que no lo tiene, sea quien fuera, y empléelo en lo que lo
> empleare. Imagine usted las aplicaciones más abominables que se pueden dar
> al dinero: el juego, la bebida, el libertinaje. Siempre resultará que corriendo,
> corriendo, y después de satisfacer necesidades ilegítimas, va a satisfacer las
> legítimas. ¡Dar a los pobres, nada más que a los pobres! Sobre que no se sabe
> nunca quiénes son los verdaderos pobres, todo lo que se da va a parar a ellos
> por un camino o por otro. Lo que importa es la efusión del alma, la piedad, el
> desprendernos de una suma que tenemos y que otro nos pide. (1798–99)

This quotation suggests that philanthropy is more to do with the good
that accrues to the giver rather than the receiver. It should be noted here
that the charitable activities of the upper classes were often motivated by
the old belief, based on providential ideas, that the rich needed the poor
as a vehicle for the fulfilment of their Christian duties, a view that Halma
seems to share and that tended to ignore economic progress. It should be
noted, however, that Halma's attitude seems to be inspired by religious
conviction rather than by mere self-aggrandisement. In this sense, she is
presented in a different light from the character of don Carlos Trujillo in
Misericordia.

In *Halma*, the introduction of the character José Antonio Urrea,
Halma's cousin, who is regarded as a parasite and a scoundrel by the
family, serves to highlight the issue of the deserving and the undeserving poor. When he finds out about Halma's charitable intentions, the
opportunist Urrea thinks of borrowing a large sum from her in order to
get a publishing business under way. To Flórez's surprise, Halma decides
to help him financially because, as she tells him, her cousin's dissolute
way of life is, in her opinion, essentially the result of his poverty. Thus,
she believes that moral indoctrination makes little sense without material
support:

> veo tras su petición un mundo de necesidades abrumadoras, de martirios
> horribles, en que igualmente gimen el alma y el cuerpo. Veo la falta de
> alimento, la estrechez de la vivienda, la persecución de los acreedores, la

vida angustiosa, llena de humillaciones y vergüenzas ocultas [...] Yo creo
que en mi primo son ciertos los propósitos de enmienda; pero demos de
barato que no lo sean; admitamos que nos engaña, que es un perdido, un
tronera lleno de vicios, entre los cuales descuella el de la postulación a
diestro y siniestro. Y ¿qué hará usted para sacarle del infierno de esa vida?
¿Predicarle? Nada se conseguirá mientras no se le ponga en condiciones de
variar de conducta, y por más que usted se devane los sesos, no hallará otra
manera de redención que darle lo que no tiene, porque su mala vida no es
más que el resultado fatal, inevitable, de la pobreza. (1799)

Contrary to the opinion of many contemporary commentators, who considered moral indoctrination as the remedy for the immorality perceived
as inherent in the poorer classes, Halma believes that Urrea – arguably
like the other poor who would have been classified as 'undeserving'
according to the criteria of the period – is innately good. He has been
corrupted by the life of destitution that he has lived: 'la orfandad, la
miseria vergonzante corrompieron aquella alma buena, que parecía
creada para el bien' (1800). This point is stressed when Urrea tells
Francisco Feramor, 'al propio tiempo que me reñía dulcemente por mi
conducta, la disculpaba, atribuyéndola, más que a perversión moral, al
inexorable despotismo de la necesidad, del hábito...' (1802). It needs to
be noted that Halma does not 'give away' her money to Urrea. As she
explains to the sceptic Flórez, she allocates him a sum that will have to be
administered by her and Flórez himself. In this sense, her practice of
charity cannot be considered as completely unthinking.

Flórez cannot completely accept Halma's anti-establishment way of
practising charity. As he exclaims,

> ¡Cuánto mejor que esta buena señora siguiera los caminos ya hechos y
> despejados, en vez de empeñarse en abrirlos nuevos, desbrozando la trocha
> salvaje! ¡Cuánto más cómodo para todos que acatara *lo establecido* y se echara
> en brazos de los que ya tienen perfectamente organizados los servicios de
> caridad, las juntas de damas, las archicofradías, las hermandades, mis colectas
> para escuelas, mis...! ¡Cuánto mejor abrazarse a *lo establecido*, Señor, que... !
> (1805)

In this quotation, the expression 'desbrozar la trocha salvaje' may be a
symbolic reference to the poor as savages, existing in a pre-civilized
state, and to Halma's attempts to civilize them. In the novel, Consuelo
Feramor and other women of her aristocratic circle are representatives of
what Flórez calls 'lo establecido'. The narrator comments,

> Consuelo Feramor, Maria Ignacia Monterones y la marquesa de San Salomó
> eran al modo de presidentas, vicepresidentas o secretarias en esas o las otras
> juntas benéficas señoriles que reunen fondos, ya por medio de limosnas, ya

con el señuelo de funciones teatrales, rifas y *kermesses*, para socorrer a los pobres de tal o cual distrito, edificar capillas o atender al inconmesurable montón de víctimas que los desatados elementos o nuestras desdichas públicas acumulan de continuo sobre la infeliz España. (1803)

When the three women try to obtain money from Halma for their upper-class charitable enterprises and Halma denies it to them, they are bewildered and angry. Consuelo Feramor associates Halma's revolutionary way of practising charity with insanity, in the same way that Flórez cannot affirm unreservedly that Nazarín is a saint because of his anti-establishment behaviour. As Consuelo Feramor tells her husband, 'Si no fuera ella quien es y nosotros quienes somos, creería yo que la residencia natural de tu hermana era un santo manicomio' (1803).

Halma's decision to help her cousin financially is disapproved of by her family and friends, including the priest Flórez, who regard Urrea as highly undeserving of her charity. Urrea appears in the eyes of many characters in the novel as undeserving because he does not work. Mirroring contemporary thought, Halma believes that his moral regeneration should be based on turning him into an honest, hard-working man. Her words to Urrea at one point in the novel are a reflection of this: 'Ya sé, ya sé que estás muy corregido. Sé que trabajas, que has sentado la cabeza' (1795). Halma's wish is that Urrea becomes a useful and self-sufficient individual: 'Has de hacerte un hombre *útil*, que viva honradamente, sin depender de nadie' (1825). The notion of self-help is emphasized when Urrea tells Nazarín that Halma wants him to achieve 'una honrada independencia' (1847). Later in the novel, when Halma allows him to stay in her institution, she advises him, 'No quiero que estés ocioso ni un momento' (1850). Unlike Angel Guerra, Halma believes that the 'asilados' should help out with the work. She points out to don Remigio, 'como tenemos tanta obra en casa, necesito que me ayuden mis buenos amigos. Hay que estar en todo, y cuantos viven aquí han de arrimar el hombro a las dificultades' (1845). Like the priest Virones in *Angel Guerra*, one of Halma's 'asilados', Ladislao, is also glad to offer his work in exchange for the charity he receives from her. As Beatriz informs Halma, 'dice que su *desiderato* sería la plaza de maestro de capilla; pero que si la señora no tiene capilla en sus estados, lo mismo le servirá de cochero que para traer leña del monte, si a mano viene' (1827).

As noted earlier, work is also used as a cure for Nazarín's insanity. Nazarín is often seen carrying out hard tasks in the fields and woods, such as wood-cutting. Interestingly, in one scene he is also seen washing floors and scrubbing corners to get the grime out. This may be connected with the narrator's portrayal of this character as a 'feminine' man.[81] Hard physical work was also employed in women's asylums as a therapy; intellectual work, however, was believed to have harmful effects on them. It is significant that in *Halma*, don Remigio engages Nazarín in the hard intellectual task of making an abstract of an eight-volume religious book (1837), which may be indicative of the different approach to male and female insanity during the period.

It could be said that Halma adopts a stricter or more rational attitude towards the dispensation of charity than Angel Guerra, although her approach would still not have been acceptable in the mentality of the period. The final moral regeneration of Urrea suggests the author's approval of Halma's attitude towards some, at least, of those classed as undeserving poor. In one scene in the novel Halma is also shown to be tolerant towards drinking in certain cases. In this scene, just before the drinker Cecilio, an old carriage driver, takes Beatriz and some other 'asilados' to Pedralba, Halma tells Beatriz,

> Oye, Beatriz. Mi buen Cecilio padece de una maldita sed que no se le quita sino con vino. Ya está tan cascado el pobre, que sería crueldad privarle de satisfacer su vicio. Durante el viaje, le permitirás que tome una copa en alguna de las ventas por donde pasen, no en todas... Fíjate bien: con tres o cuatro copas de pardillo en todo el camino tiene bastante; pero nada más, nada más... (1828)

Halma's attitude towards drinking is little different from that of Angel Guerra, who similarly believed that don Pito's drinking habits were too ingrained in him to be eradicated.

In the course of the novel the sceptic Manuel Flórez is gradually convinced by Halma's ideas – in the same way that Guerra's views change under Leré's influence. At one point he observes, '[Halma] descubre cosas que nadie ve, que si al principio parecen disparates, bien examinadas resultan con toda la hermosura y toda la grandeza de Dios' (1801). Just before his death he is shown to have been converted to Halma's beliefs regarding the undeserving poor. Thus, he admonishes his servant and his niece, both of whom are looking after him on his death-bed, to help the poor financially, whether they deserve charity or not: 'socorred a cuantos menesterosos estén a vuestro alcance, sin reparar si lo merecen o no. Todo necesitado merece dejar de serlo' (1826). Flórez's words, however, do not seem to have an effect on the two women. In a scene that takes place shortly afterwards, Flórez's servant voices the ideas expressed by the priest towards the beginning of the novel about the dangers of

---

81 Jo Labanyi, ' Representing the Unrepresentable: Monsters, Mystics, and Feminine Men in Galdós's *Nazarín*', *Journal of Hispanic Research*, 1 (1992–93), 225–38.

indiscriminate charity. Thus, when Beatriz comes to see Halma, the servant, mistaking her for a beggar, warns Halma:

> Ha entrado una mujer que quiere hablar con la señora. Debe de ser una pobre... de estas que acosan y marean con sus petitorios. Yo que vuecencia, le daría medio panecillo y la pondría en la calle, porque si nos corremos demasiado en la limosna, esto será el mesón del tío Alegría, y nos volverán locas. Trae una niña de la mano, y me da olor a trapisonda, quiero decir a sablazo de los que van al hueso. Conque póngase en guardia la señora condesa, que en eso de dar o no dar con tino está el toque, como dice nuestro pobrecito don Manuel, de la verdadera caridad. (1826)

At the end of the novel the author's message would seem to endorse Halma's idea of helping those poor whom she chooses. According to Nazarín, Halma should give up the idea of founding an institution, since in this way she will never be free from the control of the Church and the State. Thus, he advises her to marry Urrea and continue practising charity from within the family unit. This will allow her to dispense charity in the way she wants, following her own criteria and without outside interference:

> Necesita usted modificar radicalmente su sistema de practicar la caridad [...] [L]a idea de dar a Pedralba una organización pública semejante a la de los institutos religiosos y caritativos que hoy existen es un grandísimo disparate [...] ¿En qué estaba usted pensando al constituir en Pedralba un organismo semejante a los organismos sociales que vemos por ahí desvencijados, máquinas gastadas y viejas que no funcionan bien? [...] Desde el momento en que la señora se pone de acuerdo con las autoridades civil y eclesiástica para la admisión de estos o los otros desvalidos, da derecho a las autoridades para que intervengan, vigilen y pretendan gobernar aquí como en todas partes. En cuanto usted se mueve viene la Iglesia y dice: "¡Alto!", y viene el intruso Estado y dice: "¡Alto!" Una y otro quieren inspeccionar. La tutela le quitará a usted toda iniciativa.¡Cuánto más sencillo y más práctico [...] es que no funde cosa alguna, que prescinda de toda constitución y reglamentos, y se constituya en familia, nada más que en familia, en señora y reina de su casa particular! *Dentro de las fronteras de su casa libre podrá usted amparar a los pobres que quiera*, sentarlos a su mesa, y proceder como le inspiren su espíritu de caridad y su amor del bien. (1868; my emphasis)

Nazarín's words imply that once Halma becomes independent of the Church and the State, she will be able to help those poor who may have been discarded as undeserving by the authorities.[82] There is the problem,

---

82 Catherine Jagoe (*Ambiguous Angels: Gender in the Novels of Galdós* [Berkeley and Los Angeles, University of California Press, 1994], 140–55) has interpreted *Halma* in the light of the ideology on domesticity and the separate spheres of activity for the

however, that Nazarín's sanity has been questioned through the novel,[83] and therefore his advice cannot be trusted. Moreover, in *Halma*, the priest's behaviour is still surrounded with ambiguity. So, although he asserts on several occasions that he is willing to submit to the authority of the Church and to human laws at the expense of sacrificing his independence (in fact he agrees to enter Halma's institution willingly), his advice to Halma shows that he is advocating freedom and independence from social institutions. The novel's message is, therefore, ambiguous.

Misericordia: Old and New Attitudes to Mendicity

Critical studies of *Misericordia* (1897) have often focused on the character of Benina and her sublime acts of charity, and on the issue of true charity or charity as a Christian value.[84] It can be argued that, as with the other novels discussed in this chapter, it is possible to go beyond a spiritual reading of *Misericordia*. Indeed, issues of undeserving begging and indiscriminate charity are central concerns in this novel; similarly, contemporary associations of mendicity with idleness, criminality, filth, infection and disease figure prominently in the text. This section will thus examine contemporary perceptions of charity and the consequent social attitudes that developed towards mendicity, which were echoed in the discourses

genders. Women's philanthropic work was seen as an acceptable extension of their domestic role in the private sphere of the home. By the end of the century, however, this kind of 'outside' work had also begun to generate anxieties due to the large number of women engaging in it. By expanding their 'angelic' duties outside the home and into the public sphere, women were beginning to destabilize the gender-roles scheme constructed by the bourgeoisie. *Halma* is, according to Jagoe, a reflection of such anxieties. Halma is seen as going a step too far in her philanthropic mission, as she transgresses gender lines by attempting to create a female sphere beyond the private domain of the home. Therefore, patriarchal society needs to intervene at the end of the novel and impose its authority with colossal force, in order to overthrow Halma's rule. The novel, Jagoe argues, endorses the view that Halma should conform to the bourgeois model of separate gender categories by showing that the protagonist's 'true mission' in life is not philanthropy (the public sphere) and the independence that the founding of an institution could give her, but marriage and the family (the private sphere).

83 Towards the end of the novel Nazarín is considered insane by the law courts, which rule that he suffers from a kind of 'neurosis epiléptica' known as 'melancolía religiosa' (1817). This reflects the medical profession's increasing power in the law courts. As Halma tells Flórez, 'el Tribunal, haciendo suya la opinión de los facultativos, da por cierto que el santo varón no tiene la cabeza en regla' (1817).

84 See, for instance, the studies on *Misericordia* mentioned in note 1. See also, Penuel, *Charity in Galdós*, chapter IV; and Robert Russell, 'The Christ Figure in *Misericordia* (A Monograph)', *Anales Galdosianos*, II (1967), 103–30.

of the period. Attention will concentrate on how *Misericordia* reflects the survival of a paternalistic conception of charity and its coexistence with new, more rational and scientific approaches to dealing with the problem of poverty.

In spite of attempts to rationalize charitable practices through the process of discriminating between different categories of the poor, old conceptions of charity, what Bahamonde has called 'la cultura de la pobreza', persisted at the end of the century.[85] The 'cultura de la pobreza', which fostered the preservation of paternalistic attitudes towards the poor, regarded the right to be poor as a non-problematic element of the Christian doctrine – in the same way that it was the natural duty of the rich to dispense charity. As Bahamonde notes, nineteenth-century Madrid was not an entirely bourgeois centre; it was still, to a large degree, a city in transition, where charitable practices inherited from the Old Regime prevailed. Some of the measures adopted during the nineteenth century to deal with the problem of mendicity were not very different from those taken during the seventeenth and eighteenth centuries. These included cheap bread; the distribution of medicines, food or alms to the poor; the expulsion of those beggars who were not resident in Madrid; the granting by the Ayuntamiento of begging licences (which benefited mainly the disabled and the elderly); and seclusion in asylums. As Bahamonde puts it, 'un conjunto de medidas en las que se entremezclan prácticas paternalistas o represoras, adobadas de caridad cristiana o de necesidad política, según convenga'.[86] Repressive measures taken towards mendicity were reinforced as a result of the great influx of migrants towards the capital from around the 1840s. The demographic growth of Madrid considerably aggravated the problem of mendicity in a pre-industrial city whose underdeveloped economy was unable to cater for the increasing demand for work. As a result, many casual and unemployed workers were pushed into begging. This explains the vagueness of the term 'mendigo', and its linkage with associated social categories, such as 'unemployed', 'underemployed' and 'vagrant'.

It is thus important to clarify that there were two types of mendicity in nineteenth-century Madrid: firstly, workers suffering unemployment as a result of excessive population growth relative to the capital's industrial capacity; and secondly, inherited from the Old Regime, a group mostly consisting of professional beggars (those who, in spite of being physically able, refused to work) and 'pobres vergonzantes' (those who

---

85 See Bahamonde Magro, 'Cultura de la pobreza', 163–82.
86 Ibid., 164.

could not work by virtue of their sex, age or physical disability).[87] Repression was applied with greater force in respect of the unemployed, or 'mendigo coyuntural' (a product of the economic crisis), than in respect of the 'passive' beggar (the professional beggar and the 'pobre vergonzante') incorporated within the 'cultura de la pobreza', as 'el primero, aunque desarrolle muy lentamente su conciencia como clase social puede ser […] clase peligrosa, mientras que el segundo asume su papel y lo reproduce sin más cuestionamientos'.[88] This resulted in the paradox that the repression of mendicity was more intense during times of economic crisis (when the number of unemployed beggars increased considerably and when charitable activities were not sufficient to contain the problem) than during periods of economic prosperity, in spite of the abundance at such times of professional beggars available for work and the consequent disruptions that the tolerance of mendicity caused in the labour market.[89]

Bahamonde has argued that in dealing with the problem of mendicity the dominant classes did not seem to appreciate the importance of work and the need for economic expansion.[90] This stands in stark contrast to the measures taken against mendicity in Anglo-Saxon countries, where laws to control begging and vagrancy were not only directed at social stability but also at the expansion and greater flexibility of the labour market. In Spain, the problem of mendicity was fundamentally a problem of public order. The measures adopted by the authorities to address the problem of mendicity – such as the rounding up of beggars or the expulsion from Madrid of those who were not in possession of a 'carta de vecindad', and the granting of licences to beg by the Ayuntamiento – were aimed at the control or regulation of the 'mendicity market', rather than at the outright repression of mendicity; that is to say, at adjusting 'la demanda de la miseria con la oferta de las obras benéfico-caritativas'.[91] As Bahamonde has written,

> No se trata siempre de castigar las *conductas desviadas;* ni siquiera se considera siempre como tal a la mendicidad. Mientras el mendigo se sitúe en los límites de la relación paternalismo-clientismo, el burgués, el noble o las

87 Ibid., 164.
88 As argued by Bahamonde Magro, 'Cultura de la pobreza', 165. As Bahamonde notes (165, 179), the repression of the 'mendigo coyuntural' was given legal support with the reform in 1868 of Article 258 of the Penal Code of 1849 (see note 54). That same year, the asylum of San Bernardino admitted more unemployed than 'passive' beggars.
89 Ibid., 165–66.
90 Ibid., especially 164–67 and 178–79.
91 Ibid., 179.

capas medias alimentan la *cultura de la pobreza* y del derecho a ser pobre
como un elemento más de la ética cristiana.[92]

Mendicity and vagrancy were tolerated provided they were kept under
control, as was the case with prostitution. As we saw earlier, moderate
drinking may have been tolerated by some for the same reason.

The control or 'ordaining' of mendicity, as opposed to its complete
repression, is explained by the perception of mendicity as an efficient
antidote to social conflict.[93] As long as beggars accepted their role of
subordination within the giver–recipient relationship, and as long as they
did not pose a threat to social order, charity was accepted by virtue of its
efficacy as a social stabilizer compared with outright repression, which
mainly needed to be implemented in extreme circumstances. Furthermore, as we saw when discussing *Halma*, alms-giving was used as a
means for the well-to-do to prove their moral worth, a view which also
flew in the face of ideas that explained the dangers which subsidizing the
poor posed to economic progress and to the free operation of the labour
market. Bahamonde has noted in this respect,

> Toda la *élite* tiene y protege a su pobre o a sus pobres aun en las escasas
> coyunturas de abundancia de trabajo, hecho nada anormal en una *élite* cuya
> percepción de sí misma se centra en la pretensión de ser la quintaesencia de
> las virtudes cristianas como justificación de su propio quehacer diario a
> través del desempeño de actividades benéfico-caritativas.[94]

In *Misericordia*, don Carlos's thoughtless alms-giving to the church
beggars exemplifies an attitude towards poverty which, in spite of the
warnings of social observers and guardians of morality,[95] was still pre-
valent, contributing to the maintenance of the 'cultura de la pobreza'.
Thus, in keeping with these old, but prevailing, providential ideas, don
Carlos regards his distribution of alms as a duty that he, as a wealthy
man, has towards the poor. The belief that God sent the poor to try people's

92 Bahamonde Magro, 'Cultura de la pobreza', 165.
93 In 1892 a contributor to *La Epoca* wrote, 'El hambre. He aquí el engendrador de
    todos los peligros sociales […] pero la religión […] resuelve el conflicto con pedazos
    de pan y hojas de catecismo' (quoted by Bahamonde Magro, 'Cultura de la pobreza',
    166). Concepción Arenal, like other commentators during this period, regarded
    helping the unemployed and underemployed not just as a virtue but also a duty if
    social tensions had to be avoided, an attitude often echoed in *La Voz de la Caridad*.
94 Bahamonde Magro, 'Cultura de la pobreza', 167.
95 Concepción Arenal and other contributors to *La Voz de la Caridad* often criticized
    alms-givers for not making the effort to find out who the recipients of their charity
    were, thus fostering vagrancy and dissolution: see, for instance, issue of 15 August
    1876, 163; and 1 July 1877, 135. This opinion was shared by Bernaldo de Quirós and
    Llanas Aguilaneido, *La mala vida en Madrid*, 344–45.

faithfulness, charity and compassion still survived in the nineteenth century.[96] Poverty was often justified on the grounds that the rich needed the poor. It was argued that if there was no destitution, there would be no opportunity for morality and spiritual improvement. In this way, the poor became the instrument of the charity of the rich who, as a result of the dispensation of charity, were able to save their souls. Don Carlos's protectorate over the poor represents the belief that one could 'buy' entry into heaven. As doña Paca notes,

> Cree que repartiendo limosnas de ochavo, y proporcionándose por poco precio las oraciones de los humildes, podrá engañar al de arriba y estafar la gloria eterna, o colarse en el cielo de contrabando, haciéndose pasar por lo que no es, como introducía el hilo de Escocia declarándolo percal de a real y medio la vara, con marchamos falsos, facturas falsas, certificados de origen falsos también… (126)

This idea is repeated again by the narrator when he describes the San Sebastián church beggars as,

> la cuadrilla de miseria, que acecha el paso de la caridad, al modo de guardia de alcabaleros que cobra humanamente el portazgo en la frontera de lo divino, o la contribución impuesta a las conciencias impuras que van a donde lavan. (63–64)

The calculating don Carlos similarly pays his 'contribución' to God:

> [Don Carlos] repartió las perras, que iba sacando del cartucho una a una, sobándolas un poquito antes de entregarlas, para que no se le escurriesen dos pegadas; y despidiéndose al fin de la pobretería con un sermoncillo gangoso, exhortándoles a la paciencia y humildad, guardó el cartucho […] y se metió en la iglesia. (69)

His exhortation to the poor to practise patience and humility is a reflection of the proposition that the entire social order had been created and arranged by divine providence, and that the poor should therefore humbly accept their lot in life as something that had been assigned by God.[97] The beggars in the San Sebastián church, in turn – also mirroring providential ideas that label them as worthy recipients of the charity of the dutiful rich – believe they have the right to receive the money they are given. This explains why don Carlos is criticized maliciously by one of the beggars, who believes that he does not always pay what he should (72).

---

96 See Hart, 'Religion and Social Control in the Mid-Nineteenth Century', 114.

97 In *Fortunata y Jacinta*, Guillermina similarly exhorted Fortunata to patience and resignation although, in this case, not only class but also gender considerations play an important role, as seen in Chapter 2.

The right of the poor to receive alms is also voiced by Pulido, one of the beggars at the San Sebastián church, when he thinks to himself,

'[...] quieren que no *haiga* pobres, y se saldrán con la suya. Pero *pa* entonces yo quiero saber quién es el guapo que saca las ánimas del Purgatorio... Ya, ya se pudrirán allá las señoras almas, sin que la cristiandad se acuerde de ellas, porque... a mí que no me digan: el rezo de los ricos, con la barriga bien llena y las carnes bien abrigadas, no vale... por Dios vivo, que no vale'. (68)

The society of beggars in *Misericordia* has been described as 'a society within a society, a microcosm with its hierarchies and classes'.[98] Accordingly, some of the beggars regard themselves as having the right to certain privileges because of their longer years of service. But apart from distinctions based on length of service, it is significant that some beggars also establish, among themselves, the distinction between those who are deserving and those who are not. As la *Burlada*, one of the beggars in the church of San Sebastián, comments,

A Demetria le darán más [bonos][99] por ser *arrecomendada* de ese que celebra la primera misa [...] Siempre lo mismo. No hay como andar con dos o tres criaturas a cuestas para sacar tajada. Y no miran a la decencia, porque estas holgazonotas, como Demetria, sobre ser unas grandísimas pendonazas, hacen luego del vicio su comercio [...] Te digo que sin criaturas no se saca nada. Los señores no miran a la *dinidá* de una, sino a si da el pecho o no da el pecho. Les da lástima de las criaturas, sin reparar en que más *honrás* somos las que no las tenemos, las que estamos en la *senetú*, hartas de trabajos y sin poder valernos. (83–84)

It is interesting that the beggar reproduces the middle-class discourse on the undeserving poor, associating Demetria with idleness and sexual waywardness and accusing her of making a business out of mendicity. The view, often stated by Arenal and others, that false beggars were taking away what by rights belonged to true or deserving beggars is also expressed by la *Burlada* when she says, 'La *caporala* es rica, mismamente rica, tal como lo estáis oyendo, y todo lo que coge aquí nos lo quita a las que *semos* de verdadera *solenidá*' (78). A few pages later la *Burlada* criticizes cruelly and sarcastically the lame Eliseo for considering that he is in a much better financial position than the other beggars. It is ironic

98 See J. E. Varey, 'Charity in *Misericordia*', in J. E. Varey (ed.), *Galdós Studies* (London, Tamesis, 1970), 172.

99 The distribution of 'bonos', and similarly clothes and food instead of money, was favoured at the time as it was believed that alms given in the form of money could encourage mendicity and vice; see *La Voz de la Caridad* (1 November 1879), 248; and (15 August 1883), 174. In *Fortunata y Jacinta* Guillermina is seen distributing 'bonos' among the working-class families of the tenement building (I, 328).

that la *Burlada* should class herself as deserving, since she is one of the most degraded beggars depicted by Galdós. In this episode the author appears to be stressing that the classification of the poor into different categories does not always work. Most of the poor who beg for alms at the church of San Sebastián are described as depraved. As Benina herself tells Almudena, 'Son unos egoístas, corazones de pedernal... El que tiene, porque tiene; el que no tiene, porque no tiene' (87). In the context of the contemporary association of beggars with a plague, it is significant that the beggars are described, at the beginning of the novel, in terms of an infestation – as 'pulgas' and 'feroces alimañas' (65). Here once more, the fact that Galdós brings to the forefront burning social debates of the time on charity and poverty, and in particular attitudes and ideas linking mendicity with vice, disease and contamination, detracts from the general critical tendency to emphasize the novel's spiritual dimension.

The moral degradation of the beggars of San Sebastián is shown by Galdós to have been fostered by the unthinking giving of alms.[100] The calculating don Carlos Trujillo, the obvious example of unthinking alms-giving in the novel, is presented in a negative light, his charity being prompted by self-interest and self-aggrandisement. There is a scene in the novel that illustrates the link drawn by contemporaries between indiscriminate charity on the one hand, and immorality, disorder and disease on the other. This takes place when, after a wedding ceremony, the beggars at the church of San Sebastián and others who have come from surrounding areas descend on the guests as a 'terrible plaga', until finally, the 'padrino' decides to throw some money in order to get rid of them:

> Al fin los del funeral no repartieron cosa mayor; y si los del bodorrio se corrieron algo más, acudió tanta pobretería de otros cuadrantes, y se armó tal barullo y confusión, que unos cogieron por cinco, y otros se quedaron *in albis*. Al ver salir a la novia, tan emperifollada, y a las señoras y caballeros de su compañía, cayeron sobre ellos como nube de langosta, y al padrino le estrujaron el gabán, y hasta le chafaron el sombrero. Trabajo le costó al buen señor sacudirse la terrible plaga, y no tuvo más remedio que arrojar un puñado de calderilla en medio del patio. Los más ágiles hicieron su agosto; los más torpes gatearon inútilmente. La *Caporala* y Eliseo trataban de poner orden, y cuando los novios y todo el acompañamiento se metieron en los coches, quedó en las inmediaciones de la Iglesia la turbamulta mísera, gruñendo y pataleando. Se dispersaba, y otra vez se reunía con remolinos zumbadores. Era como un motín, vencido por su propio cansancio. Los últimos disparos eran: " *Tú cogiste más... me han quitado lo mío... aquí no hay decencia... cuánto pillo...*" La Burlada, que era de las que más habían

100 As observed by Varey, 'Charity in *Misericordia*', 170–72.

apandado, echaba sapos y culebras de su boca, concitando los ánimos de toda la cuadrilla contra la *Caporala* y Eliseo. Por fin intervino la policía, amenazándoles con *recogerles* si no callaban, y esto fue como la palabra de Dios. (185–86)

Here, once more, unthinking charity is not shown to spring from a genuine charitable feeling but is, rather, motivated by the padrino's need to free himself from the overwhelming swarm of beggars. Similarly, the result of the padrino's indiscriminate scattering of coins is presented negatively: the beggars become associated with animality, pre-civilized behaviour, disorder and even political rebellion. Also, it is significant that they are once more equated with a plague.

With their disorderly behaviour, the beggars in the wedding ceremony scene can be seen as having gone beyond the limits imposed by the 'cultura de la pobreza'. It then becomes essential that the police intervene to reestablish order, threatening to take them to the 'depósito' if they do not keep quiet: that is to say, as long as mendicity keeps within the limits set by authority, it does not need to be repressed. It is noteworthy that the authorities, in spite of the fact that begging was prohibited, do not arrest the beggars and are concerned only about their unruly behaviour. This kind of beggar, as described by Galdós in *Misericordia*, did not represent as much of a threat as the 'mendigo coyuntural', the unemployed or temporarily unemployed worker whose predicament resulted directly from the economic circumstances of the day. The beggars depicted by Galdós are integrated into the 'cultura de la pobreza', and thus the authorities sought their control or regulation rather than their repression. This is not to say, however, that the 'passive' beggar escaped repression entirely, as Benina's arrest later in the novel and her imprisonment in San Bernardino and El Pardo show. The fear of being rounded up is illustrated in the wedding scene by the effect that the police's warning has on the beggars.

In another scene in the novel where Benina is seen distributing bread among the beggars in 'las Cambroneras', the association of mendicity with disorder, animality and savagery is further emphasized. As the narrator notes,

La operación se dificultó en extremo, porque todos se abalanzaban a ella con furia, cada uno quería recibir su parte antes que los demás, y alguien intentó apandar dos raciones. Diríase que se duplicaban las manos en el momento de mayor barullo, o que salían otras de debajo de la tierra. Sofocada, la buena mujer tuvo que comprar más libretas, porque dos o tres viejas a quienes no tocó nada, ponían el grito en el cielo, y alborotaban el barrio con sus discordes y lastimeros chillidos. (243–44)

The brutal aspects of mendicity are underlined in a later episode, when Benina and Almudena are sitting on the rubbish tip (where Almudena is shown to be living) having something to eat. They are suddenly surrounded by some troublesome inhabitants of 'las Cambroneras', who begin to shout abuse at Benina, calling her 'ladrona' and 'santa de pega', and end up hurling stones at them (239). Like the beggars at the San Sebastián church, the poor of 'las Cambroneras' believe that it is their right to receive charity from the rich, which contradicted the new, more scientific and rational views on poverty.[101] By suggesting that begging fosters an acceptance of the state of poverty and resignation to one's lot in life, Galdós appears to legitimize ideas that stressed the importance of work, independence and self-improvement.

Varey contrasts this form of unthinking alms-giving with Guillermina Pacheco's active philanthropy.[102] However, the narrator of *Misericordia* notes through one of the beggars that Guillermina's charity was not always discriminating. When Benina is first met by the swarm of beggars of 'las Cambroneras', who mistake her for Guillermina Pacheco,[103] the narrator notes that one of them 'fue y dijo, en nombre del gremio de pordioseros allí presente, que la señora debía distribuir sus beneficios entre todos sin distinción, pues todos eran igualmente acreedores a los frutos de su inmensa caridad' (242). The beggars admit that when Guillermina was last there 'a todos les había socorrido igualmente' (242), thereby implying that she had given alms indiscriminately among them. Here, rather than criticize the indiscriminate distribution of alms, Galdós may in fact defend the view expressed by Arenal that sometimes it was impossible to know who the really deserving were and that, faced with the doubt, it was one's duty to succour anyone who appeared needy. As she wrote in *La Voz de la Caridad*, 'la caridad no puede dejar de amparar por dudar si una persona es realmente desvalida o no'.[104]

Galdós also seems to adopt this position in *Fortunata y Jacinta*, in the episode where Moreno-Isla meets a crippled beggar. In this episode

---

101 It is noteworthy in this respect that in Britain, one of the reasons put forward in the 1870s to justify the abolition of the Poor Law of 1834, according to which official charity could be dispensed only through the workhouse (though cash alms did in fact continue), was that in viewing charity as a right of the poor the state had for centuries been fostering the development of pauperism, as one contributor to *La Voz de la Caridad* remarked (15 June 1879), 111ff.

102 Varey, 'Charity in *Misericordia*', 173, 175.

103 For a comparison between the character of Guillermina Pacheco and that of Benina, see J. L. Brooks, 'The Character of Guillermina Pacheco in Galdós's Novel, *Fortunata y Jacinta*', *Bulletin of Hispanic Studies*, XXXVIII (1961), 86–94.

104 See *La Voz de la Caridad* (1 July 1877), 135.

Moreno-Isla's first reaction is one of indignation and repulsion. As the narrator notes, 'Tales espectáculos indignaban a Moreno, que al verse acosado por estos *industriales* de la miseria humana, trinaba de ira' (II, 344; my emphasis). Here, Moreno's perception of mendicity as an 'industry' shows that he is in the Protestant self-help tradition (indeed, Moreno-Isla is depicted as an Anglophile). It is significant, however, that the day before his death, Moreno repents his meanness towards the beggar, and hopes that he can meet him again and help him financially. As Moreno thinks to himself, 'El infeliz se ha de buscar la vida de alguna manera. No tiene él la culpa de que no haya en esta tierra maldita estable-cimientos de beneficencia. Si le veo mañana le doy un duro… Vaya si se lo doy…' (II, 344–45). Moreno's change of attitude towards begging is reinforced by the fact that, on the night of his death, he is once more shown to feel terrible remorse for not having given enough to a gypsy girl singing in the street (II, 361–62). The trauma caused by his recalling these two episodes seems, in a way, to precipitate his death.

From the perspective of the associations established during this period between filth and deviant groups of the population, it is significant that Almudena is seen to take refuge in a rubbish heap.[105] As the narrator comments,

> Distinguió […] Benina la inmóvil figura del ciego, en un vertedero de escorias, cascote y basuras […] en medio de una aridez absoluta, pues ni árbol ni mata, ni ninguna especie vegetal crecen allí. (235)

Later in the novel, the narrator points out,

> [Almudena] [t]rató de explicar la atracción que, en el estado de su espíritu, sobre él ejercían los áridos peñascales y escombreras en que a la sazón se encontraba. Realmente, ni él sabía explicárselo ni Benina entenderlo; pero el observador atento bien puede entrever en aquella singular querencia un caso de atavismo o de retroacción instintiva hacia la antigüedad, buscando la semejanza geográfica con las soledades pedregosas en que se inició la vida de la raza…¿Es esto un desatino? Quizás no. (240)

Here, atavism, a reversion to more primitive stages of evolution, is not linked to contemporary ideas on the degeneration of the race. In spite of this negative image of decay, Almudena's natural desire to go to the rubbish tip does not suggest that he is degenerating morally; that is, Almudena is not judged morally in this scene.[106] There is another passage

---

105 This scene is similar to the episode in *Fortunata y Jacinta* in which Mauricia is sitting on a manure heap in the Convent of Las Micaelas.

106 Also, as Hazel Gold has argued ('El nomadismo urbano y la crisis finisecular en *Misericordia*', *Actas del VI Congreso Internacional Galdosiano* [Las Palmas de Gran

in the novel in which the narrator echoes views linking poverty with filth and organic residuum (and the moral corruption each represents), a scene that is reminiscent of the description of the dwellings and streets of the 'cuarto estado' during Guillermina and Jacinta's visit there in *Fortunata y Jacinta*. As the narrator comments,

> No lejos del punto en que Mesón de Paredes desemboca en la Ronda de Toledo, hallaron el parador de Santa Casilda, vasta colmena de viviendas baratas alineadas en corredores sobrepuestos. Entrase a ella por un patio o corralón largo y estrecho, lleno de motones de basura, residuos, despojos y desperdicios de todo lo humano. (91)

Notwithstanding this negative image of the poor, and in spite of the description of the beggars at the San Sebastián church in terms of infection, animality and savagery, Benina and Almudena are associated with immorality only in the eyes of the authorities.

Although mendicity was widely regarded as leading to moral debasement and loss of dignity, there was also an awareness that some poor needed to beg – and had a natural right to do so – in order to survive, as otherwise they would die of starvation, a view Galdós appears to endorse in *Misericordia*.[107] On one occasion when doña Paca accuses Benina of not possessing 'decorum' and dignity (Benina admits to being able to cope with the humiliation and shame of owing money to everybody), Benina replies, 'Yo no sé si tengo eso; pero tengo boca y estómago natural, y sé también que Dios me ha puesto en el mundo para que viva, y no para que me deje morir de hambre' (100). The narrator shows that in fact Benina regards begging as shameful and undignified. At one point in the novel the narrator comments that, after having managed to have some money lent to her, Benina 'pensando verse libre de la vergüenza de pedir limosna, al menos por un par de días, volvió a su casa' (200), but that she has to have recourse to begging in order for her and doña Paca to survive. As the narrator states, 'la fiera necesidad le impuso el triste oficio de mendicante' (119). Galdós mocks doña Paca's impractical and unrealistic sense of dignity when he makes her say to Benina, 'Yo que tú, rechazaría la limosna. Mientras tengamos a nuestro D. Romualdo podemos permitirnos un poquito de dignidad, Nina' (128). It is worth noting here that

---

Canaria, Cabildo Insular de Gran Canaria, 2000], 387–95), Almudena is not seen to degenerate physically. In fact, his skin disease improves, as we are told at the end of the novel.

107 This opinion was expressed, for instance, by Concepción Arenal: see *La Voz de la Caridad* (1 June 1880), 78, and *El pauperismo*, I, 390–91. Galdós also seems to favour this view in *Fortunata y Jacinta*, in the previously noted scene where Moreno-Isla regrets not having financially helped two beggars whom he encounters.

Benina's lie about obtaining her money from the work she does for don Romualdo creates a 'split identity', whereby she becomes, at once, both a receiver and a giver of alms. The fact that Benina fabricates a lie in which she sees herself earning money through work (rather than by means of begging) reflects that she has internalized the work ethic and that she finds begging unacceptable. Through her lie Benina is thus constructed as a deserving beggar.

Furthermore, Benina is presented as a model of thrift, traditionally regarded as a bourgeois value that needed to be instilled in the working classes. Her thrifty habits are contrasted to doña Paca's wasteful spending, which Benina has to control. As she exclaims on one occasion, '¡Ay, si yo no mandara, bonitas andaríamos! Ya nos habrían mandado a San Bernardino o al mismísimo Pardo!' (218). Interestingly, Benina is also described as a 'sisona'. The issue of the 'sisa' in connection with domestic servants became a major concern during the second half of the century in particular, and it was often referred to in *La Voz de la Caridad*.[108] In *Misericordia*, Benina's tendency to steal some of the shopping money is not linked to dissolution and the immoral habits associated with the poor. Indeed, Benina's habits of 'sisa' are associated, rather, with her thrifty instincts:

> tenía el vicio del descuento, que en cierto modo, por otro lado, era la virtud del ahorro. Difícil expresar dónde se empalmaban y confundían la virtud y el vicio. La costumbre de escatimar una parte grande o chica de lo que se le daba para la compra, el gusto de guardarla, de ver cómo crecía lentamente su caudal de perras, se sobreponían en su espíritu a todas las demás costumbres, hábitos y placeres. (107)

Thrift was considered important for both the material and moral improvement of the working classes, individual improvement leading, in turn, to national progress. *La Voz de la Caridad* includes a considerable number of articles on thrift and how to foster it among the working classes. As one commentator writing for this journal pointed out, 'Es indispensable ahorrar, porque la mejora individual y el progreso social son imposibles sin el capital, y el capital es imposible sin el ahorro'.[109] In *Misericordia*, don Carlos's exhortation to Benina, '[c]on orden, los pobres se hacen ricos'

---

108 An article from *La Voz de la Caridad* entitled 'La sisa de las criadas' attributes this vice to the lack of moral education and religious principles in servants. The best remedy against 'la sisa' is 'imbuir esas ideas de moralidad y religión a las criadas que no las tengan o sostenerlas en quienes las tengan debilitadas' (15 May 1880), 68. Concepción Arenal stated similar views in the issue of 1 December 1878 of this journal (292), and in *El pauperismo*, I, she devoted a whole chapter to discussing the problem.

109 *La Voz de la Caridad* (15 December 1880), 251.

(131), echoes the ideology of some contemporaries. Others stated, from a more realistic perspective, the impossibility for many poor people to be thrifty when their income was barely sufficient to cover their basic needs.[110] In the novel, don Carlos's unrealistic view is ridiculed by the narrator. When he gives Benina the accounts book and tells her that doña Paca should enter in it both income and expenditure, the narrator's irony is reflected through Benina's reply: 'Pero si a la señora no le ingresa nada' (132).

Towards the end of the century, people were becoming more suspicious of alms-giving, because they were growing more aware of the fact that not all beggars were really needy.[111] This explains why it was becoming increasingly difficult for able beggars to ask for public charity, in spite of the fact that alms were very often given in an indiscriminate way, as is the case with don Carlos. This is the reason why Demetria, who has several young children, is favoured by one of the priests of the San Sebastián church. It also explains why Benina needs to resort to a disguise when begging in the streets at night:

> En la breve campaña nocturna, sacaba escondido un velo negro, viejísimo, de doña Paca, para entapujarse la cara; y con esto y unos espejuelos verdes que para el caso guardaba, hacía divinamente el tipo de señora *ciega vergon-zante*, arrimadita a la esquina de la calle de Barrionuevo, atacando con quejumbroso reclamo a media voz a todo cristiano que pasaba. (250; my emphasis)

In *Nazarín*, when describing the lodging house of *Chanfaina*, the narrator portrays the kind of deserving poor most likely to attract public charity:

> dos hombres sacaron en brazos a una vieja paralítica, que llevaba colgado del pecho un cartel donde constaba su edad, de más de cien años, buen reclamo para implorar la caridad pública, y se la llevaron a la calle para ponerla en la esquina de la Arganzuela. (11)

Moreover, beggars in the streets could not count on being shown the tolerance displayed towards those who begged outside churches. Thus, la *Burlada* owes her place in San Sebastián to the lame Eliseo, who exhorted her to come with him and beg at the church door, as la *Burlada* herself reminds him:

> '*Seña* Flora, ¿por qué no se pone a pedir en un templo, quitándose de la *santimperie*, y arrimándose al cisco de la religión? Véngase conmigo y verá cómo puede sacar un diario, sin rodar por las calles, y tratando con pobres decentes'. (81)

---

110 Concepción Arenal made this observation in *El pauperismo*, II, in which she wrote one full chapter on the issue of thrift.

111 These attitudes are echoed, for instance, in an article significantly entitled 'Desconfianza de la limosna', which Concepción Arenal wrote for *La Voz de la Caridad* (15 October 1880), 212–16.

This tolerant attitude towards begging at the church door attracted criticism. In an article published in *La Epoca* the author regrets the spectacle offered by beggars at the entrance to churches and warns against the dangers of indiscriminate charity, concluding that 'la tolerancia se ha convertido en un derecho protector de la mendicidad convertida en industria'.[112] As mentioned earlier, Arenal also expressed concern about the difficulty of eradicating in Spain such deeply rooted habits as begging at the doors of religious institutions, as these habits had been largely tolerated in the past.[113] The beggars of San Sebastián are never shown in the novel to be at risk of being arrested by the authorities (apart from the time when they break the rules and become disorderly), in spite of the prohibition on begging outside churches, as stipulated in the edicts regularly dictated by the Mayor of Madrid.[114] However, street beggars would have been exposed not only to the less lenient attitude of the public but also to the dangers of being rounded up and taken to a 'depósito de mendicidad'. On the few occasions when Benina is forced to beg in the streets because the alms which she receives outside San Sebastián are not enough, she constantly runs the risk of arrest. On one of these occasions, when she needs to win the favour of alms-givers by playing, again, the role of the 'distinctly' deserving poor, the narrator comments,

> [Benina] se puso a pedir en la esquina de la calle de San Millán, junto a la puerta del café de los Naranjeros, importunando a los transeúntes con el relato de sus desdichas: que acababa de salir del hospital, que su marido se había caído de un andamio, que no había comido en tres semanas, y otras cosas que partían los corazones. Algo iba pescando la infeliz, y hubiera cogido algo más, si no se pareciese por allí un maldito guindilla que la conminó con llevarla a los sótanos de la prevención de la Latina si no se largaba con viento fresco. (187–88)

That Benina had to use a disguise shows that people were becoming more discriminating in their alms-giving, and it implies, therefore, that some alms-givers might have regarded her as undeserving had she not disguised herself. Here, by demonstrating the difficulty of making a clear distinction between the deserving and undeserving poor, Galdós implicitly criticizes, once more, the illogicality of bourgeois strategies of classifying beggars and awarding charity in a scientific, discriminatory way: the classification of beggars into deserving and undeserving is shown by Galdós to be flawed and unjust. Also in this episode Galdós seems once

---

112 *La Epoca* (25 March 1881), in Bahamonde Magro and Toro Mérida, 'Mendicidad y paro', 367.

113 This point was also made a few decades earlier by Monlau, *Remedios del pauperismo*, 11.

114 See, for example, the edict dictated in 1884, which Bahamonde Magro ('Cultura de la pobreza', 180) gives as a model.

again to fall in behind Arenal's view that occasionally, due to the problem of deciding who the really deserving are, one had an obligation to help the needy financially, regardless of their merits or circumstances.

As the passage in which Benina is threatened with arrest shows, the rounding-up of beggars constituted an important means of regulating mendicity. This measure, along with the expulsion of the non-residents of Madrid from the capital, was regularly enacted, particularly during periods of economic crisis.[115] The sweeping-up of beggars from the streets (their arrest reflecting the association established between mendicity and criminality) separated them from the rest of the population. Once inside the 'depósito', however, a more detailed classification became necessary: between the healthy and the sick, the indigenous of Madrid and the immigrants, professional beggars and deserving beggars.[116]

Another instrument of classification used to control mendicity was the identification of beggars through the issuing of begging licences. Here, as with the rounding-up of beggars, the main objective was pragmatic control rather than outright repression to secure the existing social system at times of crisis. This measure resulted, it has been observed, from the desire of the Madrid bourgeoisie to draw up specific registers of the lower social groups[117] or, in other words, the desire to label and categorize the masses. Licences were mainly awarded to workers who had become disabled through accidents at work or to elderly people without income:[118] those who would have been classed as 'deserving'. In 1884 the Ayuntamiento required that those beggars who had been granted a permit to beg for alms should wear, in a visible place, a badge (*'un distintivo'*) marked with a number and the inscription 'mendicidad' *'para no ser confundidos* con los que carezcan de él' (my emphasis).[119] To combat promiscuity and confusion, the authorities promoted order and classification. Mendicity was to be tolerated within limits, in accordance with the rules and criteria imposed by the system. There were some deserving beggars, however, who refused to comply with the requirements – which they regarded as 'deshonrosos' – laid down by the authorities for their

---

115 Bahamonde Magro and Toro Mérida, 'Mendicidad y paro', 359.

116 Bahamonde Magro ('Cultura de la pobreza', 182) reproduced a report drawn up by the authorities on the age, geographical origin and other personal details (mostly concerning their motives for begging) of the beggars arrested in the streets of Madrid in 1868.

117 Ibid., 180

118 Bahamonde Magro and Toro Mérida, 'Mendicidad y paro', 357. As these historians note, there were also cases of 'jornaleros' applying for licences because their income was not sufficient.

119 As the edict announced by the Mayor of Madrid ordered; see Bahamonde Magro, 'Cultura de la pobreza', 180.

identification, and who subsequently had their permits removed.[120] The fact that in the scene where Benina is threatened with arrest she did not have a licence may similarly be connected with her refusal to be identified or labelled; although receiving a licence was not always easy, since it was often necessary to obtain a recommendation from the monarch or a member of the aristocracy.[121]

In spite of the fact that Benina is described in the novel as deserving or respectable regarding her poverty, begging in the streets without a licence finally leads to her arrest and her imprisonment in San Bernardino, and her subsequent transfer, after the classification process, to El Pardo. As doña Paca's son tells Ponte,

> Ese ángel está en el Pardo, que es el Paraíso a donde son llevados los angelitos que piden limosna sin licencia […] En una redada que echaron los policías, cogieron a Nina y al otro, y los zamparon en San Bernardino. De allí me les empaquetaron para el Pardo. (281)

Benina's arrest and her seclusion in El Pardo is explained by the above-mentioned legislation against vagrancy implemented earlier in the century. The narrator describes the scene of her arrest in the following terms:

> se apareció un individuo de la ronda secreta que, empujándola con mal modo, le dijo: "Ea, buena mujer, eche usted a andar para adelante … Y vivo, vivo…
> — ¿Qué dice?…
> — Que se calle y ande…
> —¿Pero a dónde me lleva?
> — Cállese usted, que le tiene más cuenta… ¡Hala!, a San Bernardino.
> —¿Pero qué mal hago yo… señor?
> —¡Está usted pidiendo!… ¿No le dije a usted ayer que el señor Gobernador no quiere que se pida en esta calle?
> — Pues manténgame el señor Gobernador, que yo de hambre no he de morirme, por Cristo… ¡Vaya con el hombre!…
> — ¡Calle usted, *so borracha*!… ¡Andando digo!
> — ¡Que no me empuje!… Yo no soy *criminala*… […]
> Se arrimó a la pared; pero el fiero polizonte la despegó del arrimo con un empujón violentísimo. Acercáronse dos de Orden público, a los cuales el de la ronda mandó que la llevaran a San Bernardino, juntamente con toda la demás pobretería de ambos sexos que en la tal calle y callejones adyacentes encontraran. (254)

Through Benina's realistic and sarcastic comment ('Pues manténgame el señor Gobernador, que yo de hambre no he de morirme'), Galdós is denouncing a system that represses mendicity without offering alternative

120 Bahamonde Magro and Toro Mérida, 'Mendicidad y paro', 359.
121 Ibid., 358.

solutions to the precariousness in which the poor lived. Like Arenal, he seems to favour begging for alms when this is the only option in a society in which both public and private charity are incapable of coping with the explosion of mendicity, in Madrid in particular. During the nineteenth century, the offer of charitable aid had become increasingly insufficient to cope with the growing numbers of beggars. Although the municipal resources devoted to charity increased, the charity of the church had been considerably cut back, particularly after the 'desamortizaciones'. As a result, charitable institutions became saturated and debased.[122] If in theory asylums had been created to instil the work ethic in beggars, in practice it became impossible to achieve this target.[123] It has also been noted that the lack of spatial and material resources of Madrid's charitable institutions was due to the fact that the city's bourgeoisie preferred direct alms-giving to the subscriptions that contributed to the maintenance of semi-official charitable institutions. Hence the failure of the 'depósito' and asylum of San Bernardino and the asylum of El Pardo. With regard to private institutions, although they had greater economic resources, their financial situation was also precarious.[124]

Of interest is the association, drawn in the episode of Benina's arrest, between mendicity, drunkenness and criminality. In the eyes of the agent of the authorities, Benina is a 'borracha'. Similarly, she is treated like a criminal. Benina, however, refuses to be associated with criminality and feels a great sense of indignation at her arrest: '¡Ser llevada a un recogimiento

122 The conditions in which the inmates had to live (many institutions lacked space, light and air) were frequently criticized by contemporary observers; see Plá et al., *El Madrid de Galdós*, 94–95. A good example of this is offered by Galdós in *Misericordia*. When Benina enters San Bernardino, the narrator comments: 'la metieron en una gran sala, ahogada y fétida, donde había ya como un medio centenar de ancianos de ambos sexos' (256).

123 Plá et al., *El Madrid de Galdós*, 179–80.

124 Bahamonde Magro and Toro Mérida, 'Mendicidad y paro', 359–60. A writer for *La Epoca* commented, 'Aunque los Asilos benéficos fuesen modelos en su género, serían ineficaces para socorrer la desgracia de gran número de desheredados. En Madrid, por ejemplo, son necesarias no pocas recomendaciones para *obtener una plaza* en cualquiera de los Asilos que aquí existen. No es tan fácil como algunos creen encontrar un sitio bajo techado donde caerse muerto' (*La Epoca* [22 December 1896], in Bahamonde Magro and Toro Mérida, 'Mendicidad y paro', 375). A private institution mentioned in *Misericordia*, the soup kitchen of El Sagrado Corazón, which is portrayed in a rather negative light, similarly failed to offer a stable means of support for the poor, as seen in the novel (233). One of the objectives of this soup kitchen was to indoctrinate the poor morally and religiously. Like other charitable institutions, this establishment was used as an instrument of social order, particularly during periods of economic crisis; see *La Epoca* (16 January 1891), in Bahamonde Magro and Toro Mérida, 'Mendicidad y paro', 373.

de mendigos callejeros como son conducidos a la cárcel los rateros y malhechores!' (255). As in *Nazarín*, Galdós is implicitly criticizing here the lumping together of different deviant groups into an undifferentiated whole, something which, ironically, ran parallel to the desire for categorization and classification. In *La Voz de la Caridad*, Arenal often attacked the abuses committed by the authorities' agents in picking up beggars, even when these were old or disabled.[125] In the passage dealing with Benina's arrest, Galdós also condemns such abuses, which were justified by the authorities on the basis of the link they established between mendicity and criminality. Furthermore, Galdós is critical of the association made by the authorities between mendicity and animality. In an episode which takes place after Benina is released from San Bernardino, she and Almudena are back to begging in the streets when the narrator notes,

> entretuvieron la primera mitad del día pordioseando en varias calles, siempre con mucho cuidado de los guindillas, por no caer nuevamente en poder de los que echan el lazo a los mendigos, cual si fueran perros, para llevarlos al depósito, donde como a perros les tratan. (308)[126]

After Benina is released from El Pardo, the narrator describes a scene that illustrates the conceptualization of beggars in terms of filth, disease and contamination. When she returns to doña Paca's house, Juliana says to her, 'La señora está aquí... Pero te dice que no pases, porque vendrás llena de miseria...' (296). At that moment Obdulia comes to the door and tells her in similar terms, 'Nina, bien venida seas; pero antes de que entres en casa, hay que fumigarte y ponerte en la colada... No, no te arrimes a mí. ¡Tantos días entre pobres inmundos!...' (296). Obdulia's words are significant from the point of view of contemporary anxieties about infection and the implementation of fumigation as a preventive measure. As we saw when discussing *Nazarín*, Galdós had attacked these measures in his journalistic writings. Fears of infection are voiced once more by doña Paca when she learns of Almudena's disease and stops Benina from coming to see her 'por temor a que nos contagie de esa peste asquerosa' (311).

After their rejection by doña Paca's family, the only alternatives left to Benina and Almudena are either begging for alms and running the risk of being arrested, or the loss of freedom and isolation that seclusion in an asylum entailed. These were, according to Arenal, the only possibilities open to beggars in nineteenth-century Madrid.[127] The option of the

125 *La Voz de la Caridad* (15 May 1880), 62–63.

126 In this respect, it has to be remembered that in *Fortunata y Jacinta*, Mauricia was treated like an animal in Las Micaelas. Similarly, Guillermina was described as 'cazando' 'fallen women' in the streets and making them enter the convent (I, 628).

127 Arenal, *El pauperismo*, I, 394.

asylum had been offered to Benina and Almudena by a 'guardabarreras' who took care of them after they were attacked in 'las Cambroneras' and who associates them with vagrants, as Benina herself notes:

> Lo que deben hacer ustedes es dejarse de andar de vagancia por calles y caminos, donde todo es ajetreo y malos pasos, y ver de meterse o que los metan en un asilo [...] Nada contestó Almudena, que amaba la libertad y la prefería trabajosa y miserable a la cómoda sujeción del asilo. Benina, por su parte, no queriendo entrar en largas explicaciones, ni desvanecer el error de aquella buena gente, que sin duda les creía asociados para la vagancia y el merodeo, se limitó a decir que no se recogían en un *establecimiento* por causa de la mucha *existencia* de pobres, y que sin recomendaciones y tarjetas de personajes no había manera de conseguir plaza. (248)

Almudena's and Benina's attitude towards entering an asylum is typical of that held by many poor people who chose the freedom of begging in the streets over the restrictions of incarceration.[128] Moreover, as Benina explains, even for those willing to be admitted to an asylum, getting a 'plaza' in one of them was not an easy task, due to the demand from Madrid's large begging population. As the narrator observes, don Romualdo is constantly bothered by beggars asking for 'recomendaciones' (269).

The fact that beggars needed a 'recomendación' to be received into an asylum meant that they would have had to be classified as deserving. When a priest friend of don Romualdo also advises Benina to abandon her life as a beggar, he makes the point that before offering her a reference, don Romualdo will need to investigate her case:

> Usted, *Doña Benigna*, bien podría dejarse de esta vida, que a su edad es tan penosa [...] ¿Por qué no entra en la *Misericordia*? Ya se lo he dicho a D. Romualdo, y ha prometido interesarse... [...] Ya le he dicho también [...] que es usted criada de una señora que vive en la calle Imperial, y prometió informarse de su comportamiento antes de recomendarla... (252–53)

At the end of the novel, in spite of doña Paca's family's interest in getting her a place in La Misericordia, Benina decides to settle with Almudena in the 'barrios bajos', thereby refusing to be categorized and effectively proclaiming her independence. This rejection of the subjection and isolation of the asylum also represents the author's reluctance to endorse an arbitrary system of labelling, segregation and containment of those social groups perceived as morally diseased and in need of spatial and social 'fixing'.

---

128 As Arenal remarked (*El pauperismo*, I, 394), 'socorro' had become synonymous with 'reclusión', which ran contrary to people's spirit of independence. Therefore, faced with the alternative of being either 'mendigos' or 'encerrados', most opted for the former.

Conclusion

In the decade covered by the novels analysed in this book – from *Fortunata y Jacinta* (1886–87) to *Misericordia* (1897) – Galdós's position remained consistent with regard to those groups of the population categorized as 'deviant' and perceived as social and moral 'filth' by many of his contemporaries. In the discussion of 'Una visita al Cuarto Estado', in *Fortunata y Jacinta*, we saw how Galdós distances himself from his bourgeois characters and the bourgeois narrator, avoiding complicity with a bourgeois system of categorization and control that associates the lower classes with immorality and filth. This position is maintained in all the other novels considered here. *Fortunata y Jacinta* also provides a clear example of Galdós's tendency to disengage himself from contemporary attitudes to prostitution and drink. Ten years after the second part of *Fortunata y Jacinta* was published, the author voiced similar views in *Misericordia* regarding the lower layers of society. In both novels he criticizes bourgeois efforts at classifying and containing those social groups – be they prostitutes, alcoholics or beggars – that represented a threat. The bourgeois attempt at categorizing and labelling social subordinates by setting up binary oppositions is shown not to work. In these novels Galdós highlights the arbitrary nature of systems of classification, showing that the dividing line between categories is often blurred. By subverting the discourses of control and the associations and categorizations produced by them, Galdós shows that such discourses are bourgeois constructions; that is, the polarized division of people into respectable/non-respectable, virtuous/immoral, deserving/undeserving, and so on, is shown to involve a system of power relations, whereby those who have been classified as abnormal or deviating from the behavioural norm become the objects of bourgeois control.

Most of the characters produced as evidence in this study, who in bourgeois and petit-bourgeois eyes are regarded, to a greater or lesser degree, as non-respectable, immoral or undeserving, and therefore in need of moral reform, are not depicted by Galdós as such. Although, on occasion, Galdós endorses contemporary ideas that associate certain groups of the population with filth and moral degradation (obvious examples being the case of the Babel sons, the beggar *Maldiciones*, or the community of beggars of *Misericordia*), he tends to present characters who do not fit neatly into any of the broad categories defined during the period, often subverting stereotypes through the use of irony and narrative point of view (as in the case of Fortunata, Mauricia, don Pito, Dulce, Gurmesinda, Urrea, Benina and Almudena). Indeed, he frequently establishes a subcategory of 'deserving' within that category of poor regarded as 'undeserving' by social commentators and observers of the period.

With regard to prostitution, we have seen how the author undermines the link between prostitutes and filth through the characters of Mauricia and Fortunata. Analysis of the panoptic strategy deployed in the convent of Las Micaelas and of the trajectories followed by these two characters later in the novel reveals how Galdós demonstrates the inefficiency of the control mechanisms implemented by the dominant classes. Also, although Galdós's association of the prostitute Andara in *Nazarín* with dirt and foul smells seemingly echoes contemporary views, such associations cannot be taken entirely at face value, given that Andara is mainly a comical figure.

In the case of alcoholism, characters such as Mauricia, Izquierdo, Dulce and don Pito are not portrayed as stereotypical drunkards. Even the violent and quarrelsome Zacarías in *Angel Guerra* is not completely stereotypical. Here, however, there is a basic difference in Galdós's treatment of male and female drinkers, derived from the contemporary bias in respect of female alcoholism. In connection with alcoholism within the specific context of the degeneration of the human race, Galdós voices contemporary debates on degeneration in his description of the Babel sons, for instance. However, he does not depict other alcoholics, such as don Pito, as morally degenerate. The author's more negative attitude towards female drinkers is partly related to his concern with the issue of degeneration. Thus, although he tends to disagree with the categorization of his working-class characters, overturning binary oppositions based on class polarities, Galdós is much more conservative when it comes to gender: the alcoholism of Mauricia and Dulce is therefore presented in much more negative terms than that of Izquierdo and don Pito. Also, Fortunata, despite rebelling against her categorization as 'non-respectable', is an essentially feminine character; that is, she is not presented as a rebel in terms of gender.

Galdós's message is less clear in respect of attitudes to the deserving and undeserving poor in the context of debates on the indiscriminate dispensation of charity and on mendicity and vagrancy. In *Angel Guerra*, the protagonist's death at the end of the novel can be read as the author's criticism of his financial aid to the Babel sons and to other characters described as morally degraded in the novel; nonetheless, the protagonist's charitable attitude to other characters who would have been regarded as undeserving by many of his contemporaries is not called into question. In this novel, as in those analysed in Chapter 4, Galdós highlights the difficulty of differentiating between those poor who are deserving of charity and those who are not, without attempting to provide an answer to this problem. Consequently, the question of how charitable funds should be administered is also left unanswered.

Nazarín is perhaps the most ambiguous of the novels focusing on the theme of begging, vagrancy and indiscriminate charity. Nazarín is presented as a challenge to dominant views, although the novel does not suggest that the author approves of Nazarín's ideas: again, the author raises issues but does not deliver solutions. In bringing up the issue of the deserving and undeserving poor, *Halma* also offers no definitive answers. The protagonist Halma's more discriminating or rational way of practising charity, as well as her endorsement of the work ethic and self-help ethos, bring her more into line than Guerra with the ideology of the period. Her imposition of work on her 'asilados' would presumably exclude from her project that unreformable category of poor represented by *Maldiciones* or the Babel sons. There is an important difference between Halma and commentators of the time, however, in that she does not regard moral indoctrination as an efficient instrument of rehabilitation, as reflected in the way she deals with Urrea. Even if her institution fails, Halma, following Nazarín's advice, is still left with the possibility of financially aiding those poor she *chooses* to assist, dispensing charity according to her own criteria and without interference from official institutions. The fact that Halma rehabilitates Urrea and also manages to convince the rational, pragmatic priest Manuel Flórez of her ideas before the latter dies would endorse her views. Although Galdós is closer to Halma's attitude to charity than to that propounded by Guerra or Nazarín, this does not necessarily imply that Galdós agrees with her determination, for Nazarín's advice to her cannot be trusted and thus at the end of the novel the reader is once more confronted with ambiguity. Galdós's reluctance to let his position be known is consistent with his demonstration of the impossibility of drawing clear demarcation lines between various groups of poor people, and with his critique of the illogicality of bourgeois social categorization strategies.

In *Misericordia*, the last of the novels examined, the issues of the deserving and the undeserving poor and of unthinking alms-giving are again problematized without any attempt to impose resolution. Through his negative portrayal of the beggars at the San Sebastián church, Galdós, voicing contemporary ideas, shows how mendicity and indiscriminate charity can lead to moral debasement and acceptance of the state of poverty. But, although the novels analysed often suggest that Galdós endorses contemporary ideas on independence and self-help and that he attacks self-imposed poverty and resignation to one's lot in life, they do not imply that he condemns begging categorically. Through characters like Benina and Almudena, Galdós criticizes a system that associates mendicity with deviancy and filth, but that does not offer alternative options for the destitute, thereby forcing them into begging in order to survive. Galdós had made this point ten years before in *Fortunata y Jacinta*, in the episode when Moreno-Isla regrets his meanness towards a crippled beggar, commenting that it was not the beggar's fault that he had to beg if there are no charitable establishments to provide for his needs. In this episode, as in *Misericordia*, when Benina had to resort to disguise in order to look distinctly 'deserving', the message is, rather, that sometimes, due to the difficulty of deciding who the really deserving were, one had an obligation to help the needy financially, regardless of their merits and circumstances, an opinion that had been voiced by Concepción Arenal, among others.

Throughout the novels examined in this study, Galdós reveals the inadequacy of the strategies advocated by contemporaries in respect of the problem of the poor, centring on the categorization, containment and 'recycling' of those social groups associated with filth. Galdós demonstrates how those considered to be in need of reform by bourgeois characters in the novel, reflecting the dominant views of the period, were often already in possession of 'respectable' values or at least had the potential to be 'respectable', and did not need to be taught to be self-reliant and independent. In those cases where such values are absent, this is shown to be the result of a lack of economic resources, or of a specific psychological case history, as with don Pito or Mauricia, rather than of an innate tendency towards degradation.

In this book I hope to have demonstrated how the study of these novels in the light of contemporary social debates and the images of filth and disease produced by them can contribute to a sensitive and illuminating reading of Galdós's work. In respect of the novels of the 1890s in particular, it has been my aim to show how Galdós echoes in them contemporary *social* concerns about the dangers posed by deviant, or 'morally diseased', groups of the population – such as alcoholics, beggars and vagrants – and about the issue of the degeneration of the race. In order to reach a better understanding of the wider implications of the novels written during this period, it is important to look beyond previous *spiritual* readings of the texts, by focusing attention on Galdós's critical engagement with contemporary discourses on deviancy and control.

Bibliography

Works by Galdós

Angel Guerra, 2 vols, Madrid, Alianza, 1986

Fortunata y Jacinta, 2 vols, ed. Francisco Caudet, Madrid, Cátedra, 1983

Halma, Obras completas, 4th edn, vol. V, ed. Federico Carlos Sainz de Robles, Madrid, Aguilar, 1965

Misericordia, ed. Luciano García Lorenzo, Madrid, Cátedra, 1993

Nazarín, Madrid, Alianza, 1984

Ghiraldo, Alberto (ed.), *Obras inéditas de Benito Pérez Galdós*, 10 vols, Madrid, Renacimiento, 1923–30

Shoemaker, W. H. (ed.), *Los artículos de Galdós en 'La Nación'*, Madrid, Insula, 1972

Shoemaker, W. H. (ed.), *Las cartas desconocidas de Galdós en 'La Prensa' de Buenos Aires*, Madrid, Cultura Hispánica, 1973

Other works

Abercrombie, Nicholas, Stephen Hill and Bryan Turner, *The Dominant Ideology Thesis*, London, George Allen & Unwin, 1980

Aldaraca, Bridget, *El ángel del hogar: Galdós y la ideología de la domesticidad en España*, Madrid, Visor, 1992

Alvarez-Uría, Fernando, 'La cárcel o el manicomio', in Julia Varela and Fernando Alvarez-Uría (eds), *El cura Galeote asesino del obispo de Madrid-Alcalá*, Madrid, La Piqueta, 1979, 149–73

——, *Miserables y locos: Medicina mental y orden social en la España del siglo XIX*, Barcelona, Tusquets, 1983

——, 'Los visitadores del pobre: Caridad, economía social y asistencia en la España del siglo XIX', in *De la beneficencia al bienestar social: Cuatro siglos de acción social*, Madrid, Siglo Veintiuno, 1993, 117–46

Andreu, Alicia, *Modelos dialógicos en la narrativa de Benito Pérez Galdós*, Amsterdam, John Benjamins, 1989

Arenal, Concepción, *Obras completas*, 2 vols, ed. Concepción Díaz Castañón, Madrid, Atlas (Biblioteca de Autores Españoles), 1993 and 1994

——, *El pauperismo*, 2 vols, Madrid, Librería de Victoriano Suárez, 1897

Bahamonde Magro, Angel, 'Cultura de la pobreza y mendicidad involuntaria en el Madrid del siglo XIX', in *Madrid en Galdós, Galdós en Madrid*, Comunidad de Madrid, Consejería de Cultura, 1988, 163–82

—— and Jesus A. Martínez, *Historia de España siglo XIX*, Madrid, Cátedra, 1994

—— and Julián Toro Mérida, *Burguesía, especulación y cuestión social en el Madrid siglo XIX*, Madrid, Siglo XXI de España, 1978

—— and Julián Toro Mérida, 'Mendicidad y paro en el Madrid de la Restauración', *Estudios de Historia Social*, 7 (1978), 353–84

—— and Luis E. Otero Carvajal (eds), *La sociedad madrileña durante la Restauración (1876–1931)*, 2 vols, Comunidad de Madrid, Consejería de Cultura, 1989

Barr, Lois Baer, 'Social Decay and Disintegration in *Misericordia*', *Anales Galdosianos*, XVII (1982), 97–104

Bell, Shannon, *Reading, Writing, and Rewriting the Prostitute Body*, Bloomington and Indianapolis, Indiana University Press, 1994

Bentham, Jeremy, *The Panopticon; or, the Inspection-House* (1791), in John Bowring (ed.), *The Collected Works of Jeremy Bentham*, Edinburgh, 1843, IV, 39–172

Berkowitz, H. Chonon, *Pérez Galdós: Spanish Liberal Crusader*, Madison, WI, University of Wisconsin Press, 1948

Bernaldo de Quirós, Constancio, and José M. Llanas Aguilaneido, *La mala vida en Madrid*, Madrid, B. Rodríguez Serra, 1901

Bernheimer, Charles, *Figures of Ill Repute: Representing Prostitution in Nineteenth-Century France*, Cambridge, MA, Harvard University Press, 1989

Blanco Aguinaga, Carlos, 'Having No Option: The Restoration of Order and the Education of Fortunata', in Peter B. Goldman (ed.), *Conflicting Realities: Four Readings of a Chapter by Pérez Galdós ('Fortunata y Jacinta' Part III, Chapter IV)*, London, Tamesis, 1984, 13–38

——, *La historia y el texto literario: Tres novelas de Galdós*, Madrid, Nuestra Cultura, 1978

Bly, Peter A., 'Fortunata y la Cava de San Miguel, No. 11', *Hispanófila*, 59 (1977), 31–48

——, '"Nazarín": '¿Enigma eterno o triunfo del arte galdosiano?', *Cuadernos Hispanoamericanos*, 124 (1981), 286–300

——, *Pérez Galdós: Nazarín*, London, Grant & Cutler, 1991

Bofill, Juan M., *Discurso pronunciado el día 7 de mayo de 1890 contra la existencia y reglamentación de las casas de mancebía*, Figueras, Imprenta de A. Garbi Matas, 1890

Booth, Charles, *Life and Labour of the People of London*, 17 vols, London, Macmillan and Co., 1902

Borderies-Guereña, Josette, 'El discurso higiénico como conformador de la mentalidad femenina (1865–1915)', in *Mujeres y hombres en la formación del Pensamiento Occidental, Actas de las VII Jornadas de Investigación Interdisciplinaria*, Madrid, Univerdidad Autónoma de Madrid, 1989, II, 299–309

Braun, Lucille V., Galdós' Re-creation of Ernestina de Villena as Guillermina Pacheco', *Hispanic Review*, XXXVIII (1970), 32–55

——, 'The Novelistic Function of Mauricia la Dura in Galdós' *Fortunata y Jacinta*', *Symposium*, 3 (Winter 1977), 277–89

Brooks, J. L., 'The Character of Guillermina Pacheco in Galdós' Novel *Fortunata y Jacinta*', *Bulletin of Hispanic Studies*, XXXVIII (1961), 86–94

Burns, Dawson, *The Temperance Dictionary* (1861–64)

Cabeza Sánchez-Albornoz, Sonsoles, 'La Constructora Benéfica 1875–1904', in Luis E. Otero Carvajal and Angel Bahamonde Magro (eds), *Madrid en la sociedad del siglo XIX*, 2 vols, Comunidad de Madrid, Consejería de Cultura, 1986, I, 136–58

Campos Marín, Ricardo, *Alcoholismo, medicina y sociedad en España (1876–1923)*, Madrid, Consejo Superior de Investigaciones Científicas, 1997

——, 'Casas para obreros: Un aspecto de la lucha antialcohólica en España durante la Restauración', *Dynamis*, 14 (1994), 111–30

——, 'Herencia biológica y medio social en el discurso antialcohólico del socialismo español (1886–1923)', in Rafael Huertas and Ricardo Campos (eds), *Medicina social y clase obrera en España (siglos XIX y XX)*, 2 vols, Madrid, Fundación de Investigaciones Marxistas, 1992, II, 67–91

——, 'La instrumentalización de la mujer por la medicina social en España a principio de siglo: Su papel en la lucha antialcohólica', *Asclepio*, 42, No. 2 (1990), 161–73

——, *Socialismo marxista e higiene pública: La lucha antialcohólica en la II Internacional (1890–1914/19)*, Madrid, Fundación de Investigaciones Marxistas, 1992

—— and Rafael Huertas, 'El alcoholismo como enfermedad social en la España de la Restauración: Problemas de definición', *Dynamis*, 11 (1991), 263–86

—— and Rafael Huertas, 'Alcoholismo y degeneración en la medicina positivista española', *Revista de la Asociación Española de Neuropsiquiatría*, 12, No. 41 (1992), 125–29

Carr, Raymond, 'A New View of Galdós', *Anales Galdosianos*, III (1968), 185–89

——, *Modern Spain: 1875–1980*, Oxford, Oxford University Press, 1980

——, *Spain 1808–1939*, Oxford, Clarendon Press, 1966

Casalduero, Joaquín, *Vida y obra de Galdós*, Madrid, Gredos, 1961

Casco Solís, Juan, 'La higiene sexual en el proceso de institucionalización de la sanidad pública española', *Asclepio*, 42, No. 2 (1990), 223–52

Castejón Bolea, Ramón, 'Enfermedades venéreas en la España del último tercio del siglo XIX: Una aproximación a los fundamentos morales de la higiene pública', *Dynamis*, 11 (1991), 239–61

Caudet, Francisco, 'José Izquierdo y el Cuarto Estado en *Fortunata y Jacinta*', *Actas del III Congreso Internacional Galdosiano*, 2 vols, Las Palmas de Gran Canaria, Cabildo Insular de Gran Canaria, 1989, II, 25–30

Cepeda Gómez, Paloma, 'La situación jurídica de la mujer en España durante el antiguo régimen y el régimen liberal', in *Ordenamiento jurídico y realidad social de las mujeres (siglos XVI a XX)*, Actas de las IV Jornadas de Investigación Interdisciplinaria, Madrid, Universidad Autónoma de Madrid, 1986, 281–58

Cervera Barat, Rafael, *Alcoholismo y civilización* (1898), in Antonio M. Rey
    González (ed.), *Estudios médico-sociales sobre marginados en la España del
    siglo XIX*, Madrid, Ministerio de Sanidad y Consumo, 1990, 107–28
Charles, A. O., *The Female Mission to the Fallen*, London, 1860
Charnon-Deutsch, Lou, *Gender and Representation: Women in Spanish Realist
    Fiction*, Amsterdam, John Benjamins, 1990
Cipolla, Carlo, *Miasmas and Disease: Public Health and the Environment in the
    Pre-Industrial Age*, New Haven, CT, Yale University Press, 1992
Classen, Constance, *Worlds of Sense: Exploring the Senses in History and across
    Cultures*, London, Routledge, 1993
——, David Howes and Anthony Synnott, *Aroma: The Cultural History of Smell*,
    London, Routledge, 1994
Cohen, Stanley, *Visions of Social Control: Crime, Punishment and Classification*,
    Cambridge, Polity Press, 1985
—— and Andrew Scull, *Social Control and the State*: *Historical and Comparative
    Essays*, Oxford, Blackwell, 1983
Colin, Vera, 'A Note on Tolstoy and Galdós', *Anales Galdosianos*, II (1967), 155–68
——, 'Tolstoy and *Angel Guerra*', in J. E. Varey (ed.), *Galdós Studies*, London,
    Tamesis, 1970, 114–35
Commenge, Oscar, *La prostitution clandestine à Paris*, Paris, Schleicher Frères, 1897
*Conclusiones relativas a la profilaxis y los medios de atenuar los efectos del cólera
    morbo epidémico*, Madrid, Rafael G. Rubio, 1890
Corbin, Alain, *Alexandre Parent-Duchâtelet: La Prostitution à Paris au XIX Siècle*,
    Paris, Seuil, 1981
——, 'Backstage', in Michelle Perrot (ed.), *From the Fires of Revolution to the
    Great War*, Cambridge, MA, Belknap Press, 1990 (vol. IV of *A History of
    Private Life*, ed. Philippe Ariès and Georges Duby), 453–667
——, 'Commercial Sexuality in Nineteenth Century France: A System of Images
    and Regulations', in Catherine Gallagher and Thomas Laqueur (eds), *The
    Making of the Modern Body*: *Sexuality and Society in the Nineteenth Century*,
    Berkeley and Los Angeles, University of California Press, 1987, 209–19
——, *The Foul and the Fragrant: Odor and the French Social Imagination*,
    Leamington Spa, Berg Publishers, 1986
——, *Time, Desire and Horror: Towards a History of the Senses*, Cambridge,
    Polity Press, 1995
——, *Women for Hire: Prostitution and Sexuality in France after 1850*, Cambridge,
    MA, Harvard University Press, 1990
Correa, Gustavo, *El simbolismo religioso en las novelas de Pérez Galdós*, Madrid,
    Gredos, 1962
Corrigan, Philip and Derek Sayer, *The Great Arch: English State Formation as
    Cultural Revolution*, Oxford, Blackwell, 1991
Cuevas de la Cruz, Matilde, 'Aproximación a la consideración social de la prosti-
    tución madrileña', in Luis E. Otero Carvajal and Angel Bahamonde Magro
    (eds), *Madrid en la sociedad del siglo XIX*, 2 vols, Comunidad de Madrid,
    Consejería de Cultura, 1986, II, 164–73

Davidoff, Leonore, *Worlds between: Historical Perspectives on Gender and Class*, Cambridge, Polity Press, 1995

De la Calle, María Dolores, *La Comisión de Reformas Sociales 1883–1903: Política social y conflicto de intereses en la España de la Restauración*, Madrid, Ministerio de Trabajo y Seguridad Social, 1989

De la Nuez, Sebastián, *Biblioteca y archivo de la Casa Museo Pérez Galdós*, Las Palmas de Gran Canaria, Cabildo Insular de Gran Canaria, 1990

Dendle, Brian J., 'Point of View in *Nazarín*: An Appendix to Goldman', *Anales Galdosianos*, IX (1974), 113–21

Díez de Baldeón, Clementina, *Arquitectura y clases sociales en el Madrid del siglo XIX*, Madrid, Siglo XXI, 1986

——, 'Barrios obreros en el Madrid del siglo XIX: ¿Solución o amenaza para el orden burgués?', in Luis E. Otero Carvajal and Angel Bahamonde Magro (eds), *Madrid en la sociedad del siglo XIX*, 2 vols, Comunidad de Madrid, Consejería de Cultura, 1986, I, 118–34

Donzelot, Jacques, *The Policing of Families: Welfare versus the State*, London, Hutchinson, 1980

Dowdle, Harold L., 'Galdós' Use of Quijote Motifs in *Angel Guerra*', *Anales Galdosianos*, XX (1985), 113–22

Dupeux, Georges, *French Society 1789–1970*, London, Methuen, 1976

Edwards, Anne R., *Regulation and Repression: The Study of Social Control*, London, Allen & Unwin, 1988

Elizalde, Ignacio, 'Angel Guerra, su vocación y su religión nacional', *Actas del IV Congreso Internacional Galdosiano*, 2 vols, Las Palmas de Gran Canaria, Cabildo Insular de Gran Canaria, 1990, II, 383–92

Eoff, Sherman H., 'The Treatment of Individual Personality in *Fortunata y Jacinta*', *Hispanic Review*, XVII (1949), 269–89

Eslava, Rafael, *La prostitución en Madrid: Apuntes para un estudio sociológico*, Madrid, Vicente Rico, 1900

Faus Sevilla, Pilar, *La sociedad española del siglo XIX en la obra de Pérez Galdós*, Valencia, Nácher, 1972

Fonssagrives, Jean Batiste, *Higiene y saneamiento de las poblaciones*, 4 vols, Madrid, El Cosmos, 1885

Foucault, Michel, *Discipline and Punish: The Birth of the Prison*, London, Penguin, 1991

——, *The History of Sexuality*, London, Penguin, 1990

——, *Madness and Civilization: A History of Insanity in the Age of Reason*, London, Routledge, 1992

Fuentes Peris, Teresa, 'Clasificando la pobreza: La caridad indiscriminada como problema social en *Angel Guerra*', *Actas del VI Congreso Internacional Galdosiano*, Las Palmas de Gran Canaria, Cabildo Insular de Gran Canaria, 2000, 344–54

——, 'The Control of Prostitution and Filth in *Fortunata y Jacinta*: The Panoptic Strategy in the Convent of Las Micaelas', *Anales Galdosianos*, XXXI–XXXII (1996–97), 35–52

——, 'Drink and Degeneration: The "Deserving" and "Undeserving" Poor in *Angel Guerra*', *Romance Studies*, 29 (Spring 1997), 7–20

——, 'Drink and Social Stability: Discourses of Power in Galdós' *Fortunata y Jacinta*', *Bulletin of Hispanic Studies* (Liverpool), LXXIII, No. 1 (January 1996), 63–77

García Arenal, Fernando, *Datos para el estudio de la cuestión social*, ed. Ramón María Alvar González, Gijón, Silverio Cañada, 1980, 42–43. (Originally published in 1885 [Gijón, Imp. del Comercio])

García Gómez-Alvarez, Alfredo, 'La sobremortalidad de la clase obrera madrileña a finales del siglo XIX (1880–1900)', in Rafael Huertas and Ricardo Campos (eds), *Medicina social y clase obrera en España (siglos XIX y XX)*, 2 vols, Madrid, Fundación de Investigaciones Marxistas, 1992, I, 145–75

Genette, Gerard, *Narrative Discourse*, Oxford, Basil Blackwell, 1980

Geremek, Bronislaw, *Poverty: A History*, Oxford, Basil Blackwell, 1994

Gilman, Stephen, 'The Consciousness of Fortunata', *Anales Galdosianos*, V (1970), 55–66

Giné y Partagás, Juan, *Curso elemental de higiene privada y pública*, 4 vols, Barcelona, Imprenta de Narciso Ramírez y Cñía, 1872

——, 'Introduction' to Prudencio Sereñana y Partagás, *La prostitución en la ciudad de Barcelona, estudiada como enfermedad social y considerada como origen de otras enfermedades dinámicas, orgánicas y morales de la población barcelonesa*, Barcelona, Imp. de los sucesores de Ramírez y Cñía, 1882

Giner de los Ríos, Francisco, 'La prohibición de la mendicidad y las Hermanitas de los Pobres', *Boletín de la Institución Libre de Enseñanza*, 5 (1881), 49–50

Golby, John M. (ed.), *Culture and Society in Britain 1850–1890: A Source Book of Contemporary Writings*, Oxford, Oxford University Press, 1987

Gold, Hazel, 'El nomadismo urbano y la crisis finisecular en *Misericordia*', *Actas del VI Congreso Internacional Galdosiano*, Las Palmas de Gran Canaria, Cabildo Insular de Gran Canaria, 2000, 387–95

Goldman, Peter B. (ed.), *Conflicting Realities: Four Readings of a Chapter by Pérez Galdós ('Fortunata y Jacinta' Part III, Chapter IV)*, London, Tamesis, 1984

——, 'Feijoo and Mr. Singer. Notes on the *aburguesamiento* of Fortunata', *Revista de Estudios Hispánicos* (Universidad de Puerto Rico), 9 (1982), 105–13

——, 'Galdós and the Aesthetic of Ambiguity: Notes on the Thematic Structure of *Nazarín*', *Anales Galdosianos*, IX (1974), 99–112

——, 'Galdós and the Nineteenth-Century Novel: The Need for an Interdisciplinary Approach', in Jo Labanyi (ed.), *Galdós*, London, Longman, 1993, 140–56. Reprinted from *Anales Galdosianos*, X (1975), 5–18

——, 'O máquina buena o mujer mala: Visión determinista y conciencia temporal en *Fortunata y Jacinta*', *Revista de Estudios Hispánicos* (University of Alabama), XXI, No. 3 (October 1987), 67–91

Granjel, Mercedes, *Pedro Felipe Monlau y la higiene española del siglo XIX*, Salamanca, Cátedra de Historia de la Medicina, Universidad de Salamanca, 1983

Guereña, Jean-Louis, 'Los orígenes de la reglamentación de la prostitución en la

España contemporánea: De la propuesta de Cabarrús (1792) al Reglamento de Madrid (1847)', *Dynamis*, 15 (1995), 401–41

Gullón, Germán (ed.), *Fortunata y Jacinta*, Madrid, Taurus, 1986

Gullón, Ricardo, 'Estructura y diseño en *Fortunata y Jacinta*', in Germán Gullón (ed.), *Fortunata y Jacinta*, Madrid, Taurus, 1986, 175–232. Reprinted from *Papeles de Son Armadans*, 143–44 (1968)

——, *Galdós, novelista moderno*, Madrid, Taurus, 1960

——, *Técnicas de Galdós*, Madrid, Taurus, 1980

Gutiérrez Sánchez, María Mercedes, 'La Beneficencia Pública en Madrid durante el último tercio del siglo XIX', in Angel Bahamonde Magro and Luis E. Otero Carvajal (eds), *La sociedad madrileña durante la Restauración (1876–1931)*, 2 vols, Comunidad de Madrid, Consejería de Cultura, 1989, II, 426–34

Hafter, Monroe Z., '"Bálsamo contra bálsamo" in *Angel Guerra*', *Anales Galdosianos*, IV (1969), 39–48

Hall, Stuart, 'The West and the Rest', in Stuart Hall and Bram Gieben (eds), *Formations of Modernity*, Cambridge, Polity Press, 1992, 275–331

Harris, José, 'Between Civic Virtue and Social Darwinism: The Concept of the Residuum', in David Englander and Rosemary O'Day (eds), *Retrieved Riches: Social Investigation in Britain 1840–1914*, Aldershot, Scolar Press, 1995, 67–87

——, *Private Lives, Public Spirit: A Social History of Britain, 1870–1914*, Oxford, Oxford University Press, 1993

——, *Unemployment and Politics: A Study in English Social Policy 1886–1914*, Oxford, Clarendon Press, 1972

Harrison, Brian, *Drink and the Victorians: The Temperance Question in England 1815–1875*, London, Faber & Faber, 1971

Hart, Jenifer, 'Religion and Social Control in the Mid-Nineteenth Century', in A. P. Donajgrodzki (ed.), *Social Control in Nineteenth-Century Britain*, London, Croom Helm, 1977, 108–33

Hauser, Philippe, *Madrid bajo el punto de vista médico-social*, 2 vols, Madrid, Establecimiento Tipográfico Sucesores de Rivadeneyra, 1902

——, 'El siglo XIX considerado bajo el punto de vista médico-social', *Revista de España*, 101 (1884), 202–24, 333–58

Himmelfarb, Gertrude, *The Idea of Poverty: England in the Early Industrial Age*, London, Faber & Faber, 1984

Hoddie, James H., '*Fortunata y Jacinta* and *The Eroica*', *Anales Galdosianos*, XIV (1979), 133–39

Howe, G. Melvyn, *Man, Environment and Disease in Britain: A Medical Geography of Britain through the Ages*, Newton Abbot, David & Charles, 1992

Huertas, Rafael, *Clasificar y educar: Historia natural y social de la deficiencia mental*, Madrid, Consejo Superior de Investigaciones Científicas, 1998

——, *Locura y degeneración*, Madrid, Consejo Superior de Investigaciones Científicas, 1987

—— and Ricardo Campos (eds), *Medicina social y clase obrera en España (siglos XIX y XX)*, 2 vols, Madrid, Fundación de Investigaciones Marxistas, 1992

Jacobus, Mary, Evelyn Fox Keller and Sally Shuttleworth (eds), *Body/Politics: Women and the Discourses of Science*, London, Routledge, 1990

Jagoe, Catherine, *Ambiguous Angels: Gender in the Novels of Galdós*, Berkeley and Los Angeles, University of California Press, 1994

——, 'La misión de la mujer', in Catherine Jagoe, Alda Blanco and Cristina Enríquez de Salamanca, *La mujer en los discursos de género: Textos y contextos en el siglo XIX*, Barcelona, Icaria, 1998

——, 'Monstrous Inversions: Decadence and Degeneration in Galdós's *Angel Guerra*', in Lou Charnon-Deutsch and Jo Labanyi (eds), *Culture and Gender in Nineteenth-Century Spain*, Oxford, Oxford University Press, 1995, 161–81

——, 'The Subversive Angel in *Fortunata y Jacinta*', *Anales Galdosianos*, XXIV (1989), 79–91

Jalland, Pat and John Hooper (eds), *Women from Birth to Death: The Female Life Cycle in Britain 1830–1914*, Atlantic Highlands, NJ, Humanities Press International, 1986

Jordanova, Ludmilla, *Sexual Visions: Images of Gender in Science and Medicine between the Eighteenth and Twentieth Centuries*, Hemel Hempstead, Harvester Wheatsheaf, 1989

Jutglar, Antoni (ed.), *Condiciones de vida y trabajo obrero en España a mediados del siglo XIX*, Barcelona, Anthropos, 1984

Krauel, Ricardo, 'Duplicidad significativa de las representaciones de ambigüedad sexual en *Fortunata y Jacinta*', *Bulletin of Hispanic Studies* (Glasgow), LXXVI (1999), 649–72

Kronik, John W., 'Galdosian Reflections: Feijoo and the Fabrication of Fortunata', *Modern Language Notes*, 97 (1982), 272–310. Reprinted in Peter B. Goldman (ed.), *Conflicting Realities: Four Readings of a Chapter by Pérez Galdós ('Fortunata y Jacinta' Part III, Chapter IV)*, London, Tamesis, 1984, 39–72

—— and Harriet S. Turner (eds), *Textos y contextos de Galdós*, Madrid, Castalia, 1994

Labanyi, Jo (ed.), *Galdós*, London, Longman, 1993

——, *Gender and Modernization in the Spanish Realist Novel*, Oxford, Oxford University Press, 2000

——, 'Introduction' to her translation of *Nazarín*, Oxford, Oxford University Press, 1993, vii–xx

——, 'The Raw, the Cooked and the Indigestible in Galdós's *Fortunata y Jacinta*', *Romance Studies*, 13 (1988), 55–66

——, 'Representing the Unrepresentable: Monsters, Mystics and Feminine Men in Galdós's *Nazarín*', *Journal of Hispanic Research*, 1 (1992–93), 225–38

Lakhdari, Sadi, *Angel Guerra de Pérez Galdós*, Paris, Editions Hispaniques, 1994

Lawrence, Christopher, *Medicine in the Making of Modern Britain (1700–1920)*, London and New York, Routledge, 1994

L'Espérance, Jean, 'Doctors and Women in Nineteenth-Century Society: Sexuality and Role', in John Woodward and David Richards (eds), *Health Care and Popular Medicine in Nineteenth-Century England*, London, Croom Helm, 1977, 105–27

Lewis, Jane, 'Women and Late-Nineteenth-Century Social Work', in Carol Smart (ed.), *Regulating Womanhood: Historical Essays on Marriage, Motherhood and Sexuality*, London, Routledge, 1992

Lida, Denah, 'Galdós y sus santas modernas', *Anales Galdosianos*, X (1975), 19–31

López de la Vega, Dr, *La higiene del hogar*, Madrid, Imp. La Guirnalda, 1878

López Piñero, José María, Luis García Ballester and Pilar Faus Sevilla, *Medicina y sociedad en la España del siglo XIX*, Madrid, Sociedad de Estudios y Publicaciones, 1964

Lowe, Jennifer, 'Structural and Linguistic Presentation in Galdós' *Angel Guerra*', *Anales Galdosianos*, X (1975), 45–53

McDowell, Linda, *Gender, Identity and Place: Understanding Feminist Geographies*, Cambridge, Polity Press, 1999

Maristany, Luis, 'Lombroso y España: Nuevas consideraciones', *Anales de Literatura Española*, 2 (1983), Universidad de Alicante, 361–81

Méndez Alvaro, Francisco, *Resumen de la discusión sobre la mortalidad en Madrid en la Sociedad Española de Higiene*, Madrid, 1882

Mesonero Romanos, Ramón de, *Escenas matritenses*, ed. María Pilar Palomo, Barcelona, Planeta, 1987 (Originally published in 1836–42.)

Miguel y Viguri, Isidoro, *Medidas de policía médica en relación con la sifílis. Discurso leído en la Academia Médico-Quirúrgica española*, Madrid, Imprenta de Enrique Teodoro, 1877

Minter, G. G., 'Halma and the Writings of St Augustine', *Anales Galdosianos*, XIII (1978), 73–97

Monlau, Pedro Felipe, *Elementos de higiene privada*, Barcelona, Imprenta de D. Pablo Riera, 1846

——, *Elementos de higiene pública*, Barcelona, Imprenta de D. Pablo Riera, 1847

——, *Higiene industrial. ¿Qué medidas higiénicas puede dictar el Gobierno a favor de las clases obreras?* (1856), ed. Antoni Jutglar, 63–143

——, *Nociones de higiene doméstica y gobierno de la casa para uso de las escuelas de primera enseñanza de niñas y colegios de señoritas*, Madrid, Imprenta de M. Rivadeneyra, 1860

——, *Remedios del pauperismo*, Valencia, Imprenta de Mariano Cabrerizo, 1846

Montesinos, José F., *Galdós*, 3 vols, Madrid, Castalia, 1969

Morón Arroyo, Ciriaco, '*Nazarín* y *Halma*: Sentido y unidad', *Anales Galdosianos*, II (1967), 67–81

Morris, Lydia, *Dangerous Classes: The Underclass and Social Citizenship*, London, Routledge, 1994

Mort, Frank, *Dangerous Sexualities: Medico-Moral Politics in England since 1830*, London, Routledge & Kegan Paul, 1987

Nash, Mary (ed.), *Mujer, familia y trabajo en España (1875–1935)*, Barcelona, Anthropos, 1983

Nash, Stanley, 'Prostitution and Charity: The Magdalen Hospital, a Case Study', *Journal of Social History*, 17 (1984), 617–28

Nead, Lynda, *Myths of Sexuality, Representations of Women in Victorian Britain*, Oxford, Basil Blackwell, 1990

Núñez Roldán, Francisco, *Mujeres públicas: Historia de la prostitución en España*, Madrid, Temas de Hoy, 1995

O'Connor, D. J., 'The Recurrence of Images in *Angel Guerra*', *Anales Galdosianos*, XXIII (1988), 73–82

Ortiz Armengol, Pedro, 'El convento de las Micaelas en *Fortunata y Jacinta*', *La Estafeta Literaria* (15 October 1974), 4–7

——, *Vida de Galdós*, Barcelona, Crítica, 1996

Otero Carvajal, Luis E. and Angel Bahamonde Magro (eds), *Madrid en la sociedad del siglo XIX*, 2 vols, Comunidad de Madrid, Consejería de Cultura, 1986

Parker, Alexander, '*Nazarín*, or the Passion of Our Lord Jesus Christ according to Galdós', *Anales Galdosianos*, II (1967), 83–101

Pearson, Geoffrey, *The Deviant Imagination: Psychiatry, Social Work and Social Change*, London and Basingstoke, Macmillan, 1975

Penuel, Arnold, *Charity in Galdós*, Athens, GA, University of Georgia Press, 1972

Pérez Baltasar, María Dolores, *Mujeres marginadas: Las casas de recogidas en Madrid*, Madrid, Gráficas Lormo, 1984

Peset, José Luis, *Ciencia y marginación: Sobre negros, locos y criminales*, Barcelona, Crítica, 1983

—— and Mariano Peset, *Lombroso y la escuela positivista italiana*, Madrid, Consejo Superior de Investigaciones Científicas, 1975

Pick, Daniel, *Faces of Degeneration*, Cambridge, Cambridge University Press, 1993

Plá, Carlos, Pilar Benito, Mercedes Casado and Juan Carlos Poyán, *El Madrid de Galdós,* Madrid, Lavapiés, 1987

Poovey, Mary, 'Speaking of the Body: Mid-Victorian Constructions of Female Desire', in Mary Jacobus, Evelyn Fox Keller and Sally Shuttleworth (eds), *Body/Politics: Women and the Discourses of Science*, London, Routledge, 1990, 29–46

Porter, Roy, 'Ever since Eve: The Fear of Contagion', *Times Literary Supplement* (27 May, 2 June 1988), 582, 597

Portero, José Antonio, *Púlpito e ideología en la España del siglo XIX*, Zaragoza, Libros Pórtico, 1978

Prats y Bosch, Antonio, *La prostitución y la sífilis: Ensayo acerca de las causas de la propagación de las enfermedades sifilíticas y los medios de oponerse a ellas*, Barcelona, Luis Tasso, 1861

Prochaska, Frank, *The Voluntary Impulse: Philanthropy in Modern Britain*, London, Faber & Faber, 1988

——, *Women and Philanthropy in Nineteenth-Century England,* Oxford, Clarendon Press, 1980

Pulido, Angel, *Bosquejos médico-sociales para la mujer*, Madrid, Imp. Víctor Saiz, 1876

Quispe-Agnoli, Rocío, 'De la mujer caída al ángel subvertido en *Fortunata y Jacinta*: Las funciones ambivalentes de Mauricia la Dura', *Bulletin of Hispanic Studies* (Glasgow), LXXV (1998), 337–54

Ramazanoğlu, Caroline (ed.), *Up against Foucault: Explorations of Some Tensions between Foucault and Feminism*, London, Routledge, 1993

Reformas Sociales, I (Información oral practicada en virtud de la Real orden de 5 de diciembre de 1883. Madrid), Madrid, Manuel Minuesa de los Ríos, 1890

Reformas Sociales, II (Información escrita practicada en virtud de la real orden de 5 de diciembre de 1883. Madrid), Madrid, Manuel Minuesa de los Ríos, 1890

Reformas Sociales, III (Información oral y escrita practicada en virtud de la Real orden de 5 de diciembre de 1883. Valencia), Madrid, Manuel Minuesa de los Ríos, 1891

Reformas Sociales, IV (Información oral y escrita practicada en virtud de la Real Orden de 5 de diciembre de 1883. Alicante, Avila, Badajoz, Burgos y Cáceres), (Madrid, 1892), ed. Santiago Castillo, Madrid, Ministerio de Trabajo y Seguridad Social, 1985

Revista de la Sociedad Española de Higiene (1883)

Riant, A., *Hygiène du cabinet de travail*, Paris, J. B. Billière et F., 1883

Ribbans, Geoffrey, 'El carácter de Mauricia la Dura en la estructura de *Fortunata y Jacinta*', *Actas del Quinto Congreso Internacional de Hispanistas*, Bordeaux, Instituto de Estudios Ibéricos e Iberoamericanos, 1977, 713–21

——, *Conflicts and Conciliations: The Evolution of Galdós's 'Fortunata y Jacinta'*, West Lafayette, IN, Purdue University Press, 1997

——, 'Notes on the Narrator in *Fortunata y Jacinta*', in Linda M. Willem (ed.), *A Sesquicentennial Tribute to Galdós 1843–1993*, Newark, DE, Juan de la Cuesta Hispanic Monographs, 1993, 88–104

——, *Pérez Galdós: Fortunata y Jacinta*, London, Grant & Cutler, 1977

——, 'Woman as Scapegoat: The Case of Dulcenombre Babel in Galdós' *Angel Guerra*', *Bulletin of Hispanic Studies* (Glasgow), LXXVI (1999), 487–97

Richer, Leon, *Le livre des femmes*, Paris, Typ. N. Blanpain, 1873

Rivière Gómez, Aurora, *'Caídas, miserables, degeneradas': Estudio sobre la prostitución en el siglo XIX*, Madrid, Dirección General de la Mujer, 1994

Roberts, Nickie, *Whores in History: Prostitution in Western Society*, London, Harper Collins, 1992

Rodríguez Ocaña, Esteban, *La constitución de la medicina social como disciplina en España (1882–1923)*, Madrid, Ministerio de Sanidad y Consumo, 1987

——, 'Paz, trabajo, higiene. Los enunciados acerca de la higiene industrial en la España del siglo XIX', in Rafael Huertas and Ricardo Campos (eds), *Medicina social y clase obrera en España (siglos XIX y XX)*, 2 vols, Madrid, Fundación de Investigaciones Marxistas, 1992, II, 383–406

Rodríguez Puértolas, Julio, *Galdós: Burguesía y revolución*, Madrid, Turner, 1975

——, '"Quien manda, manda", La ley y el orden en *Fortunata y Jacinta*', in John W. Kronik and Harriet S. Turner (eds), *Textos y contextos de Galdós*, Madrid, Castalia, 1994, 115–25

Rogers, Douglass M. (ed.), *Benito Pérez Galdós*, Madrid, Taurus, 1973

——, 'Charity in Galdós', *Anales Galdosianos*, IX (1974), 169–73

Romero Pérez, Francisco, 'The Grandeur of Galdós' Mauricia *la Dura*', *Hispanic Journal*, 3, No. 1 (Autumn 1981), 107–14

Round, Nicholas G., 'The Fictional Plenitude of *Angel Guerra*', in A. H. Clarke and E. J. Rodgers (eds), *Galdós' House of Fiction* (papers given at the Birmingham Galdós Colloquium), Llangrannog Dolphin, 1991, 145–67

——, 'Misericordia: Galdosian Realism's "Last Word"', in Linda M. Willem (ed.), *A Sesquicentennial Tribute to Galdós 1843–1993*, Newark, DE, Juan de la Cuesta Hispanic Monographs, 1993, 155–72

Russell, Robert, 'The Christ Figure in *Misericordia* (A Monograph)', *Anales Galdosianos*, II (1967), 103–30

Russet, Cynthia Eagle, *Sexual Science: The Victorian Construction of Womanhood*, Cambridge, MA, Harvard University Press, 1989

Salarich, Joaquim, *Higiene del tejedor* (1858), ed. Antoni Jutglar, 157–286

Santero, Francisco Javier, *Elementos de higiene privada y pública*, 2 vols, Madrid, El Cosmos, 1885

Sayers, Kathleen M., 'El sentido de la tragedia en *Angel Guerra*', *Anales Galdosianos*, V (1970), 81–85

Scanlon, Geraldine, *La polémica feminista en la España contemporánea 1868–1974*, 2nd edn, Madrid, Akal, 1986

Schraibman, Joseph, 'Los sueños en *Fortunata y Jacinta*', in Douglass M. Rogers (ed.), *Benito Pérez Galdós*, Madrid, Taurus, 1973, 161–68

Sereñana y Partagás, Prudencio, *La prostitución en la ciudad de Barcelona, estudiada como enfermedad social y considerada como origen de otras enfermedades dinámicas, orgánicas y morales de la población barcelonesa*, Barcelona, Imp. de los sucesores de Ramírez y Cñía, 1882

Shiman, Lilian L., *Crusade against Drink in Victorian England*, London, Macmillan, 1988

Shoemaker, W. H., *The Novelistic Art of Galdós*, 3 vols, Valencia, Albatrós Hispanófila, 1980

Showalter, Elaine, *The Female Malady: Women, Madness and English Culture, 1830–1980*, London, Virago Press, 1987

Shubert, Adrian, *A Social History of Modern Spain*, London, Unwin Hyman, 1990

Shuttleworth, Sally, 'Female Circulation: Medical Discourse and Popular Advertising in the Mid-Victorian Era', in Mary Jacobus, Evelyn Fox Keller and Sally Shuttleworth (eds), *Body/Politics: Women and the Discourses of Science*, London, Routledge, 1990, 47–68

Sieburth, Stephanie, 'Enlightenment, Mass Culture, and Madness: The Dialectic of Modernity in *La desheredada*', in Linda M. Willem (ed.), *A Sesquicentennial Tribute to Galdós 1843–1993*, Newark, DE, Juan de la Cuesta Hispanic Monographs, 1993, 27–40

Sierra Alvarez, José, '¿El minero borracho?: Alcoholismo y disciplinas industriales en Asturias', *Cuadernos del Norte*, 29 (1985), 58–63

——, *El obrero soñado: Ensayo sobre el paternalismo industrial (Asturias, 1860–1917)*, Madrid: Siglo XXI de España, 1990

Sinnigen, John H., 'Individuo, clase y sociedad en *Fortunata y Jacinta*', in Germán Gullón (ed.), *Fortunata y Jacinta*, Madrid, Taurus, 1986, 71–93. Reprinted from Robert J. Weber (ed.), *Galdós Studies* II, London, Tamesis Books, 1974

——, 'The Problem of Individual and Social Redemption in *Angel Guerra*', *Anales Galdosianos*, XII (1977), 129–40

——, 'The Search for a New Totality in *Nazarín, Halma, Misericordia*', *Modern*

Language Notes, 93, No. 2 (1978), 233–51

——, *Sexo y política: Lecturas galdosianas*, Madrid, Ediciones de la Torre, 1996

Smart, Barry, *Michel Foucault*, London, Ellis Horwood, 1985

Soubeyroux, Jacques, 'Pauperismo y relaciones sociales en el Madrid del siglo XVIII', *Estudios de Historia Social*, 12–13 (1980), 7–229

Stedman Jones, Gareth, *Outcast London*, Harmondsworth, Penguin, 1984

Summers, Anne, 'A Home from Home – Women's Philanthropic Work in the Nineteenth Century', in Sandra Burman (ed.), *Fit Work for Women*, London, Croom Helm, 1979, 33–63

Thompson, F. M. L., *The Rise of Respectable Society: A Social History of Victorian Britain (1830–1900)*, London, Fontana, 1988

——, 'Social Control in Victorian Britain', *Economic History Review*, XXXIV (May 1981), 189–208

Tolosa Latour, Manuel de, *Discursos leídos en la Real Academia de Medicina...* (Tema: concepto y fines de la Higiene Popular), Madrid, Tip. de la Vda. e Hijos de M. Tello, 1900

Topalov, Christian, 'The City as *Terra Incognita*: Charles Booth's Poverty Survey and the People of London, 1886–1891', *Planning Perspectives: An International Journal of History, Planning and the Environment*, 8 (1993), 395–425

Trinidad Fernández, Pedro, *La defensa de la sociedad: Cárcel y delincuencia en España (siglos XVIII–XX)*, Madrid, Alianza, 1991

——, 'Penalidad y gobierno de la pobreza en el Antiguo Régimen', *Estudios de Historia Social*, 48–49 (1989), 7–64

Tsuchiya, Akiko, 'The Female Body under Surveillance: Galdós's *La desheredada*', in Jeanne P. Brownlow and John W. Kronik (eds), *Intertextual Pursuits: Literary Meditations in Modern Spanish Narrative*, Lewisburg, PA, Bucknell University Press, 1998, 201–21

——, '"Las Micaelas por fuera y por dentro": Discipline and Resistance in *Fortunata y Jacinta*', in Linda M. Willem (ed.), *A Sesquicentennial Tribute to Galdós 1843–1993*, Newark, DE, Juan de la Cuesta Hispanic Monographs, 1993, 56–71

——, 'Peripheral Subjects: Policing Deviance and Disorder in *Nazarín* and *Halma*', *Letras Peninsulares*, 13, No. 1 (Spring 2000), 197–208.

Turner, Harriet S., *Benito Pérez Galdós: Fortunata and Jacinta*, Cambridge, Cambridge University Press, 1992

Ullman, Joan Connelly and George H. Allison, 'Galdós as a Psychiatrist in *Fortunata y Jacinta*', *Anales Galdosianos*, IX (1974), 7–36

Urey, Diane F., *Galdós and the Irony of Language*, Cambridge, Cambridge University Press, 1982

Valis, Noël, 'On Monstruous Birth: Leopoldo Alas' *La Regenta*', in Brian Nelson (ed.), *Naturalism in the European Novel: New Critical Perspectives*, New York, Berg, 1992, 191–209

Varela, Julia, 'Técnicas de control social en la "Restauración"', in Julia Varela and Fernando Alvarez-Uría (eds), *El cura Galeote asesino del obispo de Madrid-Alcalá*, Madrid, La Piqueta, 1979, 210–36

———, and Fernando Alvarez-Uría (eds), *El cura Galeote asesino del obispo de Madrid-Alcalá*, Madrid, La Piqueta, 1979

Varey, J. E., 'Charity in *Misericordia*', in J. E. Varey (ed.), *Galdós Studies*, London, Tamesis, 1970, 164–204.

———, (ed.), *Galdós Studies*, London, Tamesis, 1970

———, 'Man and Nature in Galdós' *Halma*', *Anales Galdosianos*, XIII (1978), 59–72

Vega Armentero, R., 'La prostitución', *Semanario de las Familias*, 2, No. 50 (10 December 1883), 432–33

Vigarello, Georges, *Concepts of Cleanliness: Changing Attitudes in France since the Middle Ages*, Cambridge, Cambridge University Press, 1988

Viñeta-Bellasierra, J., *La sífilis como hecho social punible y como una de las causas de la degeneración de la raza humana*, Barcelona, Est. tip. Edit. La Academia, 1886

Voz de la Caridad (various issues 1876–1883)

Walkowitz, Judith R., *Prostitution and Victorian Society: Women, Class, and the State*, Cambridge, Cambridge University Press, 1980

Watkins, C. Ken, *Social Control*, London, Longman, 1975

Webb, Sidney and Beatrice, *Industrial Democracy*, London, Longmans, Green and Co., 1897

Whiston, James, 'Language and Situation in Part I of *Fortunata y Jacinta*', *Anales Galdosianos*, VII (1972), 79–91

———, 'The Materialism of Life: Religion in *Fortunata y Jacinta*', *Anales Galdosianos*, XIV (1979), 65–81

Willem, Linda M., *Galdós's 'Segunda Manera': Rhetorical Strategies and Affective Response*, Chapel Hill, NC, North Carolina University Press, 1998

———, 'Jacinta's "visita al cuarto estado": The Galley Version', *Anales Galdosianos*, XXXI/XXXII (1996/1997), 97–103

——— (ed.), *A Sesquicentennial Tribute to Galdós 1843–1993*, Newark, DE, Juan de la Cuesta Hispanic Monographs, 1993

Williams, Perry, 'The Laws of Health: Women, Medicine and Sanitary Reform, 1850–1890', in Marina Benjamin (ed.), *Science and Sensibility: Gender and Scientific Enquiry 1780–1945*, Oxford, Basil Blackwell, 1991, 60–88

Wilson, Elizabeth, *The Sphinx in the City: Urban Life, the Control of Disorder, and Women*, Berkeley and Los Angeles: University of California Press, 1991

Zahareas, Anthony, 'El sentido de la tragedia en *Fortunata y Jacinta*', *Anales Galdosianos*, III (1968), 26–34

Index